Complete
Computerised
Payroll

using SAGE

A Computer Linked Tutorial in Payroll principles using SAGE Payroll Software.

Comput-Ed Ltd

Acknowledgements

During the writing of this book I made numerous telephone calls and visits to the nearest offices of the Inland Revenue and the Department of Social Security. My enquiries always met with a knowledgeable and friendly respnse for which I am happy to record my appreciation. To my friend, Andrew Nicholls, who gave advice and support during the writing and to Philip K Bird BPMA, who so carefully read and suggested alterations to the final draft of this book I acknowledge my debt. Nevertheless, if, in spite of all this assistance, there are any remaining errors the fault is mine alone.

William Murray

Advice concerning Income Tax and National Insurance

Income Tax

For advice concerning the calculation of income tax and the regulations surrounding what payments are taxable you should contact your local Tax Office - Her Majesty's Inspector of Taxes

For advice surrounding the *payment* of Income Tax you should contact the Accounts Office of the Collector of Taxes.

National Insurance

For advice concerning the deduction of National Insurance contributions and the payment of Statutory Sick Pay and Statutory Maternity Pay you should contact either your local office of the Contributions Agency (DSS) or telephone (free) the Social Security Advice Line for Employers (SSALE) on 0800 393539.

Copyright

Published 1992 Comput-Ed Ltd
        ISBN 1-874449-01-5

Contents

Contents

Introduction and Installation

The Payroll Course

At the end of this course you should be able to handle the day to day operation of a payroll for a firm. There will still be a variety of situations arising that are new to you and for which you will need assistance from the local Tax Office. Nevertheless, the bulk of the payments and deductions, the ones that are common to most firms most of the time, are covered by this course.

Requirements

In order to use this course of lessons an IBM PC compatible computer is required with the Sage Sterling Payroll II program loaded on the hard disk.

Structure of the Lessons

The book is divided into three parts.

Lessons 1 and 2 provide a detailed analysis of one person's wage packet as tax codes, National Insurance categories and the level of pay changes. By studying this section carefully you should be able to explain to an employee why the firm has deducted certain amounts from his or her pay.

Lesson 3 requires you to enter details of some of the employees of an imaginary firm called Dragon Enterprise Limited.

Lessons 4 to 15 involve you in running the payroll for Dragon Enterprise Limited's 20+ employees for a year. As you work your way through the payroll there are explanations of the deductions being made and any essential forms that are involved with employees or the Inland Revenue. For those students who are combining this with a study of double entry book-keeping an explanation of the ledger account entries that are necessary when running a payroll are included in some lessons.

By the end of the course you will be that very rare person, somebody who understands and can check their pay-slip.

At the back of this training manual are appendices showing the structure of the menu system used in the Sage Payroll II program, a list of all the people employed by Dragon and details of the rates of income tax and National Insurance deductions that are used. You will find these useful to refer to at times.

This course was written in the Summer of 1992 and the rates of income tax and National Insurance contributions used are those that applied then. If you are using these lessons after 5th April 1993 you will necessarily be using out of date rates of deductions. Some of the forms produced by the Inland Revenue or Department of Social Security may also have changed. Nevertheless, the method of running a computerised payroll is not likely to vary much and it is this that is important; the computer will look after the calculations if you look after the entries.

At the end of each lesson after Lesson Three is a summary of the payroll for the whole firm. *Before moving on to the next lesson you should check carefully that your figures agree with the ones provided here.* If they don't match you have made a mistake somewhere. You will always be able to identify which person or persons' figures are wrong so you will know where to look more closely for an error. If you have made a mess of one month's entries and you want to start that month again it is possible to load into the computer the figures that were correct at the end of the previous month.

Typographical Conventions

As you work your way through this course there will be times when you are reading information about payroll procedure. Such information will be given using this type face.

⇨ At other times you will be instructed on how to operate the computer. These instructions are given in this type face. You should endeavour to do *exactly* as stated.

You should not be operating the computer while reading paragraphs that use this typeface.

Italics are used to emphasise ideas that are particularly important. **Bold characters** are used for items that appear on the computer screen, keyboard names such as **Escape** or **Enter** and information that has to be keyed in.

Conventions of Gender

When referring to a particular employee it has been possible to use he or she, him or her. With more general comments the author has chosen to use he or him irrespective of the possible sex of an employee. This avoids the tedious 'he or she' that would add length but not clarity to an explanation. It is hoped that this shorthand will not cause offence.

Multiple or Single User

If you are a student at a training establishment you should move on to the section entitled **Starting the Sage Payroll Program** on page Intro - 7.

If you are responsible for the computer on which this training material will be used you first need to install the Sage Sterling Payroll II program.

Installing the Sage Sterling Payroll II Program

The basic steps necessary to get going are: (a) install Sage Sterling Payroll II in a directory called **PAY** *on drive C*, (b) copy a number of files from the floppy disk supplied with the course into a sub-directory within the **PAY** directory and (c) load the opening set of payroll records. All this can be done semi-automatically.

⇨ If you already have a copy of any Sage Sterling program on the computer at present you must follow the instructions in thie box below and in the box on page Intro - 4. If you do not already have such a program disregard these instructions.

At the moment your existing Sage program is probably activated by entering SAGE at the C:> system prompt. The file that starts the program must be saved and this is going to be done by renaming it.

⇨ At **C:>** type **REN SAGE.BAT SAGEONE.BAT** and press **Enter.**

You should now find that entering SAGE at the C:> system prompt will not activate the existing Sage program but that entering SAGEONE will do so.

⇨ Load the Sage Sterling Payroll II program *on drive C* by following the instructions given in your Sage Manual but when the computer suggests that the Destination Path should be **\SAGE** reject this by typing **\PAY** and pressing **Enter.** This will install the Payroll program in a directory called PAY. During this process you will be asked to enter the name of the company involved. You should key in:

DRAGON ENTERPRISE LIMITED
UNIT 10
MANNHEAD TRADING ESTATE
RENCHESTER
RR9 9RR

⇨ During the installation procedure you will be asked to enter the number of employees. Key in **30** and press **Enter.**

You will now find that entering the word **SAGE** at the **C:>** system prompt will bring the newly installed payroll program on to the screen. This is not what is wanted so:

⇨ At **C:>** type **REN SAGE.BAT PAY.BAT** and press **Enter.**

⇨ At **C:>** type **REN SAGEONE.BAT SAGE.BAT** and press **Enter.**

You should now find that entering **SAGE** at the **C:>** prompt causes the original Sage program to run while entering **PAY** will activate the Payroll II program that you have just installed.

Where to Keep the Payroll Records

It is recommended that if you have sole use of the payroll program you should keep your records on the hard disk. If more than one person will be using the program as would be the case at a training establishment the records should be kept on a floppy disk in drive A.

If floppy disks are to be used for the records the following installation procedure must be followed. If they are to be kept on the hard disk this is not needed and you can move straight on to the section entitled **Loading the Payroll Records Supplied** on page Intro - 6.

Installation Procedure

⇨ At the system prompt **(C:\PAY>)** key in the word **Install** and press **Enter** twice. You are presented with these options.

```
           SAGE SOFTWARE INSTALLATION ROUTINE

           A).  Install Terminal
           B).  Install Printer
           C).  Install Drive Letters
           D).  Edit settings

           Q).  Abandon the program
           X).  Exit from program

           Which Option ?
```

⇨ Choose **C). Install Drive Letters**. Press **C, C, Enter, A** to complete the screen as shown below (assuming that your hard disk is C drive and the floppy disk is A drive).

```
Select your disk drive configuration:

A). Single floppy drive
B). Double floppy drive
C). Hard disk drive

X). Return to Main Menu



Which drive is your hard disk ?
Drive Letter: C

Which drive is your floppy disk ?
Drive Letter: A
```

⇨ Press **Enter**.

This will return you to the **Sage Software Installation Routine** menu.

⇨ Choose **D Edit Settings** and a new list of options will appear that are not displayed here.

⇨ Choose **F). Drive Letters**. Change the values on this page to appear as shown below.

```
DRIVE SETTINGS

A). Data Drive / Stock Drive [A=0] [B=1]        0    0    0    0    0
B). Exist Drive / Repgen Drive /
    Spool Drive [A=0] [B=1]                     0    0    0    0    0
C). Hard Disk Option [Off = 0] [On = 1]         0    0    0    0    0
D). One Disk Option  [Off = 0] [On = 1]         0    0    0    0    0
```

⇨ This will involve you in pressing **A** for Line A then pressing **0** and **Enter** five times. Press **B** for Line B then **0** and **Enter** five times etc.

⇨ Press **X** three times until you are returned to the system prompt:

C:PAY>

Loading the Payroll Records Supplied

⇨ Insert the floppy disk labelled **PAYDATA** in drive A.

⇨ If you are going to keep your payroll records on the hard disk type **LOADHARD** and press **Enter.** If you are going to keep your payroll records on a floppy disk in drive A type **LOADFLOP** and press **Enter.**

The effect of this action will be to load a set of files contained on the floppy disk into the C:\PAY\COMPANY0\PAYDATA sub-directory and to bring the Sage Sterling Tutorial Menu on to the screen as shown below.

```
 ———————— Applications ————————   ┌———— Function Key's ————
                                  │
 Load Sage Payroll II Program     │  F1  -
 Load Opening Payroll Records     │  F2  -
 Load Payroll at start of Lesson Three │ F3  -
 Load Payroll at start of April   │  F4  -
 Load Payroll at end of April     │  F5  -
 Load Payroll at end of May       │  F6  -
 Load Payroll at end of June      │  F7  -
 Load Payroll at end of July      │  F8  -
 Load Payroll at end of August    │  F9  -
 Load Payroll at end of September  │  F10 -
 Load Payroll at end of October   │  F11 -
 Load Payroll at end of November  │  F12 - Change Menu
 Load Payroll at end of December   │
 Load Payroll at end of January   │  D   - DOS Command
 Load Payroll at end of February  │  P   - Path/Directory
                                  │
```

This menu can be brought to the screen at any time by entering **PAYROLL** at the **C:>** system prompt.

⇨ Before starting to run the payroll program you must load the opening set of payroll records. (If you are going to keep your payroll records on a floppy disk in drive A insert a blank floppy disk there now.) Move the cursor to **LOAD OPENING PAYROLL RECORDS** and press **Enter.**

The screen will inform you that the file containing the Payroll Records is being exploded either on the hard disk or the floppy disk as required.

If you make any mistakes during the course you can easily reload a correct set of payroll records simply by choosing the appropriate ones from the Tutorial Menu. A word of warning though - you will nearly always have to **Update the Records** immediately after doing this. That instruction may not mean much to you now but by the time you need to understand it you will.

Starting the Sage Payroll Program.

⇨ Move the cursor to **LOAD SAGE PAYROLL II PROGRAM** and press **Enter**.

The name of the company involved, Dragon Enterprise Limited, appears for a few seconds.

⇨ Enter today's date as **060492** and press **Enter**. Type in the password **LETMEIN** (Let me in!). You will be presented with this screen.

```
┌─────────────────────────────────────────────────────────────┐
│  Sage Menu Program        DRAGON ENTERPRISE                   │
└─────────────────────────────────────────────────────────────┘

              ┌────────────────────────────┐
              │                            │
              │    Payroll                 │
              │    Report Generator        │
              │    Utilities               │
              │                            │
              │    Quit                    │
              │                            │
              │                            │
              └────────────────────────────┘
```

⇨ With the cursor highlighting **Payroll** press **Enter**.

⇨ If your payroll records are on a disk in drive A press **Enter** when asked to do so.

⇨ You are now ready to start the course. Disregard the rest of this Introduction and move on to **Lesson One - National Insurance Contributions**.

About the Payroll Records Supplied

There is no need to read this section unless you are having difficulty with installing the files supplied on the floppy disk labelled PAYDATA that accompanies this course.

The floppy disk labelled PAYDATA holds the following compressed files.

PAYOPEN.EXE	to be used at start of Lesson One or Two
STARTPAY.EXE	to be used at start of Lesson Three
MARCH.EXE	can be used at start of April Lesson
APRIL.EXE	payroll records correct at end of April Lesson (but not updated)
MAY.EXE	payroll records correct at end of May Lesson (but not updated)
JUNE.EXE	payroll records correct at end of June (but not updated)
and so on....	

The **LOADHARD** and **LOADFLOP** commands copy these files into the C:\PAY\COM-PANY0\PAYDATA sub-directory. All that is needed to explode these into workable files is to go into that sub-directory and type **APRIL -o** to explode the APRIL.EXE file, **JULY -o** to explode the JULY.EXE file and so on. If the payroll records are to be kept on a floppy disk in drive A the command should be **APRIL -o A:**. This is what the Tutorial Menu does for you automatically.

The Tutorial Menu is also loaded into the same sub-directory but the appearance of the screen is determined by the SYSTM.HRD or SYSTM.FLP file that LOADHARD places in the root directory then naming it SYSTM.PAY. The loading procedure is designed so that computers that are already loaded with this tutorial's companion, *Complete Computerised Accounting using Sage*, can operate both tutorials' menus as required. Entering **PAYROLL** to run this tutorial or **DRAGON** to run the Accounting tutorial have the effect of renaming the SYSTM.PAY or SYSTM.ACC files to SYSTM.DAT so that whichever menu is in use has access to the correct SYSTM file in the root directory.

Lesson One

National Insurance Contributions

In this lesson you will learn about the various deductions that are made from most people's wage packets to pay for the National Insurance scheme. Much of this lesson involves calculations; the arithmetic is not always easy. If you find it confusing, don't worry; many people operate payrolls quite satisfactorily without being able to make these calculations. *If your main concern is to learn how to* run *a payroll program don't get bogged down in the arithmetic of this lesson.* Try to understand the general principles involved and be prepared to leave the computer to do the arithmetic.

It is assumed that you have followed the instructions contained at the end of the Introduction and that you are using a computer with the Sage Payroll II program installed and the employee files either contained on the hard disk or on a floppy disk in drive A.

You should have the Main Menu of the Sage Payroll program on the screen in front of you as shown below.

```
Sage Payroll II          DRAGON ENTERPRISE
```

```
Employee Details
Processing Payroll
Statutory Sick Pay
Statutory Maternity Pay
Government Parameters
Company Details
```

Employee Details

Before investigating the National Insurance contributions themselves you are going to learn something about the employee whose pay you will be calculating.

⇨ The words **Employee Details** should be highlighted. Use the **arrow keys** on the right hand side of the keyboard to move the highlight (cursor) up and down the menu. This is how you select the part of the payroll program that you want to work with. With the highlight over **Employee Details** press **Enter** (or **Return**). This sub-menu is presented to you.

```
┌─────────────────────────────────────────────────────────────┐
│  Sage Payroll II          Employee Details                    │
└─────────────────────────────────────────────────────────────┘
              ┌──────────────────────────────────┐
              │                                  │
              │   Amend Employee Details          │
              │   Add a New Employee              │
              │   Remove an Employee              │
              │   P11 Deduction Card              │
              │   Absence Report                  │
              │                                  │
              └──────────────────────────────────┘
```

⇨ With the cursor highlighting **Amend Employee Details** press **Enter** again and then press **Enter** while **Full Details** is displayed. You are presented with a screen onto which you have to enter some information. By pressing **Enter** now you are accepting the **1** that is offered to you. Do this. The other number that is then offered to you - **30,** can also be accepted by pressing **Enter**. Do this.

Onto the screen appears information about our company's single employee as displayed below.

```
┌─────────────────────────────────────────────────────────────┐
│  Sage Payroll II              Full Details                    │
└─────────────────────────────────────────────────────────────┘


   Employee No. :   1      On HOLD : NO       Start Date : 120777
                                              Leave Date :
       Forenames : John                    Holiday Return :
         Surname : Smith
                                               Tax Code : 2200L
         Address :                        Effective from : 060492
            .. :                            N.I. Number : AG354291A
            .. :                          N.I. Category : A
            .. :                         Contracted-Out : N
                                             SCON Ref. : 0
    Works Number : 000001                 Effective from : 060492
    Payment Type : CW
    Pension Ref. : 0                       Marital Status : S
     Auto SSP/SMP : Y                        Male/Female : M
   Date of Birth : 210948                      Director : N
```

The screen tells us some obvious information about the employee such as name and date of birth together with the details:

Payment Type: CW - Paid by cash weekly

Pension Ref: 0 = Not involved in a pension scheme

Auto SSP/SMP: Y = Yes, Smith is automatically entitled to Statutory Sick Pay (SSP). As a man he does not, of course qualify for Statutory Maternity Pay (SMP).

Smith's Tax Code is **2200L**. This is a very unusual and high tax code. It is being used in this lesson to avoid any Income Tax (PAYE) calculations being made. It has been at this level since 6th April 1992 **(060492).**

Smith's National Insurance No. is given.

Smith's **NI Category** is **A**, i.e. Smith is aged between 16 and 65 and contributes to the State Earnings Related Pension Scheme (SERPS).

⇨ If you press the **down arrow cursor key** when **Director: N** is highlighted or the **Page Down** key at any time you will move on to this page of further information about Smith.

```
┌─────────────────────────────────────────────────────────────────────────┐
│ Reference : 1     Name : John Smith               Pay Type : CW          │
└─────────────────────────────────────────────────────────────────────────┘

    ┌───────────────────────────────────────────────────────────────────┐
    │        Department :   0  : BLANK                                    │
    │     Qualifying Days :  1  : NQQQQQN NQQQQQN NQQQQQN NQQQQQN          │
    └───────────────────────────────────────────────────────────────────┘

    ┌──────── Rates of Pay ────────┐   ┌──────── Adjustments ────────┐
    │                              │   │                             │
    │  2  : Basic Hourly  :  1.0000│   │ 1 : Salary Advance          │
    │  0  : BLANK         :  0.0000│   │ 2 : Salary Refund           │
    │  0  : BLANK         :  0.0000│   │ 3 : Expenses                │
    │  0  : BLANK         :  0.0000│   │ 4 : Additions/Taxed         │
    │  0  : BLANK         :  0.0000│   │ 5 : Union Dues              │
    │                              │   │ 0 : BLANK                   │
    │                              │   │ 0 : BLANK                   │
    │                              │   │ 0 : BLANK                   │
    │                              │   │ 0 : BLANK                   │
    │                              │   │ 0 : BLANK                   │
    └──────────────────────────────┘   └─────────────────────────────┘
```

Disregard **Qualifying Days** for the time being, this will be explained later on.

Rates of Pay tells you that Smith is paid at the rate of **£1** per hour. This value is included at this stage for convenience of calculation rather than realism. Additionally you learn that five types of adjustment may be made to Smith's pay. You will learn more about these adjustments in the next Lesson.

⇨ Press **Page Down** for a further page full of information which has been left blank as it is not relevant at this stage of the course.

⇨ Press **Page Down** again, a further screen of blank information appears. Press **Escape** and you are returned to the first page of details about Smith. Keep pressing **Escape** until you return to the Main Menu.

Government Parameters

Using these basic details about the firm's only employee it is now time to investigate the terms under which the Government imposes contributions by nearly all employees and employers to its National Insurance scheme. National Insurance contributions (NIC's) are made in order to finance benefits when people are out of work either because they are unable to get a job, because they are sick or because they have retired. A part of the NIC's help to finance the National Health Service but the majority of the NHS's income is generated by general taxation.

⇨ With the Cursor highlighting **Government Parameters** press **Enter**. This screen appears.

```
┌─────────────────────────────────────────────────────────────────┐
│  Sage Payroll II         Government Parameters                    │
└─────────────────────────────────────────────────────────────────┘



              ┌─────────────────────────────────────┐
              │                                     │
              │   Tax Bandwidths & Rates            │
              │   NI Bandwidths                     │
              │   NI Categories                     │
              │   NI Rates                          │
              │   SSP Parameters                    │
              │   SSP Rates                         │
              │   SMP Rates                         │
              │                                     │
              │                                     │
              │                                     │
              └─────────────────────────────────────┘
```

⇨ Move the cursor to **NI Categories** and press **Enter**. You are presented with this screen.

```
┌─────────────────────────────────────────────────────────────┐
│  Sage Payroll II              NI Categories                   │
└─────────────────────────────────────────────────────────────┘

                          Category   Contracted
                          letter       -out

                    1 :      A           N
                    2 :      B           N
                    3 :      C           N
                    4 :      C           Y
                    5 :      D           Y
                    6 :      E           Y
                    7 :      X           N
                    8 :                  N
                    9 :                  N
                   10 :                  N
```

Disregarding Category X you notice that there are 6 different categories of people within the National Insurance scheme. The first three categories are concerned with people who have chosen to take part in the State Earnings Related Pension Scheme (SERPS). The second three are used by people who have chosen to *contract out* of the scheme.

Most people will be either category A, i.e. people who have *not contracted out* of SERPS or Category D - people who have *contracted out* of the scheme.

People will only be allowed to contract out if they have arranged with their employers to pay into a company pension scheme. All employed people except those on very low incomes either pay into SERPS or a company or private pension scheme. People who have *not contracted out* of SERPS (in other words those who have *contracted in*) will make higher NIC's than those who are paying for a pension in some other way.

Categories B and E are used for some married women or widows (a diminishing number) who have chosen to pay National Insurance at reduced rate for which, of course, they receive reduced benefits. The employee must obtain a *Certificate of Election* before changing from Category A or D to one of these categories.

Category C applies to women over the age of 60 and men over the age of 65 or to people who have made other arrangements with the Contributions Agency, an executive agency of the Department of Social Security, concerning how they will pay their contributions. These people will not have any NIC's deducted from their salaries by their employers although the employers will have to make some contributions on their behalf. An employee must obtain documentation from the DSS before being allowed to change to Category C.

Smith has contracted in to SERPS.

⇨ Press **Escape** to return to the **Government Parameters** menu. Choose **NI Rates** and press **Enter**. On to the screen appears the following table.

```
┌─────────────────────────────────────────────────────────────────┐
│  Sage Payroll II                    NI Rates                      │
└─────────────────────────────────────────────────────────────────┘

                        Category :  A

           ++++++ BANDS ++++++     Employer's     Employee's
            From        To        < min  > min   < min  > min

            54.00  -   89.99  :    4.60   4.60    2.00   9.00
            90.00  -  134.99  :    6.60   6.60    2.00   9.00
           135.00  -  189.99  :    8.60   8.60    2.00   9.00
           190.00  -  405.00  :   10.40  10.40    2.00   9.00
           405.01  -  excess  :   10.40  10.40    0.00   0.00
```

This tells you that no National Insurance contributions are made by either the employee or the employer where the weekly wage is less than £54.00.

A person earning between £54.00 and £89.99 will contribute 2% of the first £54.00 of their earnings and 9% of the difference between their earnings and £54.00. The employer will pay 4.6% of the total wage.

A person earning between £90.00 and £134.99 will pay in the same manner as described above; 2% on £54.00 and 9% on the wage above £54.00. The employer will pay 6.6% of the entire wage.

And so on.

Running the Payroll

You are now going to pay Smith £53.99. According to the table above Smith should not be stopped any money as National Insurance contributions.

⇨ Press **Escape** until you get back to the Main Menu. Choose **Processing Payroll** by highlighting this and pressing **Enter**. Key in the payroll run date **100492**, (10th April 1992). The screen should appear as shown below.

```
┌─────────────────────────────────────────────────────────────┐
│ Sage Payroll II          Processing Payroll                   │
└─────────────────────────────────────────────────────────────┘
```

```
┌─────────────────────────────────────────────────────────────┐
│                                                               │
│            Payroll Run Date  : (100492)                       │
│                                                               │
│                                                               │
│               Tax week :  1    Tax month :  1                 │
│                                                               │
└─────────────────────────────────────────────────────────────┘
```

```
                Current Tax Year is  92  to  93
```

```
            ┌─────────────────────────────────┐
            │    Is this correct : No Yes     │
            └─────────────────────────────────┘
```

⇨ Press **Y** for **Yes** to confirm that the above information is correct. The screen should changes and you should use the arrow keys to highlight **Weekly** against the word **Process**

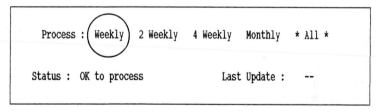

```
┌─────────────────────────────────────────────────────────────┐
│                                                               │
│     Process : ( Weekly )  2 Weekly   4 Weekly   Monthly  * All *│
│                                                               │
│   Status :  OK to process          Last Update :    --        │
│                                                               │
└─────────────────────────────────────────────────────────────┘
```

⇨ There will have been no previous update of the payroll as this is the first week of the year. Press **Enter** and complete the screen as shown below by pressing **Enter** twice.

```
┌─────────────────────────────────────────────────────────────┐
│ Sage Payroll II          Processing Payroll                   │
└─────────────────────────────────────────────────────────────┘

       Lower Employee No.          1            :    1

       Upper Employee No.          30           :    30

            ┌─────────────────────────────────────┐
            │    Clear payments file : No Yes     │
            └─────────────────────────────────────┘
```

⇨ Accept the **No** that is highlighted in **Clear payments file : No Yes** by pressing **Enter** and you are presented with this screen.

```
Sage Payroll II          Processing Payroll


         Enter Payments        Payslips
         Payment Summary       Print Giro's
         Cash Analysis         Print Cheques
         Cheque Analysis       COMPS min-payment
         Giro Analysis         Collector of Taxes
         Average Earnings      Update Records

```

⇨ Accept **Enter Payments** by pressing **Enter** while this is highlighted. Enter **£53.99** as shown below and press **Enter**.

```
Reference : 1     Name : John Smith              Pay Type : CW


Basic Hourly :( 53.9900 )    :    53.99   P.A.Y.E. (TAX) :    0.00
       BLANK :   0.0000   :     0.00
       BLANK :   0.0000   :     0.00   NATIONAL INS. :    0.00
       BLANK :   0.0000   :     0.00
       BLANK :   0.0000   :     0.00

             Pre-Tax Add/n :   0.00   Post-Tax Add/n :    0.00
             Pre-Tax Ded/n :   0.00   Post-Tax Ded/n :    0.00
                   Pension :   0.00

        Statutory Sick Pay :   0.00   NETT PAY (1) :     53.99
    Statutory Maternity Pay :  0.00   Rounding B/F :      0.00

                                      NETT PAY (2) :     53.99
          Total Holiday Pay :  0.00   Rounding C/F :      0.00

        TAXABLE GROSS PAY :   53.99
          TOTAL GROSS PAY :   53.99   TOTAL NETT PAY :   53.99
```

You will notice that there is nothing stopped for tax, of which more later, but nothing stopped for NI contributions which is what you would have expected because Smith is being paid less than the £54.00 *Minimum Earnings Level* at which NIC's start. If Smith is paid one penny more you can expect some deduction.

➪ Using the **arrow keys** move the cursor to the top left hand corner of the screen again. Key in **54** and press **Enter**.

Immediately the NI contribution changes to **£1.08**, i.e. 2% of £54.00. This £1.08 will be deducted from Smith's gross pay of £54.00 to arrive at the net pay of £52.92 shown at the bottom of the screen.

➪ Press the **Page Down** key. Here you will notice the employer's contribution is shown as **£2.48**, i.e. 4.6% of £54.00.

These 2% and 4.6% deductions are the ones displayed in the NI Rates table shown previously.

If Smith was paid £72.00 you would expect the firm to pay 4.6% of £72.00. But Smith's contribution would be more complicated: 2% of £54.00 + 9% of £18.00 (£72.00 - £54.00).

Employer's contribution:	4.6% of £72.00=		£3.31
Smith's contribution:	2% of £54.00 =	£1.08	
	plus 9% of £18.00=	£1.62	
		£2.70	

➪ Press **Page Up** and enter Smith's pay as £72.00 and check that the correct figures appear.

The figures that appear on the screen are slightly different to this. This is because *the Sage Payroll program produces the figures that are used by those people who run their payroll manually.* In order to simplify the task for these people sets of tables are supplied by the Contributions Agency (DSS) and the values of people's earnings are rounded off to the nearest £1 below. This is called a person's *Standard Earnings.* For the purpose of *calculating* a person's NIC though the standard earnings are increased by 50p. Thus a person who earns £72 a week will pay National Insurance contributions as if he was earning £72.50. Likewise people earning £72.99 will pay National Insurance contributions as if they were earning £72.50.

Under these circumstances the calculations become as shown below.

Employer's contribution	4.6% of £72.50 =		£3.33
Smith's contribution	2% of £54.00 =	£1.08	
	9% of £18.50 =	£1.66	
		£2.74	

These figures of £3.33 and £2.74 are the ones that are calculated by Sage.

Not all computerised payroll programs use this method of calculation. Some will simply take the first set of figures that we calculated and arrive at values of £3.31 and £2.70.

At first it might seem that the Sage method of contribution will be unfair to some people. A 'swings and roundabouts' approach is taken. Sometimes a person will gain a couple of pence and sometimes they will lose it.

⇨ Test this yourself by changing Smith's wages from **£72.00** to **£72.50**. There is no change in his or his employer's National Insurance contribution.

⇨ Change it to **£72.99** - still there is no change.

⇨ Change it to **£73.00** and the National Insurance contribution for Smith rises to **£2.83** - an increase of 9p or 9% of the extra £1.00 he is earning. His employer's contribution will rise to £3.38 - an increase of approximately 4.6% of the extra £1.00.

⇨ Increase Smith's salary to **£73.99** - no change in the NI contribution.

⇨ Change it to **£74.00** and his contribution goes up to **£2.92**.

Work out for yourself what National Insurance contributions there would be if Smith earns £84.99. If you need a calculator to do this press F2. and one will appear on the screen for you. To get rid of it just press Escape. When using the screen calculator use the * for multiply and the / for divide.

⇨ Now enter Smith's pay as **£84.99** and check your arithmetic.

Although Smith earns £84.99 the calculation is made as if he had earned £84.50, i.e. rounded to the nearest 50p below.

Employer's contribution	4.6% of £84.50=		£3.89
Smith's contribution	2% of £54.00 =	£1.08	
	9% of £30.50 (£84.50 - £54.00) =	£2.74	
		£3.82	

If Smith was to earn between £135.00 and £189.99 (say £154.00) per week his pay would be in a higher band so the NI contributions would be calculated in the following manner.

Employer's contribution:	8.6% of £154.50 =		£13.29
Smith's contribution:	2% of £54.00 =	£1.08	
	9% of £100.50 (£154.50 - £54.00) =	£9.04	
		£10.12	

⇨ Check this for yourself by entering Smith's pay as £**154.00**.

Now try testing yourself on the arithmetic so far.

Calculate the employee's and employer's contributions at wages of £120.00, £190.80, £304.30 and £410.99. A word of warning though. On earnings in excess of £405.00 the rounding is done to the nearest £ below - not to the 50p intervals. £410.99 will therefore be treated as £410.00.

⇨ When you have done the calculations - and not before - feed these values into the computer and check that your answers are correct.

You should now understand how the National Insurance contributions are made at all levels of earnings. However, we have concerned ourselves so far only with Smith who has contracted in (usually described as not being contracted out) and therefore a Category A employee. Let us see the effect of Smith deciding to contract out of SERPS because he has joined a company pension scheme.

⇨ Press **Escape** until you get back to the Main Menu. Choose **Employee Details - Amend Employee Details - Full Details**. Press **Enter** twice to accept the **1** and **30** that are offered you.

⇨ Move the cursor to **NI Category: A** and change this to **D**. This will result in a menu of Categories appearing on the screen as shown below.

```
┌─────────────────────────────────────────────────────────────────────┐
│   Reference : 1     Name : John Smith              Pay Type : CW      │
└─────────────────────────────────────────────────────────────────────┘


    Employee No. :   1      On HOLD : NO        Start Date : 120777
                                                Leave Date :
      Forenames : John      ┌─────────────────┐ day Return :
        Surname : Smith     │ 1   Category A  │
                            │ 2   Category B  │  Tax Code : 2200L
        Address :           │ 3   Category C  │ ctive from : 060492
             .. :           │ 4   Category C  c/o .I. Number : AG354291A
             .. :           │ 5   Category D  c/o . Category : A
             .. :           │ 6   Category E  c/o racted-Out : N
                            │ 7   Category X  │  SCON Ref. :  0
                            └─────────────────┘ ctive from : 120777
   Works Number : 000001
   Payment Type : CW
   Pension Ref. :  0                         Marital Status : S
   Auto SSP/SMP : Y                            Male/Female : M
  Date of Birth : 210948                         Director : N
```

⇨ Highlight **5 Category D c/o** and press **Enter**. A **SCON Reference** (to be explained later) will appear. Press **Enter** again to accept this. Ensure that the date of this change is **060492** so that your screen looks as is shown below.

```
┌─────────────────────────────────────────────────────────────────────┐
│  Sage Payroll II              Full Details                            │
└─────────────────────────────────────────────────────────────────────┘


      Employee No. :   1      On HOLD : NO        Start Date : 120777
                                                  Leave Date :
           Forenames : John                   Holiday Return :
           Surname : Smith

                                                    Tax Code : 2200L
           Address :                            Effective from : 060492
               .. :                              N.I. Number : AG354291A
               .. :                            N.I. Category : D
               .. :                           Contracted-Out : Y
                                                  SCON Ref. :  1
      Works Number : 000001                   Effective from : 060492
      Payment Type : CW
      Pension Ref. : 0                        Marital Status : S
      Auto SSP/SMP : Y                          Male/Female : M
      Date of Birth : 210948                       Director : N
```

⇨ Press **Escape** and when the word **Post** is highlighted press **Enter**.

⇨ Go back to the Main Menu. Choose **Processing Payroll**. The payroll run date is **100492** again and when you get through to John Smith's screen enter £154.00 as his pay.

His National Insurance is £8.11 and the contribution made by his employer is £9.46. This is different from the situation that we have seen before. When you entered this wage with Smith as a Category A employee the NIC's were £10.12 and £13.29 respectively. This time they are lower because Smith now falls into Category D and pays National Insurance contributions at different rates than he would have done before. Smith is now only paying for sickness benefit, unemployment benefit and a basic pension. Previously, being a not contracted out employee his contributions would have been larger in order to pay for an earnings related pension.

Category D contributions are based on this table.

```
┌─────────────────────────────────────────────────────────────┐
│ Sage Payroll II              NI Rates                        │
└─────────────────────────────────────────────────────────────┘

                    Category :  D      Contracted-Out

        ++++++ BANDS ++++++   Employer's    Employee's
          From       To       < min  > min  < min  > min

          54.00  -   89.99 : 4.60   0.80   2.00   7.00
          90.00  -  134.99 :  6.60   2.80   2.00   7.00
         135.00  -  189.99 :  8.60   4.80   2.00   7.00
         190.00  -  405.00 : 10.40   6.60   2.00   7.00
         405.01  -  excess  : 10.40   6.60   0.00   0.00
```

You notice that the employee still has to pay the basic 2% on the first £54.00 of earnings but his contributions are now 7% rather than 9% on earnings above that. The situation for the employer has changed more dramatically. For a category A employee the employer's contribution is a constant percentage of the earnings. Now, however, the employer will pay, for example, 4.6% on earnings up to £54 but on any earnings between £54.00 and £89.99 only 0.8%.

If an employee earns say £100.00 the employer will pay 6.6% of the first £54 and 2.8% on the remaining £46.50 (£100.50 - £54.00).

Now turn your attention back to John Smith.

⇨ Enter **£54.00** as Smith's salary.

His NI contribution is still £1.08 as before, 2% of £54.00 and the employer's contribution is still £2.48 (4.6% of £54.00).

⇨ However, now give Smith a salary of **£72.00**.

His National Insurance contribution is now £2.37 whereas it was £2.70 when he was a Category A employee.. The employer's contribution is now £2.63 where it was previously £3.31. These figures are calculated as follows.

Employer's contribution:
4.6% of £54.00 =   £2.48
0.8% of £18.50 =   £0.15
TOTAL   £2.63

Smith's contribution:

2% of £54.00 =	£1.08
7% of £18.50 =	£1.29
TOTAL	£2.37

You will notice that the rounding to the nearest 50p does not occur at £54.00 itself but it does occur at all values above this.

Now that you are aware of the various categories and the rates at which people pay you should be able to calculate the National Insurance contribution for any employee at any level of salary once you know the category of that employee.

Try to calculate the contributions made by
  (a) a category B employee earning £150.00,
  (b) a category C (contracted out) employee earning £310.00 and
  (c) a category E employee earning £100.00.

The rates of contribution of the various categories can be found in Appendix 2 at the back of this book.

⇨   Enter these values yourself to see if you were right. The calculations behind these answers are given below.

Answers

(a)

Employer's contribution:
  8.6% of £150.50 =£12.94

Employee's contribution:
  3.85% of £150.50 =   £5.79

(b)

Employer's contribution:

10.4% of £54.00 =	£5.62
6.6% of £256.50 =	£16.93
	£22.55

Employee's contribution:
  0.00% of £310.50 =   £0.00

(c)

Employer's contribution:

6.6% of £54.00 =	£3.56
2.8% of £46.50 =	£1.30
	£4.86

Employee's contribution:

3.85% of £100.50 =	£3.87

Monthly Deductions

All calculations introduced so far have been made on a weekly basis. Some employees though are paid monthly and whilst the principles of their calculations are the same the method is slightly different.

Firstly, it must be recognised that the weekly income bands can be restated as monthly income bands. Here is a comparison of the weekly and monthly figures.

Weekly Bands		Monthly Bands	
54.00 -	89.99	234.00 -	389.99
90.00 -	134.99	390.00 -	584.99
135.00 -	189.99	585.00 -	823.99
190.00 -	405.00	824.00 -	1,755.00
405.01 -	excess	1,755.01 -	excess

You are aware that for calculation purposes all wages are based upon the nearest £ below. Thus wages of £94.00 and £94.99 will both be treated as *standard earnings* of £94.00 but the actual calculation of employer's and employee's contributions will be based on £94.50, i.e. the midway point between these two extremes.

When wages are paid monthly instead of being rounded off to the nearest £ below they are rounded off to the nearest £4 below. Thus wages of £998.00 and £1,001.99 will both be treated as standard earnings of £998.00 but the calculation of contribution will be based on £1,000.00, i.e. the midway point between £998.00 and £1,001.99. You will note that this is £2.00 above the standard earnings. Once again it should be stated that the purpose of this complication is to enable the Sage program to produce the same values as those produced when using the Tax Tables.

It is not immediately obvious to what value a wage of say £761.90 should be rounded down. Should it be £761.00, £760.00, £759.00 or £758.00. Fortunately it is seldom necessary to know but it is possible to find out. It will not be an odd number so that excludes £761.00 and £759.00. It will not be an even number that when divided by 4 produces a whole number so as £760.00 / 4 = exactly £190.00 that excludes £760.00.

The standard earnings is therefore £758.00 and the calculation will be based on a value £2.00 above this, namely £760.00.

Yes, it is complicated - it's all about matching those NI Tables. Be aware though that comparatively few people who run payrolls understand this either because everybody relies on the Tax Tables or their computer to get it right.

⇨ Just one calculation will be made on a monthly basis but to do this you must first go back and choose **Employee Details - Amend Employee Details - Full Details**. Change the **Payment Type** to CM (cash monthly) as shown below. Make sure also that the **NI Category** is **A** as depicted below.

```
┌──────────────────────────────────────────────────────────────────────┐
│  Sage Payroll II              Full Details                             │
└──────────────────────────────────────────────────────────────────────┘

   Employee No. :   1      On HOLD : NO        Start Date : 120777
                                               Leave Date :
       Forenames : John                     Holiday Return :
         Surname : Smith
                                                 Tax Code : 2200L
         Address :                        Effective from : 060492
            ..   :                         N.I. Number  : AG354291A
            ..   :                         N.I. Category : A
            ..   :                         Contracted-Out : N
                                              SCON Ref. :  0
   Works Number : 000001                  Effective from : 060492
   Payment Type : CM
   Pension Ref. : 0                       Marital Status : S
   Auto SSP/SMP : Y                          Male/Female : M
  Date of Birth : 210948                       Director : N
```

⇨ Go into **Processing Payroll**. Enter the date as **300492** and ensure that **Monthly** is highlighted at the bottom of the screen. Press **Enter** and choose **Enter Payments**.

⇨ Enter **£761.90** as shown below.

The NI contribution for Smith is **£52.02** and for the employer **£65.36**.

```
┌────────────────────────────────────────────────────────────────────┐
│ Reference : 1    Name : John Smith              Pay Type : CM        │
└────────────────────────────────────────────────────────────────────┘

    Basic Hourly : 761.9000  :    761.90   P.A.Y.E. (TAX) :      0.00
           BLANK :   0.0000  :      0.00
           BLANK :   0.0000  :      0.00   NATIONAL INS. :    ( 52.02 )
           BLANK :   0.0000  :      0.00
           BLANK :   0.0000  :      0.00

              Pre-Tax Add/n :      0.00   Post-Tax Add/n :      0.00
              Pre-Tax Ded/n :      0.00   Post-Tax Ded/n :      0.00
                    Pension :      0.00
```

```
┌──────────────────────── Employer's ───────────────────────────────┐
│                                                                    │
│  National Ins. :    ( 65.36 )      Pension :      0.00             │
│                                                                    │
└────────────────────────────────────────────────────────────────────┘
```

The calculations of these deductions are:

Employee	2% of £234.00	4.68
	9% of £526.00 (£760 - £234)	47.34
		52.02
Employer	8.6% of £760.00	65.36

A further example of a monthly calculation of NIC appears in Lesson Four - April.

Lesson Two (Income Tax) starts on the facing page.

Lesson Two

Income Tax

In this lesson you will learn how income tax deductions are calculated. Whilst the *principles* of these calculations are fairly straightforward the reality is a good deal more complicated. *If your main concern is to learn how to* run *a payroll program don't get bogged down in the arithmetic of this lesson* - it will be easy to estimate to within a few pence how much tax a person should pay. The first part of this lesson in particular is concerned with getting the calculation right to the nearest penny.

Everybody is allowed to earn a certain amount of money before the Government starts to take a share of his earnings. At the time of writing (April 1992) a single person had an allowance of £3445 per year. Thus a person earning £3445.00 would pay no tax but a person earning £3446.00 would (in theory) pay tax on the £1 that his earnings exceed the *tax threshold.*

In these circumstances:

£3446.00 would be the *Gross Pay*
£3445.00 would be the *Tax Free Pay*
£1.00 would be the *Taxable Pay*

Government Parameters

Before entering a variety of payments for John Smith it is necessary to look a the rates at which the Government levies Income Tax.

⇨ Go into the **Government Parameters - Tax Bandwidths and Rates.**

You are presented with the following screen.

```
┌─────────────────────────────────────────────────────────┐
│ Sage Payroll II      Tax Bandwidths & Rates              │
└─────────────────────────────────────────────────────────┘


        No. of Bandwidths :  2      Basic rate band :   2



           Bandwidth      ++ From ++   +++ To +++   %-tax

       1 :   2000.00          0.01  -   2000.00  : 20.00
       2 :  21700.00       2000.01  -  23700.00  : 25.00  <-- BR band
       3 : * excess *     23700.01  - * excess * : 40.00
```

This tells you that 20% of the first £2,000 of taxable pay will be deducted as income tax. On the next £21,700 worth of taxable pay a rate of 25% will be charged and on any pay in excess of this 40% must be paid.

⇨ Take a printout of this so that you can refer to it during this lesson. This is easily done by pressing the **Pr**(int) **Scr**(een) key. This may involve you in holding down the **shift** key at the same time.

Before studying the effect of changes in the level of pay and of tax codes you must ensure that your records agree with the ones used by the author at this stage.

⇨ Now go back to the Main Menu and into **Employee Details - Amend Employee Details - Full Details**. Press **Enter** twice to accept the **1** and **30** that you are offered.

You need to ensure that your screen looks like the one depicted below.

⇨ Change the payment type to **CW** (Cash weekly).

⇨ Move the cursor to **Tax Code** and change this to **344L**. (You will need to depress the space bar to overwrite the 'L' of 2200L). After pressing **Enter** you are asked **Confirm Amendments: No Yes**. Press **Y** for Yes and you must key in the date of the amendment as **060492** and press **Enter**.

⇨ Change the **N I Category** to **A** if necessary.

⇨ Press **Escape** then **Enter** again to **Post** the information in the records.

```
Sage Payroll II            Full Details

Employee No. :   1      On HOLD : NO        Start Date : 120777
                                            Leave Date :
       Forenames : John              Holiday Return :
        Surname : Smith

         Address :                       Tax Code : 344L
            ..   :                  Effective from : 060492
            ..   :                     N.I. Number : AG354291A
            ..   :                   N.I. Category : A
                                    Contracted-Out : N
                                        SCON Ref. : 0
  Works Number :  000001             Effective from : 060492
  Payment Type :  CW
  Pension Ref. :  0                  Marital Status : S
  Auto SSP/SMP :  Y                    Male/Female : M
  Date of Birth : 210948                   Director : N
```

Running the Payroll

⇨ Go back to the Main Menu and this time choose **Processing Payroll**. The date is **100492**. Choose **Enter Payments**.

Personal allowances are always rounded off to the nearest £ and these are then converted into Tax Codes rounded off to the nearest £10 below. Thus, a person who receives allowances of £3440 or £3449 would be given a Tax Code of 344. The Tax Code doesn't distinguish between these two figures and so the calculations are based upon the assumption that a person with a Tax Code of 344 actually has a personal allowance at the top of this tax band, i.e. £3449.

£3449 per annum divided by 52 = £66.33 per week. It follows therefore that a person earning this amount should not pay any tax.

⇨ Enter **£66.33** as the pay given to John Smith. You notice that the tax that must be paid is **£0.00**. This is depicted in the screen printed below.

```
┌────────────────────────────────────────────────────────────────────┐
│  Reference : 1     Name : John Smith              Pay Type : CW      │
└────────────────────────────────────────────────────────────────────┘

    Basic Hourly :   66.3300  :    66.33   P.A.Y.E. (TAX) :      0.00
           BLANK :    0.0000  :     0.00
           BLANK :    0.0000  :     0.00   NATIONAL INS. :      2.20
           BLANK :    0.0000  :     0.00
           BLANK :    0.0000  :     0.00

            Pre-Tax Add/n :     0.00   Post-Tax Add/n :      0.00
            Pre-Tax Ded/n :     0.00   Post-Tax Ded/n :      0.00
                  Pension : 0.00
        Statutory Sick Pay :     0.00   NETT PAY (1) :       64.13
    Statutory Maternity Pay :    0.00   Rounding B/F :        0.00

                                        NETT PAY (2) :       64.13
          Total Holiday Pay :     0.00  Rounding C/F :        0.00

        TAXABLE GROSS PAY :    66.33
          TOTAL GROSS PAY :    66.33   TOTAL NETT PAY :     64.13
```

Lower Rate Tax (20%)

⇨ Now increase the wage to **£67.33**.

The tax that must be paid on this is £0.20, i.e. 20% of the pay over and above the weekly minimum on which tax has to be paid of £66.33.

You would expect that a person who earns an extra £1.00 would pay an extra £0.20 in tax.

⇨ Enter **£68.33** and prove that this is the case. The tax jumps from 20p to 40p as you expected.

Pay between £67.33 and £68.33 does not increase by 1p for each 5p. As with the National Insurance contributions the Sage program follows the values that appear in the Tax and National Insurance Tables that are used by people who keep their payroll without the aid of a computer. These calculations are all rounded off to the nearest £1. The effect of this is that a wage of £67.32 does not attract any tax but one of £67.33, as you have seen, is taxed at 20p.

Smith will go on paying another 20p on every £1 he earns on the next £2,000 per annum. In other words any pay between £3,449 and £5,449 will attract tax at the rate of 20p in the £. Any pay in excess of £5,449 and below £27,149 (£2,000 + £21,700 + £3,449) will attract tax at the rate of 25p in the £.

£5449 divided by 52 = £104.79 per week. This is the highest rate at which Smith can earn and only be charged tax at the rate of 20p in the £.

⇨ Enter **£104.79** as Smith's basic hourly pay.

The PAYE (Tax) figure becomes **£7.60**. The calculation of this value is this:

Gross wage	104.79
less Tax free pay	66.33
Taxed pay	38.46
20% of £38.00 (£38.46 rounded down to nearest £)	7.60

Standard Rate Tax (25%)

Once Smith's taxable pay (i.e. pay after deduction of allowances) exceeds £2,000 per annum (£38.46 per week) he will start to pay income tax at 25% - not on all his wage but on the part of his taxable pay that exceeds £38.46. When his free pay of £66.33 per week (£3,449 per annum) is taken into account it means he can earn up to £104.79 before starting to pay tax at the standard rate. The calculation of tax above this level though is a little strange. The tax is calculated at 25% on all the taxable pay and then a rebate of 5% on the first £38.46 (equivalent to £2,000 per annum) is deducted from this.

Here is an example.

Gross wage		209.14
less Tax free pay		66.33
Taxable pay		142.81
25% of £142.00	35.50	
less 5% of £38.46	1.93	
Tax due	33.57	

⇨ Enter this wage of £209.14 for yourself and confirm the above calculation.

A wage of £400 would produce a tax calculation as follows:

Gross wage		400.00
less Tax free pay		66.33
Taxable pay		333.67
25% of £333.00	83.25	
less 5% of £38.46	1.93	
Tax due	81.32	

⇨ Enter this wage of £400.00 to confirm the above calculations.

Calculate the tax due on a wage of £378.87.

⇨ Enter this wage of £378.87 to check your arithmetic.

The calculation would be:

Gross wage		378.87
less Tax free pay		66.33
Taxable pay		312.54
25% of £312.00	78.00	
less 5% of £38.46	1.93	
Tax due	76.07	

Higher Tax Rate (40%)

If Smith's taxable pay was to exceed £23,700 per annum (£455.77 pw) - this represents a gross pay of £27,149 per annum, (£3,449 allowance + £2,000 at 20% + £21,700 at 25%) - he must pay tax at the rate of 40% on all earnings in excess of this. Thus a weekly wage of £600 would attract tax as follows.

Gross wage	600.00
less Tax free pay	66.33
Taxable pay	533.67

The first £456 (£23,700 per annum) is taxed in the way described above. The remaining £77.00 (£533.00 - £456.00) is taxed at 40%.

£456 at 25%	114.00
less 5% of £38.46	1.93
	112.07
plus (explained below)	0.04
plus £77.00 at 40%	30.80
Tax due	142.91

The only thing that is odd about the above calculation is the extra £0.04 added near the end. This arises once again because of the Sage program emulating the Tax Table calculations. In the tables, taxable pay of £456 requires PAYE of £112.07, however, at any higher taxable pay that same £456 is taxed at £112.11 - a 4p increase. All of this is a consequence of the rounding off that is done in the tables to make the computation of tax easier when done manually.

⇨ Enter this wage of **£600** for yourself to check the above.

Calculate the tax you would expect Smith to pay if his wage was to be £660.85 per week.

⇨ Enter this wage of **£660.85** to check your calculation.

The calculation would be:

Gross wage		660.85
less Tax free pay		66.33
		594.52
less		456.00
		138.52
Tax on £456.00	112.11	
plus £138.00 @ 40%	55.20	
	167.31	

Changing the Tax Code

You have seen the effect of the 20%, 25% and 40% tax rates on various levels of pay. It is now time to change Smith's taxable allowance to see its effect on the tax he must pay.

At the time of writing this course of lessons married men were given an extra allowance of £1,720 over and above their personal allowance of £3,445, i.e. a total allowance of £5,165. This, of course, will produce a Tax Code of 516. Smith's tax code must now be changed to this figure.

⇨ Go into **Employee Details - Amend Employee Details - Full Details** and enter a new tax code of **516H** as shown below. (The 'H' after 516 indicates that Smith is receiving the married person's allowance.) You will have to confirm this by accepting the **Yes** that is offered and make sure that the effective date of this change is **060492**.

```
┌─────────────────────────────────────────────────────────────────┐
│  Sage Payroll II            Full Details                          │
└─────────────────────────────────────────────────────────────────┘


   Employee No. :   1        On HOLD : NO        Start Date : 120777
                                                 Leave Date :
      Forenames : John                       Holiday Return :
        Surname : Smith
                                                  Tax Code : 516H
        Address :                         Effective from : 060492
             .. :                             N.I. Number : AG354291A
             .. :                           N.I. Category : A
             .. :                          Contracted-Out : N
                                                SCON Ref. : 0
   Works Number : 000001                   Effective from : 060492
   Payment Type : CW
   Pension Ref. : 0                         Marital Status : S
   Auto SSP/SMP : Y                           Male/Female : M
  Date of Birth : 210948                         Director : N
```

⇨ Press **Escape** to post this information.

As in the previous situation, although Smith's tax free pay is £5,165 it will be assumed, for calculation purposes, that he is receiving an allowance of £5,169.

£5,169.00 per annum = £99.40 per week. At any wage below this figure you would not expect Smith to pay any tax.

⇨ Go into **Processing Payroll**, enter the Run Date as **100492** again and enter a payment to Smith of **£99.40**.

No tax is recorded as shown below.

```
┌─────────────────────────────────────────────────────────────────────────┐
│ Reference : 1      Name : John Smith                    Pay Type : CW     │
└─────────────────────────────────────────────────────────────────────────┘

         Basic Hourly :   99.4000  :      99.40    P.A.Y.E. (TAX) :       0.00
                BLANK :    0.0000  :       0.00
                BLANK :    0.0000  :       0.00    NATIONAL INS. :        5.17
                BLANK :    0.0000  :       0.00
                BLANK :    0.0000  :       0.00

                   Pre-Tax Add/n :     0.00    Post-Tax Add/n :       0.00
                   Pre-Tax Ded/n :     0.00    Post-Tax Ded/n :       0.00
                       Pension : 0.00
```

⇨ Now enter a wage of **£100.40** (i.e. an increase of £1.00). No tax is still required.

You would expect Smith to pay 20p in tax. In fact he is not required to pay tax until his pay is £100.58. This odd situation arises, once again, because of Sage producing the same values as the tax tables. Whereas the tax tables show that a tax code of 344 gives tax free pay of £66.33 (£3,449 / 52) it gives no value for a tax code of 516. (The highest tax code contained in the tables is 480.) The code of 516 involves the user in applying a code of 258 twice.

258 gives tax free pay of   £49.79   (£2589 / 52)

                                                x 2

therefore tax free pay for code 516 =   £99.58

(Note how £5169 / 52 is £99.40. The gain to the employee of 18p arises from the allowance being rounded up by £9 twice.)

⇨ Enter a wage of **£100.58**, i.e. £1.00 above the £99.58 level at which no tax would be levied.

The tax due is 20p as shown below.

```
┌──────────────────────────────────────────────────────────────────────┐
│   Reference : 1      Name : John Smith            Pay Type : CW        │
└──────────────────────────────────────────────────────────────────────┘
```

Basic Hourly :	100.5800	:	**100.58**	P.A.Y.E. (TAX) :	**0.20**
BLANK :	0.0000	:	0.00		
BLANK :	0.0000	:	0.00	NATIONAL INS. :	5.26
BLANK :	0.0000	:	0.00		
BLANK :	0.0000	:	0.00		

Pre-Tax Add/n :	0.00	Post-Tax Add/n :	0.00
Pre-Tax Ded/n :	0.00	Post-Tax Ded/n :	0.00
Pension : 0.00			

Statutory Sick Pay :	0.00	NETT PAY (1) :	95.12
Statutory Maternity Pay :	0.00	Rounding B/F :	0.00

⇨ Try entering a wage £35.00 higher, i.e. **£135.58** and you would expect the tax to go up by 20% of £35.00 = £7.00 Do this yourself now and see the tax liability come out at this new figure of **£7.20**.

Tax Codes

Smith's tax code is 516H. The letter(s) after the 516 could be any of **H, L, P, T or V.** These letters indicate the following:

   L - single person's allowance
   H - married person's allowance (in addition to single person's allowance)
   P - age allowance for a single person
   V - age allowance for a married person
   T - used by the Inland Revenue where it is not appropriate to use either suffix L or
      H. This could be for a number of reasons such as:
         A special coding to recover the previous underpayment of tax
         The tax office has identified an underpayment that is to be collected at a
         later stage
         The tax payer has requested that neither L or H is used, thereby not
         advising the employer of his marital status

These letters (or *suffixes)* do not have any effect on the Sage Payroll program calculations.

⇨ Try changing Smith's Tax Code to **516L, 516P, 516T or 516V** and see for yourself that the PAYE figure does not alter.

There are two codes, BR and NT, that will affect the tax that must be paid in the week or month under consideration. More will be explained about these later in the course. Similarly a prefix letter of D or F is occasionally used.

When this course was written it was possible for either the husband or wife to claim the married person's allowance of £1720 or for this to be shared betwen them. It is clear therefore that the act of getting married will have an effect on at least one of the partner's tax liability.

It is the Tax Office that issues tax codes - not the employer. If an employee is given a new tax code by the Tax Office the firm will change the tax code in their computer program as you have already done for Smith and the tax will be calculated automatically at the new rate. The employer cannot change a tax code and must not assume that such a change will be made by the Tax Office.

⇨ Before attempting the rest of the Lesson go to **Employee Details - Amend Employee Details - Full Details** and give Smith a Tax Code of **344L** with effect from **060492**.

Pre-tax and Post -tax Deductions

You are now going to study the effect of further deductions from the employee's earnings. Throughout this section Smith's earnings are taxed at the lower rate of 20%.

⇨ Go into **Processing Payroll** and enter a wage for Smith of **£80.00**. Use the **Print Screen (Prt Scr)** key on your computer to take a printout of this.

```
Reference : 1     Name : John Smith                    Pay Type : CW

      Basic Hourly : 80.0000    :    ( 80.00 )   P.A.Y.E. (TAX) :    ( 2.60 )
             BLANK :  0.0000    :      0.00
             BLANK :  0.0000    :      0.00      NATIONAL INS. :     ( 3.46 )
                  Pre-Tax Add/n :      0.00      Post-Tax Add/n :      0.00
                  Pre-Tax Ded/n :      0.00      Post-Tax Ded/n :      0.00
                       Pension :      0.00

          Statutory Sick Pay :      0.00         NETT PAY (1) :       73.94
      Statutory Maternity Pay :      0.00         Rounding B/F :        0.00

                                                 NETT PAY (2) :       73.94
             Total Holiday Pay :      0.00         Rounding C/F :        0.00

             TAXABLE GROSS PAY :     80.00
               TOTAL GROSS PAY :     80.00      TOTAL NETT PAY :    ( 73.94 )
```

Smith's Net Pay after deduction of **£2.60** tax and **£3.46** National Insurance contribution is **£73.94.** This is the figure against which the following changes will be compared

Non-allowable Deductions

It is now decided that Smith's employers should deduct £2.00 per week from his pay and send this straight to his trade union. It is a fairly painfree way of paying such bills. Paying a trade union subscription does *not* affect Smith's tax liability.

⇨ Press **Page Down** and enter the **£2.00** Union Dues as shown below.

```
 ┌────────────────────────────────────────────────────────────────────────┐
 │  Reference : 1     Name : John Smith              Pay Type : CW          │
 └────────────────────────────────────────────────────────────────────────┘

          Pre-Tax Adjustments      ANP        Post-Tax Adjustments      ANP

   Salary Advance :    0.00  : +YY        Expenses :     0.00   : +NN
    Salary Refund :    0.00  : -YY      Union Dues :     2.00   : -NN
  Additions/Taxed :    0.00  : +YN              ** :     0.00   :
```

⇨ Press **Page Up** or **Escape** and check that Smith's tax and NIC remain as before but that his take home pay has fallen by £2.00 to **£71.94.**

Union dues, in this case, are a post-tax deduction i.e. the union dues are deducted *after* the employee's liability to tax is calculated. Union Dues were defined as a post-tax deduction in the Company Details part of the Sage Payroll II program. Check this now for yourself.

⇨ From the Main Menu choose **Company Details - Adjustment Types** and you will notice that there is a '**N**' against **Union Dues** for **Tax, NI** and **Pen**(sion). In other words these deductions are *not* affected by a Trade Union subscription.

Tax Allowable Deductions

The next change in Smith's circumstances is for him to join a pension scheme. Under the company pension scheme the employee pays 6% of his income towards a pension while the employer adds a further 5%.

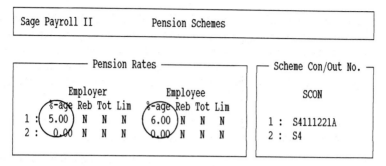

```
┌─────────────────────────────────────────────────────────────────┐
│ Sage Payroll II          Pension Schemes                          │
└─────────────────────────────────────────────────────────────────┘

  ┌──────────── Pension Rates ────────────┐  ┌── Scheme Con/Out No. ──┐
  │                                        │  │                        │
  │     Employer            Employee       │  │         SCON           │
  │   %-age Reb Tot Lim    %-age Reb Tot Lim│ │                        │
  │ 1 : 5.00  N   N   N    6.00  N   N   N  │  │ 1 :  S4111221A         │
  │ 2 : 0.00  N   N   N    0.00  N   N   N  │  │ 2 :  S4                │
  └────────────────────────────────────────┘  └────────────────────────┘
```

This table showing these deductions could be found by going into **Company Details - Pension Schemes** (but don't bother to do this now).

⇨ Go into **Employee Details - Amend Details - Full Details** and change the **Pension Ref** to 1.

```
┌─────────────────────────────────────────────────────────────────┐
│  Sage Payroll II          Full Details                            │
└─────────────────────────────────────────────────────────────────┘


  Employee No. :   1      On HOLD : NO        Start Date : 120777
                                              Leave Date :
       Forenames : John                    Holiday Return :
         Surname : Smith

                                              Tax Code : 344L
    Works Number : 000001              Effective from : 060492
    Payment Type : CW
    Pension Ref. :   1                   Marital Status : S
    Auto SSP/SMP : Y                        Male/Female : M
   Date of Birth : 210948                      Director : N
```

⇨ Go into **Processing Payroll** and leave Smith's earnings of **£80.00** as before but remove the Union Dues as shown below.

```
┌─────────────────────────────────────────────────────────────────┐
│  Reference : 1    Name : John Smith              Pay Type : CW    │
└─────────────────────────────────────────────────────────────────┘


       Pre-Tax Adjustments        ANP      Post-Tax Adjustments       ANP

   Salary Advance : 0.00        : +YY        Expenses :    0.00    : +NN
    Salary Refund :     0.00    : -YY      Union Dues :    0.00    : -NN
  Additions/Taxed :     0.00    : +YN              ** :    0.00    :
```

This time you notice that Smith's income tax deduction has fallen to £1.60 - a reduction of £1.00. When he paid something towards a Trade Union subscription his tax was not affected, when he paid towards his pension his tax went down. The more pension contribution he pays (up to 15% of his earnings) the lower will be his tax bill. In this case he is paying nearly £5.00 (actually £4.80) towards a pension so his tax falls by 20% of £5.00.

Contributions towards an approved *pension scheme are tax deductible, i.e. the tax liability is calculated* after *the pension scheme payment is deducted.*

Smith's take home pay has gone down by £4.80 because of the contributions he makes to a pension scheme and up by £1.00 because his tax bill has gone down for the very same reason. People are not taxed on pension contributions while they are making them but they are taxed on the income they receive from a pension later in life.

Here is a detailed calculation of Smith's take home pay at this stage.

Gross earnings	80.00		
less Pension Contributions		4.80	
Taxable Gross Earnings			75.20
less tax free pay			66.33
= Taxable pay			8.87
Tax at 20% of £8.00		1.60	
NIC (2% of £54.00 + 9% of £26.50)		3.46	
TOTAL DEDUCTIONS	9.86		
Take home pay	70.14		

The adjustment that you have just made is, in fact, unrealistic. Smith has paid into an approved pension scheme yet has remained a Category A employee - he should have been Category D. This alteration was avoided here because it would have created two changes in his deductions; one because of his pension contribution and another because of the change in his NI Category. Because his NI Category did not change Smith's NI contribution has not changed. *National Insurance calculations are not affected by the size of pension contributions.* The *amount* of NIC that he pays is calculated on his *gross earnings* of £80.00 - not his taxable gross earnings of £75.20.

⇨ Before considering the effect of any additions to Smith's pay go back to **Employee Details - Change Employee Details - Full Details** and change Smith's **Pension Ref:** back to **0** as illustrated below.

```
┌─────────────────────────────────────────────────────────────────────┐
│  Sage Payroll II              Full Details                            │
└─────────────────────────────────────────────────────────────────────┘
```

Employee No. :   1   On HOLD : NO   Start Date : 120777
                                                 Leave Date :
        Forenames : John   Holiday Return :
        Surname : Smith

                                                   Tax Code : 344L
                                               Effective from : 060492
     Works Number : 000001   N.I. Number : AG354291A
     Payment Type : CW
     Pension Ref. : 0   Marital Status : S
     Auto SSP/SMP : Y   Male/Female : M
     Date of Birth : 210948   Director : N

Pre-tax and Post-tax Additions

Non-allowable Expenses

It frequently arises that extra money is added to an employee's salary to cover expenses that the employee has incurred in connection with the firm's business. Some firms will provide their employees with working clothing, others will give an allowance to enable the employee to buy his own. People who are regularly away from the firm's premises at lunch time and so forced to use restaurants may be paid an allowance to cover this. If the employee ceases to need these allowances because the nature of his job changes they will simply be removed without there being any adjustment to the person's actual salary. Such payments are usually not allowable against tax. In other words if a person is paid a *round sum allowance* of £10 per week to cover the cost of, for example, meals eaten in restaurants so far as the Inland Revenue is concerned his earnings have risen by £10 and so tax on an extra £10 must be paid. You can see the effect of this on the payroll.

⇨ Go into **Processing Payroll**. On the first page of Smith's details change the **Pension: 4.80** to **0.00**.

```
┌─────────────────────────────────────────────────────────────────────┐
│  Reference : 1     Name : John Smith              Pay Type : CW       │
└─────────────────────────────────────────────────────────────────────┘
```

     Basic Hourly :   80.0000 :   80.00   P.A.Y.E. (TAX) :   2.60
            BLANK :   0.0000 :   0.00
            BLANK :   0.0000 :   0.00   NATIONAL INS. :   3.46
                     Pre-Tax Add/n :   0.00   Post-Tax Add/n :   0.00
                     Pre-Tax Ded/n :   0.00   Post-Tax Ded/n :   0.00
                          Pension :   0.00

⇨ Enter **£10.00** on page two against **Additions/Taxed** and change the **Employer's Pension: 4.00** to **0.00** as shown below.

```
┌────────────────────────────────────────────────────────────────────┐
│  Reference : 1    Name : John Smith              Pay Type : CW       │
└────────────────────────────────────────────────────────────────────┘


        Pre-Tax Adjustments       ANP     Post-Tax Adjustments      ANP

   Salary Advance : 0.00         : +YY       Expenses :    0.00   : +NN
   Salary Refund :       0.00    : -YY      Union Dues :    0.00   : -NN
   Additions/Taxed :   ( 10.00 ) : +YN            ** :    0.00   :
             ** :       0.00     :              ** :    0.00   :
             ** :       0.00     :              ** :    0.00   :
             ** :       0.00     :              ** :    0.00   :
             ** :       0.00     :              ** :    0.00   :
             ** :       0.00     :              ** :    0.00   :
             ** :       0.00     :              ** :    0.00   :
             ** :       0.00     :              ** :    0.00   :

┌──────────────────────── Employer's ─────────────────────────────────┐
│                                                                      │
│     National Ins. :      5.97         Pension  ( 0.00 )              │
│                                                                      │
└──────────────────────────────────────────────────────────────────── ┘
```

When you studied the details of these Adjustment Types (see also Appendix Two at the back of the book) you saw that **Additions/Taxed** had a 'Y' against it so far as Tax and National Insurance Contributions were concerned to indicate that any extra payment made to cover these expenses would affect the PAYE and NIC. However, the 'N' under **Pen**sion showed that the pension would not be affected by such a payment.

⇨ Go back to page one.

Smith's tax has now increased by **£2.00** (20% of the extra £10.00) and his NIC by 90p (9% of the extra £10) above the original figures of £2.60 and £3.46 respectively. Note that his total nett pay is £81.04 - £10.00 more because of the Addition but £2.90 less because of the extra deductions.

```
┌─────────────────────────────────────────────────────────────────┐
│  Reference : 1     Name : John Smith              Pay Type : CW   │
└─────────────────────────────────────────────────────────────────┘
```

Basic Hourly : 80.0000	:	80.00	P.A.Y.E. (TAX) :	4.60
BLANK : 0.0000	:	0.00		
BLANK : 0.0000	:	0.00	NATIONAL INS. :	4.36
BLANK : 0.0000	:	0.00		
BLANK : 0.0000	:	0.00		
Pre-Tax Add/n :		10.00	Post-Tax Add/n :	0.00
Pre-Tax Ded/n :		0.00	Post-Tax Ded/n :	0.00
Pension :		0.00		
Statutory Sick Pay :		0.00	NETT PAY (1) :	81.04
Statutory Maternity Pay :		0.00	Rounding B/F :	0.00
			NETT PAY (2) :	81.04
Total Holiday Pay :		0.00	Rounding C/F :	0.00
TAXABLE GROSS PAY :		90.00		
TOTAL GROSS PAY :		90.00	TOTAL NETT PAY :	81.04

Tax Allowable Expenses

There can be other additions to a person's pay for expenses that the employee has paid
on behalf of the firm and for which he is to be recompensed. A sales representative who
pays for petrol to go into the firm's car and the cost of parking the vehicle is a good
example for which such additions to his salary are a regular feature. These additions to
his pay do not represent any advantage to the employee in a personal sense; only the
firm benefits from such expenditure. In such cases these additions to salary payments are
tax deductible.

⇨ Go into Processing Payroll (if you are not already there) and this time enter
£**20.00** Expenses on page two of Smith's details but remove the £10
Additions/Taxed that was there previously.

```
┌─────────────────────────────────────────────────────────────────┐
│  Reference : 1     Name : John Smith              Pay Type : CW   │
└─────────────────────────────────────────────────────────────────┘
```

Pre-Tax Adjustments		ANP	Post-Tax Adjustments		ANP
Salary Advance :	0.00	: +YY	Expenses :	20.00	: +NN
Salary Refund :	0.00	: -YY	Union Dues : 0.00		: -NN
Additions/Taxed :	0.00	: +YN	** :	0.00	:
** :	0.00	:	** :	0.00	:

You will remember that when you first looked at the details of the Additions and Deductions using the Company Details - Adjustment Types routine Expenses had three 'N's' against it to indicate that such expenses did not have any effect on the Tax, National Insurance or Pension payments that were to be made.

⇨ Go back to page one and you see that Smith's Net Pay has risen by £20.00 above the original value - the full amount of the expense, just as predicted. His tax and NIC have not changed.

```
┌─────────────────────────────────────────────────────────────────────────┐
│  Reference : 1     Name : John Smith                    Pay Type : CW     │
└─────────────────────────────────────────────────────────────────────────┘

      Basic Hourly : 80.0000     :      80.00   P.A.Y.E. (TAX) :     2.60
             BLANK :  0.0000     :       0.00
             BLANK :  0.0000     :       0.00   NATIONAL INS. :     3.46
             BLANK :  0.0000     :       0.00
             BLANK :  0.0000     :       0.00

              Pre-Tax Add/n :     0.00   Post-Tax Add/n :    20.00
              Pre-Tax Ded/n :     0.00   Post-Tax Ded/n :     0.00
                    Pension :     0.00

        Statutory Sick Pay :      0.00   NETT PAY (1) :    93.94
    Statutory Maternity Pay :     0.00   Rounding B/F :     0.00

                                         NETT PAY (2) :    93.94
          Total Holiday Pay :     0.00   Rounding C/F :     0.00

          TAXABLE GROSS PAY :    80.00
            TOTAL GROSS PAY :   100.00   TOTAL NETT PAY :    93.94
```

Summary

Let us now summarise what has been included in these first two lessons so far.

A person's deductions from his pay packet are affected by:

(a) The deductions he *chooses* to make such as pension contributions and trade union subscriptions.

Some of these deductions will be made *before* his PAYE is calculated but some will be made *after* his deductions have been calculated.

National Insurance contributions are always based on the gross pay - no deductions are allowed before this figure is calculated.

(b) Deductions that go to the Government.

There are generally two of these; NIC and PAYE.

National Insurance contributions are always paid by the employer where earnings are above the Lower Earnings Limit (LEL) (at April 1992 this was £54.00 per week). The employee will also pay providing they are not a female over the age of 60 or a male over the age of 65 at the day of payment.

There may also be additions that the employer makes to a pay packet. Such additions could arise because the employee reaps some benefit from them (in which case he will almost always have to pay tax on the addition) or the extra money could simply be a reimbursement for an expense incurred on behalf of the business but paid for by the employee (in which case no tax would be liable).

The wonderful thing about a computerised payroll is that all these calculations are made for you. Nevertheless, whilst computers seldom make mistakes, the figures that are entered may be wrong and employees often want to know how their deductions are calculated. It is therefore desirable that a person with responsibility for running a company's payroll is able to explain just how these deductions are arrived at.

Cumulative Effects.

So far in this course you have only dealt with the first week of the Tax Year. It is now time to see how the deductions for the second and subsequent weeks are calculated but before studying this it is important that you start this section from the position used by the author to illustrate this.

⇨ Go back into **Employee Details - Amend Details - Full Details** and make sure that you start this section with the following information about Smith.

NI Category **A**
Tax Code **344L**
Pension Ref : **0**

⇨ Go back into **Processing Payroll** at **100492**. Record earnings of **£105.00** and ensure that there are no adjustments previously entered on Smith's second page.

Satisfy yourself that these are the details that appear on Smith's payslip.

PAYE:	£7.60	NIC:	£5.71	Net Pay:	£91.69

Until now you have never gone beyond entering data and you have always been able to alter that data. It is now time to assume that Smith has actually been paid this amount. You need to go into the routine for permanently recording this information in the computer records. Do this as shown below.

⇨ Go into **Processing Payroll - Payment Summary.** Accept the **P** for Print that is offered by pressing **Enter** and then **Enter** to start the printer.

This should produce a set of three tables that look like those displayed on the next page.

⇨ If your summaries do not agree with these look again at the entries you have made for Smith, correct them and produce the Payment Summary again. When your tables agree with those displayed here move the cursor down to **Update Records** and press **Enter**. This screen will appear.

```
Sage Payroll II        Update - Check Report
```

```
  Payroll date : 100492   Tax week :  1   Tax month :  1



         Weekly    - ok to update
```

```
Print check report : No Yes
```

⇨ Press **Enter** and you are asked

```
Do you want to BACKUP your data files : No Yes
```

⇨ Press **Enter** to accept the **No.**

⇨ On the next screen press **Y** to indicate that you do want to update the records. When this has been done **Press any key to continue...**

DRAGON ENTERPRISE LIMITED
Tax week 01

P A Y M E N T S   S U M M A R Y - P A R T 1
<< Weekly >>

Date : 100492
Page : 1

Ref.	Total Gross Pay	Taxable Gross Pay	Pre-Tax Addition	Pre-Tax Deduct'n	Pension	P.A.Y.E.	Nat.Ins.	S.S.P.	S.M.P.	Post-Tax Addition	Post-Tax Deduct'n	Amount B/F	Amount C/F	Nett Pay
1	105.00	105.00	0.00	0.00	0.00	7.60	5.71	0.00	0.00	0.00	0.00	0.00	0.00	91.69
1 employees	105.00	105.00	0.00		0.00	7.60	5.71	0.00	0.00	0.00	0.00	0.00	0.00	91.69

P A Y M E N T S   S U M M A R Y - P A R T 2
*** N A T I O N A L   I N S U R A N C E ***

Ref.	Name	Standard Earnings	Total Contr'n	Emp'ees Contr'n	Con/out Earnings	Con/out Contr'n	Employers Nat.Ins.	Pension	Tax Code	Nat.Ins. Category
1	J.Smith	105.00	12.67	5.71	0.00	0.00	6.96	0.00	344L	A
Total values for 1 employees		105.00	12.67	5.71	0.00	0.00	6.96	0.00		

P A Y M E N T S   S U M M A R Y - P A R T 3
*** Y E A R   T O   D A T E ***

Ref.	Name	Total Gross Pay	Taxable Gross Pay	P.A.Y.E.	National Insurance Employees	National Insurance Employers	S.S.P.	S.M.P.	Pension Employee	Pension Employer
1	J.Smith	105.00	105.00	7.60	5.71	6.96	0.00	0.00	0.00	0.00
Total values for 1 employees		105.00	105.00	7.60	5.71	6.96	0.00	0.00	0.00	0.00

It is now time to enter the details for the payment to Smith at the end of the second week of the year.

⇨ Go back to the Main Menu and into **Processing Payroll** and this time enter the date as **170492**. It should indicate that you are working on Tax week 2. Press **Y** to produce this screen.

```
┌─────────────────────────────────────────────────────────────┐
│ Sage Payroll II          Processing Payroll                  │
└─────────────────────────────────────────────────────────────┘

┌─────────────────────────────────────────────────────────────┐
│                                                               │
│            Payroll Run Date  : 170492                         │
│                                                               │
│                                                               │
│                 Tax week :  2    Tax month :  1               │
│                                                               │
└─────────────────────────────────────────────────────────────┘

┌─────────────────────────────────────────────────────────────┐
│                                                               │
│    Process :  Weekly   2 Weekly   4 Weekly   Monthly  * All * │
│                                                               │
│   Status :  OK to process              Last Update :  100492  │
│                                                               │
└─────────────────────────────────────────────────────────────┘
```

⇨ Make sure the cursor is highlighting **Weekly** and press **Enter** three times.

At the bottom of the screen it states:

```
┌─────────────────────────────────┐
│ Clear payments file : No Yes     │
└─────────────────────────────────┘
```

⇨ Answering **Yes** would mean that the pay of £105.00 made to Smith last week would be removed so that you would have to type it in again. Smith's pay is not going to change so just press **Enter** to accept the **No** that is highlighted.

⇨ Choose **Enter Payments**. Smith's page appears like this.

```
┌─────────────────────────────────────────────────────────────────┐
│  Reference : 1      Name : John Smith            Pay Type : CW    │
└─────────────────────────────────────────────────────────────────┘
```

Basic Hourly : 105.0000	:	105.00	P.A.Y.E. (TAX) :	7.80
BLANK : 0.0000	:	0.00		
BLANK : 0.0000	:	0.00	NATIONAL INS. :	5.71
BLANK : 0.0000	:	0.00		
BLANK : 0.0000	:	0.00		
Pre-Tax Add/n :		0.00	Post-Tax Add/n :	0.00
Pre-Tax Ded/n :		0.00	Post-Tax Ded/n :	0.00
Pension :		0.00		
Statutory Sick Pay :		0.00	NETT PAY (1) :	91.49
Statutory Maternity Pay :		0.00	Rounding B/F :	0.00
			NETT PAY (2) :	91.49
Total Holiday Pay :		0.00	Rounding C/F :	0.00
TAXABLE GROSS PAY :		105.00		
TOTAL GROSS PAY :		105.00	TOTAL NETT PAY :	91.49

You will notice that his pay was the same but his tax liability has changed. The reason for this is that tax calculations are always made on a cumulative basis. This involves calculating the *total pay to date* during the year, the *total tax due to date* at that pay day then subtracting the tax that has actually been paid so far from the total tax due. Here is this particular calculation.

	Week 1	Week 2	Total
Total pay	105.00	105.00	210.00
Tax free pay (£3449 / 52 x 2 weeks)			132.65
Taxable pay			77.35
20% tax on £77.00			15.40
less tax already paid			7.60
Tax due in week 2			7.80

This is more than the PAYE in the previous week because the benefit of rounding down the taxable pay to the nearest £ is now spread over two weeks instead of being concentrated in just one. Tax computations are made in this way; calculating the tax liability for the year and subtracting the tax paid to date unless the tax code is a Week 1 or Month 1 as described in Lesson Eight. Further examples of cumulative calculations will be given later in the course.

This is sufficient study of tax calculations - you are now in a position to make the preparations for running a company's payroll for a year.

Do not be deterred if you have found these two lessons difficult. It is an advantage to understand just how the various deductions are calculated but it is not *essential* to being able to run a payroll. The remainder of the course is easier than the part that you have just completed!

Lesson Three (Entering Employee Details) starts on the facing page

Lesson Three

Entering Employee Details

Having made a detailed study of the arithmetic that underlies the deductions from earned income it is time to run a payroll for Dragon Enterprise Limited for a year.

Details of all the employees employed by Dragon Enterprise Limited are given in Appendix Three at the end of the book. It would be possible for you to enter all these details for yourself but this would be very time-consuming. Instead you are going to load the records of the first seventeen employees into the computer and merely add the information about the last three.

⇨ Move the cursor to highlight **LOAD PAYROLL RECORDS AT START OF LESSON THREE** on the Tutorial Menu and press **Enter**.

⇨ Ensure that the Main Payroll Menu is on the screen in front of you.

It will only be necessary for you to enter the information about three extra employees.

⇨ Go into **Employee Details - Add a New Employee**. Press **Enter** twice to accept the 1 and 30 that you are offered. Complete the screen as shown below and when you press **Enter** while the cursor is resting on **Director : Y** a new screen will appear. When you enter the Surname: **Long** on the screen it will be necessary for you to press the spacebar a few times afterwards to overwrite the **O's** that appear on the screen when you start. The same must be done for the Works Number.

```
┌─────────────────────────────────────────────────────────────────────┐
│  Sage Payroll II          Add a New Employee                          │
└─────────────────────────────────────────────────────────────────────┘

  Employee No. :   18      On HOLD : NO        Start Date : 120181
                                                Leave Date :
        Forenames : Rachel                   Holiday Return :
        Surname : Long
                                                  Tax Code : 216L
          Address :                          Effective from : 060492
              .. :                             N.I. Number : TD784445B
              .. :                            N.I. Category : A
              .. :                          Contracted-Out : N
                                                 SCON Ref. : 0
    Works Number : 30                        Effective from : 120181
    Payment Type : GM
     Pension Ref. : 0                         Marital Status : S
     Auto SSP/SMP : Y                           Male/Female : F
    Date of Birth : 150642                        Director : Y
```

```
┌────────────────────────────────────────────────────────────────────┐
│ Reference : 18    Name : Rachel Long              Pay Type : GM      │
└────────────────────────────────────────────────────────────────────┘
```

```
┌────────────────────────────────────────────────────────────────────┐
│        Department : 3    : Management                                │
│     Qualifying Days :   1  : NQQQQQN NQQQQQN NQQQQQN NQQQQQN         │
│                                                                      │
└────────────────────────────────────────────────────────────────────┘
```

```
┌──────── Rates of Pay ────────┐   ┌───── Adjustments ─────┐
│                              │   │                       │
│  1 : Monthly Pay  : 2500.0000│   │  1 : Salary Advance   │
│  4 : Bonus        :    1.0000│   │  2 : Salary Refund    │
│  0 : BLANK        :    0.0000│   │  3 : Expenses         │
│  0 : BLANK        :    0.0000│   │  4 : Additions/Taxed  │
│  0 : BLANK        :    0.0000│   │  5 : Union Dues       │
│                              │   │                       │
└──────────────────────────────┘   └───────────────────────┘
```

⇨ When you get to the end of the adjustments section press **Enter** and a third screen will appear. Alternatively, after entering adjustment No. 5 you can simply press the **Page Down** key. Complete this third screen as shown below.

```
┌────────────────────────────────────────────────────────────────────┐
│ Reference : 18    Name : Rachel Long              Pay Type : GM      │
└────────────────────────────────────────────────────────────────────┘
```

```
┌──────────────────── Banking Information ────────────────────┐
│                                                             │
│           Bank name : Coopers Bank                          │
│    Branch Address 1 : King Street                           │
│         Address 2 : Benton                                  │
│                                                             │
│     Branch Sort Code : 65-16-12                             │
│                                                             │
│       Account Name : R. Long                                │
│     Account Number : 78782456                               │
│                                                             │
└─────────────────────────────────────────────────────────────┘
```

```
┌─ Previous Employment (P45) ─┐   ┌───── Current Employment ─────┐
│                             │   │                              │
│ Taxable Gross Pay :   0.00  │   │ Gross Pay for NI :    0.00   │
│        Tax Paid :     0.00  │   │     Rounding C/F :    0.00   │
│                             │   │                              │
└─────────────────────────────┘   └──────────────────────────────┘
```

⇨ When this page is complete press **Enter** and you will be presented with a new screen for employee No. 18. You need to press the **F10** key twice, once to get back to the first screen and then to say you want to move onto another employee. You are given the opportunity of posting it which you accept by pressing **Enter** and the first page for the next employee appears on the screen. The details for the other two employees are given by the screen images below.

```
┌──────────────────────────────────────────────────────────────────────────┐
│  Sage Payroll II          Add a New Employee                               │
└──────────────────────────────────────────────────────────────────────────┘

   Employee No. :   19      On HOLD : NO          Start Date : 191077
                                                  Leave Date :
          Forenames : Kirstie                 Holiday Return :
            Surname : Farmer
                                                    Tax Code : 344L
            Address :                         Effective from : 060492
                 .. :                            N.I. Number : GR133645A
                 .. :                          N.I. Category : A
                 .. :                         Contracted-Out : N
                                                   SCON Ref. :  0
   Works Number : 42                          Effective from : 120181
   Payment Type : GM
   Pension Ref. :  0                          Marital Status : S
   Auto SSP/SMP : Y                              Male/Female : F
   Date of Birth : 230933                          Director : N

┌──────────────────────────────────────────────────────────────────────────┐
│  Reference : 19    Name : Kirstie Farmer              Pay Type : GM         │
└──────────────────────────────────────────────────────────────────────────┘

┌──────────────────────────────────────────────────────────────────────────┐
│       Department : 1    : Printshop                                         │
│   Qualifying Days :  1  : NQQQQQN NQQQQQN NQQQQQN NQQQQQN                    │
└──────────────────────────────────────────────────────────────────────────┘

┌───────── Rates of Pay ─────────┐    ┌───── Adjustments ─────┐
│                                │    │                       │
│   1 : Monthly Pay  : 1100.0000 │    │  1 : Salary Advance   │
│   2 : Basic Hourly :    7.0500 │    │  2 : Salary Refund    │
│   4 : Bonus        :    1.0000 │    │  3 : Expenses         │
│   0 : BLANK        :    0.0000 │    │  4 : Additions/Taxed  │
│   0 : BLANK        :    0.0000 │    │  5 : Union Dues       │
│                                │    │                       │
└────────────────────────────────┘    └───────────────────────┘
```

```
Reference : 19    Name : Kirstie Farmer            Pay Type : GM
```

```
──────────────── Banking Information ────────────────

              Bank name : Midfield Bank
       Branch Address 1 : Arch Street
              Address 2 : Renchester

       Branch Sort Code : 12-12-33

           Account Name : K. Farmer
         Account Number : 33351212
```

```
── Previous Employment (P45) ──      ──── Current Employment ────

Taxable Gross Pay :      0.00        Gross Pay for NI :      0.00
         Tax Paid :      0.00        Rounding C/F :          0.00
```

```
Sage Payroll II          Add a New Employee
```

```
Employee No. :   20      On HOLD : NO        Start Date : 191077
                                             Leave Date :
   Forenames : John                       Holiday Return :
     Surname : Nibbs
                                                Tax Code : 516H
     Address :                          Effective from : 060492
          .. :                             N.I. Number : WW773334A
          .. :                           N.I. Category : A
          .. :                          Contracted-Out : N
                                              SCON Ref. : 0
Works Number : 67                       Effective from : 191077
Payment Type : GM
Pension Ref. : 0                        Marital Status : M
Auto SSP/SMP : Y                          Male/Female : M
Date of Birth : 220470                        Director : N
```

```
Reference : 20    Name : John Nibbs              Pay Type : GM
```

```
      Department : 1    : Printshop
  Qualifying Days :   1  : NQQQQQN NQQQQQN NQQQQQN NQQQQQN
```

```
┌──────── Rates of Pay ─────────┐   ┌──── Adjustments ────┐
│                               │   │                     │
│  1 : Monthly Pay      :  870.0000 │  1 : Salary Advance  │
│  2 : Basic Hourly     :    5.5800 │  2 : Salary Refund   │
│  3 : Time and a half  :    8.9700 │  3 : Expenses        │
│  4 : Bonus            :    1.0000 │  4 : Additions/Taxed │
│  0 : BLANK            :    0.0000 │  5 : Union Dues      │
│                               │   │                     │
└───────────────────────────────┘   └─────────────────────┘
```

```
Reference : 20    Name : John Nibbs              Pay Type : GM
```

```
┌──────────────────── Banking Information ────────────────────┐
│                                                             │
│         Bank name : Midfield Bank                            │
│  Branch Address 1 : Arch Street                              │
│         Address 2 : Renchester                               │
│                                                             │
│  Branch Sort Code : 12-12-33                                 │
│                                                             │
│      Account Name : J. Nibbs                                 │
│    Account Number : 26549812                                 │
│                                                             │
└─────────────────────────────────────────────────────────────┘
```

```
┌─ Previous Employment (P45) ─┐   ┌──── Current Employment ────┐
│                             │   │                            │
│ Taxable Gross Pay :   0.00  │   │ Gross Pay for NI :   0.00  │
│          Tax Paid :   0.00  │   │      Rounding C/F :   0.00 │
│                             │   │                            │
└─────────────────────────────┘   └────────────────────────────┘
```

⇨ When you have completed entering the information for these three employees go back to the Main Menu.

In case any of these employees is off sick in the near future it is desirable to enter their *past* absences through sickness. The computer will then know what Statutory Sick Pay they are entitled to. There are, in fact, only absences to be entered for Farmer (19).

⇨ Go into **Statutory Sick Pay - Initialise SSP Diary** and enter **19** as the **Lower** and **Upper Employee No.**. Enter the dates as shown on the printout below. When you enter **A** against **Type**, meaning that this is legitimate absence owing to illness, you will be invited to **Block Fill** the dates involved. Accept the **Yes**. The dates of the absence the previous Autumn will be recorded.

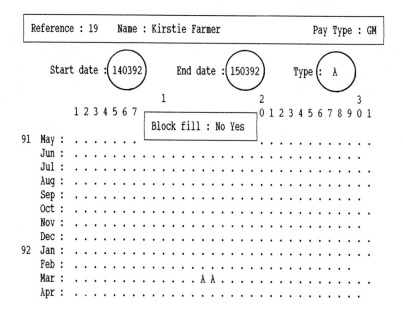

⇨ Press **Escape** three times to get back to the initial menu.

An Overview

You are now in a position to start running the payroll for the year commencing April 1992 but before doing so it is useful to realise the relationship between all the information that is in the computer and from which the monthly payroll will be run.

Some of the information is decided by the Government. This can be found in **Government Parameters**. It includes things like PAYE deduction rates and NIC categories. This information will usually only change once a year (after Budget Day) and will not be changed at all during this course.

Some of the information is decided by the firm. This can be found in **Company Details**. It includes things like pension scheme details and methods of pay such as 'per hour' or 'per month'. This information will seldom change and it is only when the firm introduces superannuation, Save as You Earn and Payroll Giving schemes that you will be required to make such changes during the following lessons..

Some of the information is specific to each employee. This can be found in **Employee Details**. It will include such things as the person's NI category, the hourly or monthly rate of pay and the department in which that person works. The information will change quite often e.g. if a person gets a pay rise, joins a pension scheme or has his tax code changed. You will make a number of such changes during the following lessons.

Each month, when the payroll is run, the pay for each employee needs to be entered, their absences recorded and so on. This you will do using the part of the program called **Processing Payroll**. This is what you will spend most of your time doing.

During nearly every month of the year for which you will be running the payroll you will be required to make some changes. Try to be aware of where, in the Sage Payroll II program, you are making the changes.

Lesson Four (April) starts on the facing page.

Lesson Four

Month One - April

Running the Payroll

You are now in a position to run the first payroll. Ensure that you are using the employee records that you completed in Lesson Three or, if you are not happy with these, choose LOAD PAYROLL AT START OF APRIL from the Tutorial Menu.

The Government's tax year starts on the 6th April so to tie in with this we are starting this course with the April payroll run.

⇨ Choose **Processing Payroll** from the Main Menu and key in the Payroll Run Date as **300492** (30th April 1992). Press **Y** to indicate that it is correct and the screen changes to this.

```
┌─────────────────────────────────────────────────────────────┐
│  Sage Payroll II        Processing Payroll                   │
│                                                              │
└─────────────────────────────────────────────────────────────┘

┌─────────────────────────────────────────────────────────────┐
│                                                              │
│         Payroll Run Date  : 300492                           │
│                                                              │
│                                                              │
│               Tax week :  4    Tax month :  1                │
│                                                              │
└─────────────────────────────────────────────────────────────┘

┌─────────────────────────────────────────────────────────────┐
│                                                              │
│     Process :  Weekly   2 Weekly   4 Weekly   Monthly  * All *│
│                                                              │
│   Status :  OK to process          Last Update :    --       │
│                                                              │
└─────────────────────────────────────────────────────────────┘
```

The bottom half of this screen indicates that it is possible to run the payroll **Weekly, Fortnightly**, every **4 Weeks** or every calendar **Month** - or you could run **All** of them at the same time.

⇨ Dragon Enterprise Limited only pays its employees at the end of the month so move the cursor to **Monthly**.

Against **Status** appears **O.K. to Process** and against **Last Update** no date appears at all. This is the first month of the year so there are no records of any previous payments for the year entered in the system at the moment.

⇨ Press **Enter** and accept the **1** and **30** that appear on the screen by pressing the **Enter** key twice. Press **Enter** a third time where it says **Clear Payments File: No Yes** and you are presented with the Processing Payroll menu.

```
┌────────────────────────────────────────────────────────────┐
│  Sage Payroll II          Processing Payroll                │
│                                                              │
└────────────────────────────────────────────────────────────┘
```

```
┌─────────────────────────────────────────────────┐
│                                                   │
│     Enter Payments        Payslips                │
│     Payment Summary       Print Giro's            │
│     Cash Analysis         Print Cheques           │
│     Cheque Analysis       COMPS min-payment       │
│     Giro Analysis         Collector of Taxes      │
│     Average Earnings      Update Records           │
│                                                   │
└─────────────────────────────────────────────────┘
```

⇨ Accept **Enter Payments** by pressing **Enter**.

⇨ The first screen for Fred Adams, employee No. 1 appears. The cursor will be flashing in the top left hand corner against **Monthly Pay**. Key in **1** to indicate that Adams is paid one month's pay and press **Enter**. You notice that the £**720** monthly pay that he receives appears immediately to the right. His NIC is £**48.42**.

You will remember that when you entered the information about the last three employees using the Employee Details - Add a New Employee routine you had to type in the Monthly, Hourly, Time and a Half and Bonus rates of pay. It is from this record that the information is retrieved to include on the page you are now working on.

The PAYE and National Insurance contributions are calculated automatically as you have already learned.

⇨ Press **F10** to move on to the next employee. You are presented with a similar screen for James Joyce, employee No. 2. Key in **1** for 1 month's pay.

Joyce is paid the same amount as Adams. However, this time there is no National

Insurance contribution. The reason for this is that Joyce is a pensioner. He was born in 1925 and has supplied Dragon with a Certificate of Age Exemption from Paying National Insurance. This is the documentation that qualifies Joyce as a Category C (contracted in) employee.

⇨ Press **F10** to move on to the next employee. Enter **1** against **Monthly Pay** and so on through all the employees until you have done this for all 20 people.

*Throughout the Sage Sterling Payroll II program pressing **F10** will move you on to the next employee, pressing **F9** will move you back to the previous employee.*

After entering the pay for John Nibbs you will be returned to the Processing Payroll sub-menu.

Whilst the majority of employees are paid by Giro some of them, Nos. 1, 2, 9 and 10 are paid in cash. This, of course, means that Dragon's wages office must go to the bank to collect the necessary notes and coins at the end of each month. How many notes and coins of each denomination are required for each employee and therefore the total for all the employees who are paid on a cash basis is calculated by the computer program.

⇨ Move the cursor to **Cash Analysis** and press **Enter**. Accept the **P** that is offered you on the next screen and press **Enter** again when you are sure that the printer is switched on and on-line. You should have a printout that is self explanatory. An abbreviated copy of this is displayed below.

```
DRAGON ENTERPRISE LIMITED                 Cash Analysis
Tax (Week-04 Month-01)

Ref. Employee name   Nett pay   #50     #20     #10     #5      #1     Totals
---- -------------- --------- ------- ------- ------- ------- ------- ---------
   1 F.Adams          572.00      11       1       0       0       2        14
   2 J.Joyce          657.00      13       0       0       1       2        16
   9 A.Ball           707.00      14       0       0       1       2        17
  10 M.English        653.00      13       0       0       0       3        16
                                ------- ------- ------- ------- ------- ---------
            Quantities :-            51       1       0       2       9        63
                                ======= ======= ======= ======= ======= =========
            Values     :-       2550.00   20.00    0.00   10.00    9.00   2589.00
```

⇨ Go back to **Enter Payments** in the Processing Payroll Menu and look at Fred Adams' first screen. It appears below.

```
┌─────────────────────────────────────────────────────────────────────┐
│  Reference : 1      Name : Fred Adams                Pay Type : CM     │
└─────────────────────────────────────────────────────────────────────┘
```

Monthly Pay :	1.0000	:	720.00	P.A.Y.E. (TAX) :	99.66
Basic Hourly :	0.0000	:	0.00		
Time and a half :	0.0000	:	0.00	NATIONAL INS. :	48.42
Bonus :	0.0000	:	0.00		
BLANK :	0.0000	:	0.00		
Pre-Tax Add/n :			0.00	Post-Tax Add/n :	0.00
Pre-Tax Ded/n :			0.00	Post-Tax Ded/n :	0.00
Pension :			0.00		
Statutory Sick Pay :			0.00	NETT PAY (1) :	571.92
Statutory Maternity Pay :			0.00	Rounding B/F :	0.00
				NETT PAY (2) :	571.92
Total Holiday Pay :			0.00	Rounding C/F :	0.08
TAXABLE GROSS PAY :			720.00		
TOTAL GROSS PAY :			720.00	TOTAL NETT PAY :	572.00

You will notice that the Net Pay to which Adams is entitled amounts to £571.92. For the ease of making up the pay packets though Dragon rounds all such payments off to the nearest £1 above. Adams is therefore going to receive £572.00 and the 8p extra that he is being paid will be deducted from next month's payslip. Similar situations arise with the other employees who are paid in cash. The remaining employees are paid by Bank Giro.

⇨ Press **Escape** to go back to the Processing Payroll menu and choose **Giro Analysis** from the Processing Payroll Menu and press **Enter** and once again **Enter** twice more in order to get a printout of these bank giro payments. A printout of this appears on the next page and should be self-explanatory.

⇨ From the Processing Payroll menu choose **Payment Summary**. Using the usual routine produce a summary of the April payroll run. This should look like the one that is printed on the three pages following the Giro Analysis.

```
DRAGON ENTERPRISE LIMITED                    Giro Analysis
Tax (Week-04 Month-01)
```

Ref.	Employee name	Nett pay	Bank name / Sort Code	Bank Address	Account Name
3	G.Rose	670.74	Midfield Bank 121233	Arch Street Renchester	G. Rose 33380934
4	J.Gieves	670.74	Midfield Bank 121233	Arch Street Renchester	J. Gieves 23784491
5	B.King	822.72	Barland Bank 010532	May Road Benton	B. KIng 23986343
6	W.Lansdown	987.54	Midfield Bank 121233	Arch Street Renchester	W. Lansdown 99734563
7	A.Fisher	1089.54	Eastern Bank 091043	High Road Renchester	A. Fisher 33982487
8	C.Young	941.34	Midfield Bank 121233	Arch Street Renchester	C. Young 22324567
11	M.Perkins	571.92	Eastern Bank 091043	High Road Renchester	M. Perkins 4562782
12	P.Corke	607.92	Eastern Bank 091043	High Road Renchester	P. Corke 27893345
13	R.Reagan	1699.68	Midfield Bank 121233	Arch Street Renchester	R. Reagan 20202011
14	W.Tasker	670.74	Barland Bank 010532	May Road Benton	W. Tasker 32145123
15	J.Wilson	471.38	Barland Bank 010532	May Road Benton	J. Wilson 39902334
16	D.Carver	1868.19	Midfield Bank 121233	Arch Street Renchester	D. Carver 22248971
17	W.Bridges	706.74	Coopers Bank 651612	King Street Benton	W. Bridges 28978712
18	R.Long	1876.99	Coopers Bank 651612	King Street Benton	R. Long 78782456
19	K.Farmer	822.72	Midfield Bank 121233	Arch Street Renchester	K. Farmer 33351212
20	J.Nibbs	706.74	Midfield Bank 121233	Arch Street Renchester	J. Nibbs 26549812

```
                    ============
Grand Total :-         15185.64
```

DRAGON ENTERPRISE LIMITED

Tax month 01

Date : 300492
Page : 1

P A Y M E N T S   S U M M A R Y - P A R T 1

<< Monthly >>

Ref.	Total Gross Pay	Taxable Gross Pay	Pre-Tax Addition	Deduct'n	Pension	P.A.Y.E.	Nat.Ins.	S.S.P.	S.M.P.	Post-Tax Addition	Deduct'n	Amount B/F	C/F	Nett Pay
1	720.00	720.00	0.00	0.00	0.00	99.66	48.42	0.00	0.00	0.00	0.00	0.00	0.08	572.00
2	720.00	720.00	0.00	0.00	0.00	63.66	0.00	0.00	0.00	0.00	0.00	0.00	0.66	657.00
3	870.00	870.00	0.00	0.00	0.00	137.16	62.10	0.00	0.00	0.00	0.00	0.00	0.00	670.74
4	870.00	870.00	0.00	0.00	0.00	137.16	62.10	0.00	0.00	0.00	0.00	0.00	0.00	670.74
5	1100.00	1100.00	0.00	0.00	0.00	194.66	82.62	0.00	0.00	0.00	0.00	0.00	0.00	822.72
6	1350.00	1350.00	0.00	0.00	0.00	257.16	105.30	0.00	0.00	0.00	0.00	0.00	0.00	987.54
7	1450.00	1450.00	0.00	0.00	0.00	246.16	114.30	0.00	0.00	0.00	0.00	0.00	0.00	1089.54
8	1100.00	1100.00	0.00	0.00	0.00	158.66	0.00	0.00	0.00	0.00	0.00	0.00	0.00	941.34
9	870.00	870.00	0.00	0.00	0.00	101.16	62.10	0.00	0.00	0.00	0.00	0.00	0.26	707.00
10	870.00	870.00	0.00	0.00	0.00	217.50	0.00	0.00	0.00	0.00	0.00	0.00	0.50	653.00
11	720.00	720.00	0.00	0.00	0.00	99.66	48.42	0.00	0.00	0.00	0.00	0.00	0.00	571.92
12	720.00	720.00	0.00	0.00	0.00	63.66	48.42	0.00	0.00	0.00	0.00	0.00	0.00	607.92
13	2300.00	2300.00	0.00	0.00	0.00	458.66	141.66	0.00	0.00	0.00	0.00	0.00	0.00	1699.68
14	870.00	870.00	0.00	0.00	0.00	137.16	62.10	0.00	0.00	0.00	0.00	0.00	0.00	670.74
15	500.00	500.00	0.00	0.00	0.00	0.00	28.62	0.00	0.00	0.00	0.00	0.00	0.00	471.38
16	2500.00	2500.00	0.00	0.00	0.00	631.81	0.00	0.00	0.00	0.00	0.00	0.00	0.00	1868.19
17	870.00	870.00	0.00	0.00	0.00	101.16	62.10	0.00	0.00	0.00	0.00	0.00	0.00	706.74
18	2500.00	2500.00	0.00	0.00	0.00	623.01	0.00	0.00	0.00	0.00	0.00	0.00	0.00	1876.99
19	1100.00	1100.00	0.00	0.00	0.00	194.66	82.62	0.00	0.00	0.00	0.00	0.00	0.00	822.72
20	870.00	870.00	0.00	0.00	0.00	101.16	62.10	0.00	0.00	0.00	0.00	0.00	0.00	706.74
20 employees	22870.00	22870.00	0.00	0.00	0.00	4023.88	1072.98	0.00	0.00	0.00	0.00	0.00	1.50	17774.64
1	2	3	4	5	6	7	8	9	10	11	12	13	14	15

4 - 6

DRAGON ENTERPRISE LIMITED
Tax month 01

Date : 300492
Page : 2

PAYMENTS SUMMARY - PART 2

<< Monthly >>

| Ref. | Name | Standard Earnings | *** NATIONAL INSURANCE *** | | | | Employers | | Tax Code | Nat.Ins. Category |
			Total Contr'n	Emp'ees Contr'n	Con/out Earnings	Con/out Contr'n	Nat.Ins.	Pension		
1	F.Adams	718.00	110.34	48.42	0.00	0.00	61.92	0.00	344L	A
2	J.Joyce	0.00	61.92	0.00	0.00	0.00	61.92	0.00	516V	C
3	G.Rose	870.00	152.79	62.10	0.00	0.00	90.69	0.00	344L	A
4	J.Gieves	870.00	152.79	62.10	0.00	0.00	90.69	0.00	344L	A
5	B.King	1098.00	197.02	82.62	0.00	0.00	114.40	0.00	344L	A
6	W.Lansdown	1350.00	245.91	105.30	0.00	0.00	140.61	0.00	344L	A
7	A.Fisher	1450.00	265.31	114.30	0.00	0.00	151.01	0.00	516H	A
8	C.Young	0.00	114.40	0.00	0.00	0.00	114.40	0.00	516V	C
9	A.Ball	870.00	152.79	62.10	0.00	0.00	90.69	0.00	516H	A
10	M.English	0.00	90.69	0.00	0.00	0.00	90.69	0.00	BR	C
11	M.Perkins	718.00	110.34	48.42	0.00	0.00	61.92	0.00	344L	A
12	P.Corke	718.00	110.34	48.42	0.00	0.00	61.92	0.00	516H	A
13	R.Reagan	1756.00	380.86	141.66	0.00	0.00	239.20	0.00	516H	A
14	W.Tasker	870.00	152.79	62.10	0.00	0.00	90.69	0.00	344L	A
15	J.Wilson	498.00	61.62	28.62	0.00	0.00	33.00	0.00	NT	A
16	D.Carver	0.00	0.00	0.00	0.00	0.00	0.00	0.00	189L	A
17	W.Bridges	870.00	152.79	62.10	0.00	0.00	90.69	0.00	516H	A
18	R.Long	0.00	0.00	0.00	0.00	0.00	0.00	0.00	216L	A
19	K.Farmer	1098.00	197.02	82.62	0.00	0.00	114.40	0.00	344L	A
20	J.Nibbs	870.00	152.79	62.10	0.00	0.00	90.69	0.00	516H	A
Total values for 20 employees		14624.00	2862.51	1072.98	0.00	0.00	1789.53	0.00		
		16	17	18	19	20	21	22	23	24

DRAGON ENTERPRISE LIMITED

Tax month 01

Date : 300492
Page : 3

PAYMENTS SUMMARY - PART 3

<< Monthly >>

Y E A R   T O   D A T E

Ref.	Name	Total Gross Pay	Taxable Gross Pay	P.A.Y.E.	National Insurance Employees	National Insurance Employers	S.S.P.	S.M.P.	Pension Employee	Pension Employer
1	F.Adams	720.00	720.00	99.66	48.42	61.92	0.00	0.00	0.00	0.00
2	J.Joyce	720.00	720.00	63.66	0.00	61.92	0.00	0.00	0.00	0.00
3	G.Rose	870.00	870.00	137.16	62.10	90.69	0.00	0.00	0.00	0.00
4	J.Gieves	870.00	870.00	137.16	62.10	90.69	0.00	0.00	0.00	0.00
5	B.King	1100.00	1100.00	194.66	82.62	114.40	0.00	0.00	0.00	0.00
6	W.Lansdown	1350.00	1350.00	257.16	105.30	140.61	0.00	0.00	0.00	0.00
7	A.Fisher	1450.00	1450.00	246.16	114.30	151.01	0.00	0.00	0.00	0.00
8	C.Young	1100.00	1100.00	158.66	0.00	114.40	0.00	0.00	0.00	0.00
9	A.Ball	870.00	870.00	101.16	62.10	90.69	0.00	0.00	0.00	0.00
10	M.English	870.00	870.00	217.50	0.00	90.69	0.00	0.00	0.00	0.00
11	M.Perkins	720.00	720.00	99.66	48.42	61.92	0.00	0.00	0.00	0.00
12	P.Corke	720.00	720.00	63.66	48.42	61.92	0.00	0.00	0.00	0.00
13	R.Reagan	2300.00	2300.00	458.66	141.66	239.20	0.00	0.00	0.00	0.00
14	W.Tasker	870.00	870.00	137.16	62.10	90.69	0.00	0.00	0.00	0.00
15	J.Wilson	500.00	500.00	0.00	28.62	33.00	0.00	0.00	0.00	0.00
16	D.Carver	2500.00	2500.00	631.81	0.00	0.00	0.00	0.00	0.00	0.00
17	W.Bridges	870.00	870.00	101.16	62.10	90.69	0.00	0.00	0.00	0.00
18	R.Long	2500.00	2500.00	623.01	0.00	0.00	0.00	0.00	0.00	0.00
19	K.Farmer	1100.00	1100.00	194.66	82.62	114.40	0.00	0.00	0.00	0.00
20	J.Nibbs	870.00	870.00	101.16	62.10	90.69	0.00	0.00	0.00	0.00
	Total values for 20 employees	22870.00	22870.00	4023.88	1072.98	1789.53	0.00	0.00	0.00	0.00
		25	26	27	28	29	30	31		

The Payment Summary

Study these three printouts carefully before reading any further. There are a number of features of Dragon's payroll that can be gleaned from such a study. Each column has been given a letter at the bottom for reference during the following explanation.

Part 1

This part lists the values that will appear on each employee's payslip. Gross Pay (Col 2) is the total amount being paid by Dragon to each of its employees. This will *include*, to be introduced later in the course, the values for Pre-Tax (Col 4) and Post-Tax (Col 11) Additions, Statutory Sick Pay (Col 9) and Statutory Maternity Pay (Col 10). The amount the employee actually gets will be this value less the PAYE (Col 7), the NIC (Col 8) and any Pre-Tax (Col 5) and Post-Tax (Col 12) deductions after being adjusted, if the employee is paid in cash, for any money brought forward (overpaid) from the previous week (Col 13) and any small overpayment during the current week (Col 14).

Part 2

Part Two contains information about Dragon's contribution towards its employees' National Insurance contributions (and, later in the course, pensions). You will remember from Lesson One that National Insurance contributions are based on the nearest £ below for weekly paid employees and the nearest £4 below for monthly paid employees. The Standard Earnings (Col 16) are these rounded down figures. The values in Column 18 are the same as in Column 8 in Part 1 but to these must be added the NIC's made by the employer as listed in Column 21. Columns 23 and 24 are self-explanatory.

Part 3

Part Three lists some cumulative figures for the year. As this is the first month all these figures will also appear in Parts 1 and 2; Col 25 is the same as Col 2, Col 26 = Col 3, Col 27 = Col 7, Col 28 = Col 8 and Col 29 = Col 21. Next month you will be able to see more clearly the cumulative nature of the values in Part Three.

Specific Employees

Five employees, Nos. 2, 8, 10, 16 and 18 display no standard earnings in the National Insurance table. The first three of these, Joyce (2), Young (8) and English (10) are all pensioners and therefore not required to make National Insurance contributions themselves. In spite of their having passed normal retirement age however, Dragon is still required to make National Insurance contributions in their name.

Carver (16) and Long (18) are the directors of the company and as such their National

Insurance contributions are assessed in a different way. Ordinary employees (i.e. not directors) are assumed to be earning at a more or less steady rate throughout the year so each month's National Insurance contribution is based on that month's earnings. Directors, on the other hand, often obtain their earnings in irregular amounts. Their NIC's are therefore cumulative. This means that their earnings during the first month of the year are too small to make them liable for NIC's - so they pay none. Their month's earnings are being treated as their year's earnings. You will find that in May the extra month's salary will put them into the income group that will involve them in paying NIC's. This will be looked at again at the end of the May payroll run.

English (10) pays more than twice as much P.A.Y.E. as Ball (9) in spite of the fact that they earned the same amount. This arises because of their respective tax codes. Ball's tax code is 516H - the normal allowance for a married man. English's though is BR, or *Basic Rate on everything*. English has retired from one job and receives a good pension from that employer and pays tax on that pension. Because her earnings from Dragon are taxed *on top of* those other earnings she is not entitled to another allowance. She therefore has to pay the basic rate of 25% on all the money she earns from Dragon. She is not entitled to pay tax at 20% on the first £2,000.00 of taxable pay. In this case she pays £217.50 which is 25% of her gross earnings of £870.00.

Wilson (15) is on a much higher salary yet has paid no tax at all. Once again the explanation can be found in her tax code. It is NT, meaning *No Tax* to be deducted. Although Wilson works at Dragon Enterprise Limited this is only on a part-time consultancy basis because she has a number of ways in which she earns money. She is a consultant to one other firm, she writes books and she serves on an industrial arbitration panel. The Inland Revenue has defined her as being self-employed and therefore she is to be taxed not by Pay-as-you-earn but by Schedule D. This involves her in making a report to the Inland Revenue each year about her earnings. She then receives an invoice for her Income Tax. No similar declaration has been made on behalf of the DSS so National Insurance must still be deducted.

Consider the figures for just one employee and satisfy yourself that these are what you would expect based on the Tax and National Insurance tables that you studied in the first part of the course.

Here are the calculations for just one employee William Lansdown (6) - monthly salary £1,350.00.

National Insurance contribution

Employer's contribution   10.4% of £1352.00   £140.61

Employee's contribution	2% of £234.00	£4.68
	9% of £1,118.00 (£1352 - £234)	£100.62
		£105.30

PAYE

Gross wage =	£1,350.00
less Tax free pay (1/12 of £3449)	£287.42
	£1,062.58
Tax £1,062.00 @ 25%	265.50
less 5% of £166.16	£8.34
	£257.16

None of these employees or directors are in a company pension scheme. They have all contracted-in to the SERPS therefore there is no entry in any of the summaries in connection with a pension and there is no deduction from their gross pay before their taxable pay is calculated. Some of the employees will join a pension scheme in Lesson Ten (October) when you will be able to see the effect of this.

Updating the Payroll

There is nothing that you have so far entered that could not be altered or removed. The process of updating the records enters these permanently on your computer disk and they cannot subsequently be changed. You need to bear this in mind. *Once the records have been updated they cannot subsequently be changed.*

⇨ If you are not already at this stage go into **Processing Payroll - Update Records.** You are presented with this screen.

```
┌─────────────────────────────────────────────────────────────┐
│  Sage Payroll II        Update - Check Report                 │
└─────────────────────────────────────────────────────────────┘

    ┌──────────────────────────────────────────────────────┐
    │                                                        │
    │   Payroll date : 300492    Tax week :   4    Tax month :   1 │
    │                                                        │
    │                                                        │
    │             Monthly    - ok to update                  │
    │                                                        │
    │                                                        │
    │                                                        │
    └──────────────────────────────────────────────────────┘

           ┌──────────────────────────────────┐
           │  Print check report : No Yes      │
           └──────────────────────────────────┘
```

⇨ Move the cursor to **Yes** and accept this by pressing **Enter**. Press **Enter** twice more and you are given a printed report of what details the computer intends to record permanently. A copy of this printout is not given here and you will not be required to produce a printout of this **Update Records Report** in later lessons. When this has been done you will revert to this screen that asks if you want to back up (take a copy of) your data files.

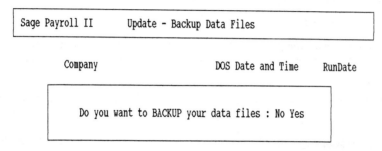

```
Sage Payroll II      Update - Backup Data Files


     Company                         DOS Date and Time    RunDate


         Do you want to BACKUP your data files : No Yes
```

If you were actually keeping these records for a company you must do this. If your computer was to break down and all your payroll records were lost in the computer you would have great difficulty in recreating them. However, as this is a training situation there is no need to keep a record of your files.

⇨ Accept the **No** that you are offered.

The screen changes to include this question

```
     Update Records : No Yes
```

⇨ Move the cursor to **Yes** and press **Enter** (or just press **Y** for **Yes**).

⇨ When the computer has finished its task go back to **Processing Payroll - Payment Summary** and once again take a printout.

Compare these figures with your first printout of the payment Summary. They are not the same. Therefore, beware of taking a Payment Summary *after* updating a particular payroll run. The figures will not be reliable. If, during this course, you produce a Payment Summary that is as different from the one you expect as this one is always check to see if you are producing a summary based upon a period that has already been updated. This is very easily done in a training situation.

In all subsequent lessons the Payment Summary for the month will appear at the end of the lesson to enable you to check your entries.

Lesson Five

Month Two - May

Keeping the Same Entries
Cumulative Effect of PAYE
Paying the Inland Revenue

If you need to reload the payroll records at this stage use LOAD PAYROLL AT END OF APRIL. You must remember to update the records at 300492 before you enter the payments for May.

This will be the simplest month's payroll run that you will make. Nothing is going to change.

⇨ Go into **Processing Payroll** from the Main Menu and enter the date **310592**.

⇨ The screen tells you that this is Tax Month 2. You accept this by pressing **Y** for **Yes**.

⇨ On the lower part of the screen ensure that **Monthly** is highlighted in which case the **Status** will be **O.K. to Process** and the **Last Update** will be **300492**. The screen should look like this.

```
Sage Payroll II          Processing Payroll
```

```
        Payroll Run Date  : 310592


             Tax week :  8    Tax month :  2
```

```
   Process :  Weekly   2 Weekly   4 Weekly   Monthly   * All *

  Status :  OK to process            Last Update :  300492
```

⇨ Press **Enter** and accept the **1** and **30** that you are offered by pressing **Enter** and press **Enter** to accept the **No** against **Clear Payments File**.

⇨ There are no changes so you can immediately print the Payment Summary. Choose this from the menu and produce a printed copy of the figures shown at the end of this lesson.

The Payments Summary

The Cumulative Effect of PAYE

Compare the Payments Summary for this month with the one for last month. All the payments have been the same but if you compare the two PAYE Columns (7) you will notice that for nearly everyone there is a slight variation between the tax this month and the tax payable in April. This arises because of the cumulative nature of the calculations as described on pages 2 - 19 to 2 - 23. Here are the calculations for just one employee, Perkins (11) to illustrate this.

	Month 1	Month 2	Total
Total pay	720.00	720.00	1,440.00
Tax free pay (£3,449 / 12 x 2)			574.83
Taxable pay			865.17
Tax at 25% of £865.00			216.25
less 5% of £333.33 (£2,000 / 12 X 2)			16.67
Tax due to date			199.58
less Tax paid in April			99.66
Tax to be paid during May			99.92

Rounding Up Cash Payments

Another difference has arisen because a few employees last month had their pay rounded up to the nearest £1. These were the employees who were paid in cash - Nos. 1, 2, 9 and 10. You will notice roundings of 8p. 66p and 26p and 50p. This month those values have to be deducted from their pay but there is still a certain rounding that is carried forward again. Here is the effect on Adams' pay.

April net pay =	£571.92
Actual pay =	£572.00
Overpayment =	£0.08
May net pay =	£571.66
less April overpayment =	£0.08
	£571.58
Actual pay =	£572.00
Overpayment =	£0.42

The Non-cumulative Effect of NIC's

A similar comparison of the NIC's (Col 8) does not show the same disparities. With the exception of the two directors the figures for the two months are the same. This is because NIC's are not calculated on a cumulative basis so the same salary will result in the same NIC.

Directors' NIC's

The Directors, Carver and Long, are this month paying significant National Insurance contributions. Their income in April, when viewed as *total annual eanings* was not sufficient to require them to make National Insurance contributions. By the end of two months (April and May) they have already earned enough this year to put them above the National Insurance threshold. Their contributions this month are calculated as follows.

Category A contributions are based on these values that you have already been introduced to.

Category: A

Bands		Employer's		Employee's	
From	To	<min	>min	<min	>min
54.00	89.99	4.60	4.60	9.00	9.00
90.00	134.99	6.60	6.60	2.00	9.00
135.00	189.99	8.60	8.60	2.00	9.00
190.00	405.00	10.40	10.40	2.00	9.00
405.01	excess	10.40	10.40	0.00	0.00

When these weekly figures are multiplied by 52 to arrive at annual values the table becomes like this.

Category: A

Bands		Employer's		Employee's	
From	To	<min	>min	<min	>min
2808.00	4679.99	4.60	4.60	9.00	9.00
4680.00	7019.99	6.60	6.60	2.00	9.00
7020.00	9879.99	8.60	8.60	2.00	9.00
9880.00	21060.00	10.40	10.40	2.00	9.00
21060.01	excess	10.40	10.40	0.00	0.00

Each director's earnings this year to date are £5,000.00 so they fall into the second band. i.e. they have to pay 2% of their first £2,808.00 and 9% of £2,192.00 in National

Insurance contributions while the employers have to pay the equivalent of 6.6% of their
earnings also.

2% of £2,808.00 =	£56.16
9% of £2,192.00 =	£197.28
	£253.44
6.6% of £5,000 =	£330.00

⇨   Assuming that your Payment Summary agrees with the one at the end of
this lesson go through the **Update Records** routine. You do not need to print
the Update Records Check Report.

Paying the Inland Revenue

Make sure that you have updated the records before proceeding with the remainder of
this lesson.

⇨   Go back to the Processing Payroll Menu and choose **Collector of Taxes**.
Complete the screen as shown below.

Sage Payroll II	Collector of Taxes			
Lower Employee No.	1	:	1
Upper Employee No.	30	:	30
By Month/Week/Date/Auto	M	:	M
Enter Tax Month from	1	:	2
Enter Tax Month to	2	:	2
Display, Print or File	D	:	P

Your printer should present you with the printout shown on the following page. This
can be used to complete the Inland Revenue Payslip (Form P30) which you are required
to send to the Accounts Office of the Collector of Taxes along with the PAYE and NIC
contributions that Dragon has had to pay and which Dragon has deducted from its
employee's pay packets. This payment together with the form P30B must reach the
Collector of Taxes by the 19th June. The P30 is shown on page 5 - 6.

DRAGON ENTERPRISE LIMITED   Collector of Taxes (Monthly Payslip Returns)   Date : 310592

Record of deductions from gross National Insurance

	(1) S.S.P.	(2) NIC comp'n	(3) S.M.P.	(4) NIC comp'n	(5) Total Ded.
Weekly	0.00	0.00	0.00	0.00	0.00
2 Weekly	0.00	0.00	0.00	0.00	0.00
4 Weekly	0.00	0.00	0.00	0.00	0.00
Monthly	0.00	0.00	0.00	0.00	0.00
Totals	0.00	0.00	0.00	0.00	0.00

Record of Payments

	(1) Income Tax	(2) Gross N.I.	(3) Total Ded.	(4) Net N.I.	(5) Total Due
Weekly	0.00	0.00	0.00	0.00	0.00
2 Weekly	0.00	0.00	0.00	0.00	0.00
4 Weekly	0.00	0.00	0.00	0.00	0.00
Monthly	4028.46	4029.39	0.00	4029.39	8057.85
Totals	4028.46	4029.39	0.00	4029.39	8057.85

NIC compensation percentage

S.S.P. : 0.00   S.M.P. : 4.50

Employee range   0001 - 0030

Date range   Week : 060592 - 050692   Month : 060592 - 050692

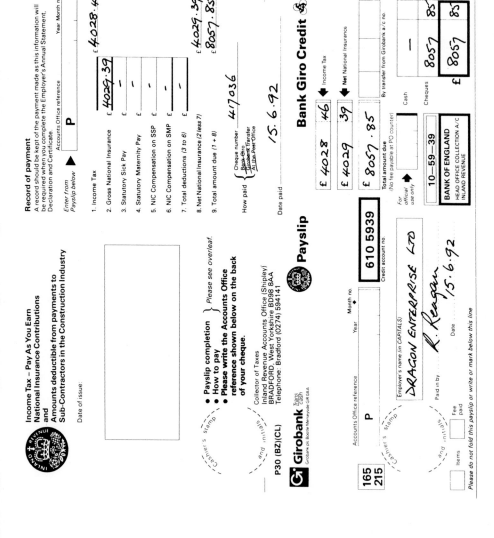

DRAGON ENTERPRISE LIMITED
Tax month 02

P A Y M E N T S   S U M M A R Y   -   P A R T   1
===

<< Monthly >>

Date : 310592
Page : 1

Ref.	Total Gross Pay	Taxable Gross Pay	Pre-Tax Addition	Deduct'n	Pension	P.A.Y.E.	Nat.Ins.	S.S.P.	S.M.P.	Post-Tax Addition	Deduct'n	Amount B/F	C/F	Nett Pay
1	720.00	720.00	0.00	0.00	0.00	99.92	48.42	0.00	0.00	0.00	0.00	0.08	0.42	572.00
2	720.00	720.00	0.00	0.00	0.00	63.92	0.00	0.00	0.00	0.00	0.00	0.66	0.58	656.00
3	870.00	870.00	0.00	0.00	0.00	137.42	62.10	0.00	0.00	0.00	0.00	0.00	0.00	670.48
4	870.00	870.00	0.00	0.00	0.00	137.42	62.10	0.00	0.00	0.00	0.00	0.00	0.00	670.48
5	1100.00	1100.00	0.00	0.00	0.00	194.92	82.62	0.00	0.00	0.00	0.00	0.00	0.00	822.46
6	1350.00	1350.00	0.00	0.00	0.00	257.42	105.30	0.00	0.00	0.00	0.00	0.00	0.00	987.28
7	1450.00	1450.00	0.00	0.00	0.00	246.42	114.30	0.00	0.00	0.00	0.00	0.00	0.00	1089.28
8	1100.00	1100.00	0.00	0.00	0.00	158.92	0.00	0.00	0.00	0.00	0.00	0.00	0.00	941.08
9	870.00	870.00	0.00	0.00	0.00	101.42	62.10	0.00	0.00	0.00	0.00	0.00	0.78	707.00
10	870.00	870.00	0.00	0.00	0.00	217.50	0.00	0.00	0.00	0.00	0.00	0.26	0.00	652.00
11	720.00	720.00	0.00	0.00	0.00	99.92	48.42	0.00	0.00	0.00	0.00	0.50	0.00	571.66
12	720.00	720.00	0.00	0.00	0.00	63.92	48.42	0.00	0.00	0.00	0.00	0.00	0.00	607.66
13	2300.00	2300.00	0.00	0.00	0.00	458.92	141.66	0.00	0.00	0.00	0.00	0.00	0.00	1699.42
14	870.00	870.00	0.00	0.00	0.00	137.42	62.10	0.00	0.00	0.00	0.00	0.00	0.00	670.48
15	500.00	500.00	0.00	0.00	0.00	0.00	28.62	0.00	0.00	0.00	0.00	0.00	0.00	471.38
16	2500.00	2500.00	0.00	0.00	0.00	632.22	253.44	0.00	0.00	0.00	0.00	0.00	0.00	1614.34
17	870.00	870.00	0.00	0.00	0.00	101.42	62.10	0.00	0.00	0.00	0.00	0.00	0.00	706.48
18	2500.00	2500.00	0.00	0.00	0.00	623.02	253.44	0.00	0.00	0.00	0.00	0.00	0.00	1623.54
19	1100.00	1100.00	0.00	0.00	0.00	194.92	82.62	0.00	0.00	0.00	0.00	0.00	0.00	822.46
20	870.00	870.00	0.00	0.00	0.00	101.42	62.10	0.00	0.00	0.00	0.00	0.00	0.00	706.48
20 employees	22870.00	22870.00	0.00	0.00	0.00	4028.46	1579.86	0.00	0.00	0.00	0.00	1.50	1.78	17261.96
	1	2	3	4	5	6	7	8	9	10	11	12	13	14	15

5 - 7

DRAGON ENTERPRISE LIMITED
Tax month 02

Date : 310592
Page : 2

PAYMENTS SUMMARY - PART 2

<< Monthly >>

*** NATIONAL INSURANCE ***

Ref.	Name	Standard Earnings	Total Contr'n	Emp'ees Contr'n	Con/out Earnings	Con/out Contr'n	Employers Nat.Ins.	Employers Pension	Tax Code	Nat.Ins. Category
1	F.Adams	718.00	110.34	48.42	0.00	0.00	61.92	0.00	344L	A
2	J.Joyce	0.00	61.92	0.00	0.00	0.00	61.92	0.00	516V	C
3	G.Rose	870.00	152.79	62.10	0.00	0.00	90.69	0.00	344L	A
4	J.Gieves	870.00	152.79	62.10	0.00	0.00	90.69	0.00	344L	A
5	B.King	1098.00	197.02	82.62	0.00	0.00	114.40	0.00	344L	A
6	W.Lansdown	1350.00	245.91	105.30	0.00	0.00	140.61	0.00	344L	A
7	A.Fisher	1450.00	265.31	114.30	0.00	0.00	151.01	0.00	516H	A
8	C.Young	0.00	114.40	0.00	0.00	0.00	114.40	0.00	516V	C
9	A.Ball	870.00	152.79	62.10	0.00	0.00	90.69	0.00	516H	A
10	M.English	0.00	90.69	0.00	0.00	0.00	90.69	0.00	BR	C
11	M.Perkins	718.00	110.34	48.42	0.00	0.00	61.92	0.00	344L	A
12	P.Corke	718.00	110.34	48.42	0.00	0.00	61.92	0.00	516H	A
13	R.Reagan	1756.00	380.86	141.66	0.00	0.00	239.20	0.00	516H	A
14	W.Tasker	870.00	152.79	62.10	0.00	0.00	90.69	0.00	344L	A
15	J.Wilson	498.00	61.62	28.62	0.00	0.00	33.00	0.00	NT	A
16	D.Carver	5000.00	583.44	253.44	0.00	0.00	330.00	0.00	189L	A
17	W.Bridges	870.00	152.79	62.10	0.00	0.00	90.69	0.00	516H	A
18	R.Long	5000.00	583.44	253.44	0.00	0.00	330.00	0.00	216L	A
19	K.Farmer	1098.00	197.02	82.62	0.00	0.00	114.40	0.00	344L	A
20	J.Nibbs	870.00	152.79	62.10	0.00	0.00	90.69	0.00	516H	A
	Total values for 20 employees	24624.00	4029.39	1579.86	0.00	0.00	2449.53	0.00		
		16	17	18	19	20	21	22	23	24

DRAGON ENTERPRISE LIMITED

Tax month 02

Date : 310592
Page : 3

P A Y M E N T S   S U M M A R Y   -   P A R T   3

<< Monthly >>

Y E A R   T O   D A T E

Ref.	Name	Total Gross Pay	Taxable Gross Pay	P.A.Y.E.	National Insurance Employees	Employers	S.S.P.	S.M.P.	Pension Employee	Employer
1	F.Adams	1440.00	1440.00	199.58	96.84	123.84	0.00	0.00	0.00	0.00
2	J.Joyce	1440.00	1440.00	127.58	0.00	123.84	0.00	0.00	0.00	0.00
3	G.Rose	1740.00	1740.00	274.58	124.20	181.38	0.00	0.00	0.00	0.00
4	J.Gieves	1740.00	1740.00	274.58	124.20	181.38	0.00	0.00	0.00	0.00
5	B.King	2200.00	2200.00	389.58	165.24	228.80	0.00	0.00	0.00	0.00
6	W.Lansdown	2700.00	2700.00	514.58	210.60	281.22	0.00	0.00	0.00	0.00
7	A.Fisher	2900.00	2900.00	492.58	228.60	302.02	0.00	0.00	0.00	0.00
8	C.Young	2200.00	2200.00	317.58	0.00	228.80	0.00	0.00	0.00	0.00
9	A.Ball	1740.00	1740.00	202.58	124.20	181.38	0.00	0.00	0.00	0.00
10	M.English	1740.00	1740.00	435.00	0.00	181.38	0.00	0.00	0.00	0.00
11	M.Perkins	1440.00	1440.00	199.58	96.84	123.84	0.00	0.00	0.00	0.00
12	P.Corke	1440.00	1440.00	127.58	96.84	123.84	0.00	0.00	0.00	0.00
13	R.Reagan	4600.00	4600.00	917.58	283.32	478.40	0.00	0.00	0.00	0.00
14	W.Tasker	1740.00	1740.00	274.58	124.20	181.38	0.00	0.00	0.00	0.00
15	J.Wilson	1000.00	1000.00	0.00	57.24	66.00	0.00	0.00	0.00	0.00
16	D.Carver	5000.00	5000.00	1264.03	253.44	330.00	0.00	0.00	0.00	0.00
17	W.Bridges	1740.00	1740.00	202.58	124.20	181.38	0.00	0.00	0.00	0.00
18	R.Long	5000.00	5000.00	1246.03	253.44	330.00	0.00	0.00	0.00	0.00
19	K.Farmer	2200.00	2200.00	389.58	165.24	228.80	0.00	0.00	0.00	0.00
20	J.Nibbs	1740.00	1740.00	202.58	124.20	181.38	0.00	0.00	0.00	0.00
	Total values for 20 employees	45740.00	45740.00	8052.34	2652.84	4239.06	0.00	0.00	0.00	0.00

Lesson Six (June) starts on the facing page.

Lesson Six

Month Three - June

Salary Increases
Hourly Rates of Pay
Double Entry Book-keeping

If you need to reload the payroll records at this stage use LOAD PAYROLL AT END OF MAY. You must remember to update the records at 310592 before you enter the payments for June.

Dragon Enterprise Limited is experiencing difficult trading conditions and wishes to cut down on its total wage bill. The obvious target for these reductions are the three pensioners employed by the company - Joyce (2), Young (8) and English (10). It is therefore decided that instead of paying these people on a monthly basis their pay will, in future, be calculated on an hourly rate and they will only attend work when asked to do so by the company.

Adjusting the Records

The first task is to change the records for these three employees.

⇨ Go into **Employee Details - Amend Employee Details - Full Details**. You are concerned only with employees between 2 and 10 so enter enter **2** and **10** as shown in the screen below.

Sage Payroll II	Full Details		
Lower Employee No.	1	:	2
Upper Employee No.	2	:	10

⇨ Joyce's second screen should be changed to appear as the one below., i.e. with the monthly pay blanked out.

```
┌─────────────────────────────────────────────────────────────────────┐
│  Reference : 2     Name : James Joyce              Pay Type : CM      │
└─────────────────────────────────────────────────────────────────────┘
```

```
┌─────────────────────────────────────────────────────────────────────┐
│        Department :   1  : Printshop                                  │
│        Qualifying Days :  1  : NQQQQQN NQQQQQN NQQQQQN NQQQQQN         │
│                                                                       │
└─────────────────────────────────────────────────────────────────────┘
```

```
┌──────── Rates of Pay ────────┐   ┌──────── Adjustments ────────┐
│                              │   │                             │
│    0  : BLANK       : 0.0000 │   │  1  : Salary Advance        │
│    2  : Basic Hourly : 4.6400│   │  2  : Salary Refund         │
│    3  : Time and a half : 6.9600│ 3  : Expenses              │
│    4  : Bonus       : 1.0000 │   │  4  : Additions/Taxed       │
│    0  : BLANK       : 0.0000 │   │  5  : Union Dues            │
│                              │   │  0  : BLANK                 │
│                              │   │  0  : BLANK                 │
│                              │   │  0  : BLANK                 │
│                              │   │  0  : BLANK                 │
│                              │   │  0  : BLANK                 │
└──────────────────────────────┘   └─────────────────────────────┘
```

⇨ Press **F10** twice then **Enter** to post this information. The screen for employee no. 3 appears. Press **F10** 5 times to bring you to the screen for Claude Young.

⇨ Change Young's second screen similarly, post this by pressing **F10** twice then **Enter** then **F10** afterwards and you will be moved on to the screen for Mollie English. You should delete her monthly pay rate in the same way. Press **F10** twice and **Enter** to post this information. You will return to the Amend Employee Details sub-menu.

Employees Adams (1) and Rose (3) are to be given a 4% pay rise.

⇨ Go back to the **Main Menu** and choose **Employee Details - Amend Employee Details - Full Details** and accept Employees Nos. 1 and **30** that you are offered and move the cursor on Fred Adams second screen so that it is highlighting £720.00 against 1 : **Monthly Pay**. Press **F2** and the calculator appears on the screen.

⇨ Key in **720*** (the * appears above the 8 on most computers) **104%** and your screen should look like the one depicted below.

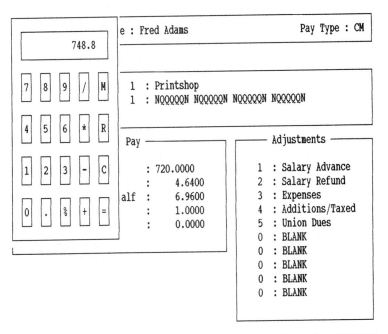

⇨ Now press the **Enter** key and this value of £**748.8** will replace the £**720.00**.

⇨ Press **Enter** again and the cursor will move down one place over the £**4.64** Basic hourly rate. This, of course, must also be changed.

⇨ Use the **F2** key to bring the calculator on to the screen again. Press **C** to clear the value from the calculator then **4.64*104%** and press **Enter**. The value **4.8256** appears. Press **Enter** again.

⇨ Alter the **Time and a half** figure by 4% in the same way to £**7.2384**. When you have completed the alterations to Adams' pay the screen should look like this.

```
┌──────────────────────────────────────────────────────────────────┐
│  Reference : 1    Name : Fred Adams        Pay Type : CM           │
└──────────────────────────────────────────────────────────────────┘
┌─────────── Rates of Pay ───────────┐   ┌──── Adjustments ─────┐
│                                     │   │                      │
│   1 : Monthly Pay      :  748.8000  │   │  1 : Salary Advance  │
│   2 : Basic Hourly     :    4.8256  │   │  2 : Salary Refund   │
│   3 : Time and a half  :    7.2384  │   │  3 : Expenses        │
│   4 : Bonus            :    1.0000  │   │  4 : Additions/Taxed │
│   0 : BLANK            :    0.0000  │   │  5 : Union Dues      │
│                                     │   │                      │
└─────────────────────────────────────┘   └──────────────────────┘
```

Notice that there is no change to the Bonus Rate - this remains at 1.00 because any bonus paid will be in multiples of £1.00.

⇨ The other employee to receive a similar rise is Gladys Rose (3). Post the new rate of pay for Adams (1) and use the **F10** key to get to the record for Rose. Bring the second page of her details on to the screen and alter her pay rates in the same way that you did for Adams until they appear as on the screen below. Post these details.

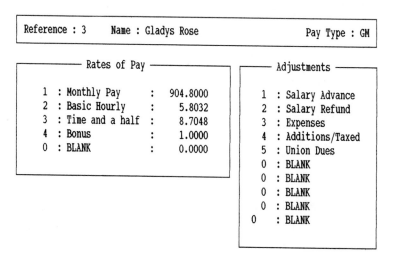

```
Reference : 3      Name : Gladys Rose              Pay Type : GM

┌──────── Rates of Pay ────────┐   ┌──── Adjustments ────┐

   1 : Monthly Pay       :  904.8000      1 : Salary Advance
   2 : Basic Hourly      :    5.8032      2 : Salary Refund
   3 : Time and a half   :    8.7048      3 : Expenses
   4 : Bonus             :    1.0000      4 : Additions/Taxed
   0 : BLANK             :    0.0000      5 : Union Dues
                                          0 : BLANK
                                          0 : BLANK
                                          0 : BLANK
                                          0 : BLANK
                                       0  : BLANK
```

Now that the changes have been made in the Employees' Personal Details the payroll can be run.

Running the Payroll

⇨ Go back to the Main Menu and choose **Processing Payroll**. Enter the date **300692**. This time, where it says **Clear Payments File : No Yes** press **Y**(es) and you will be advised by the screen that the old values are being cleared from the records.

⇨ Go into **Enter Payments** and you will notice that when Adams' first page appears on the screen there are no payments recorded. On the top right hand corner the screen says **PAYE (Tax) -£80.33**. This is an indication that if Adams is not paid any money this month he will be entitled to a refund of £80.33 overpayment of tax. However, Adams is to be paid this month so enter **1** and the screen changes to the one shown below.

```
┌─────────────────────────────────────────────────────────────────────┐
│  Reference : 1     Name : Fred Adams              Pay Type : CM       │
└─────────────────────────────────────────────────────────────────────┘
```

Monthly Pay :	1.0000	:	748.80	P.A.Y.E. (TAX) :	106.92
Basic Hourly :	0.0000	:	0.00		
Time and a half :	0.0000	:	0.00	NATIONAL INS. :	50.94
Bonus :	0.0000	:	0.00		
BLANK :	0.0000	:	0.00		
Pre-Tax Add/n :			0.00	Post-Tax Add/n :	0.00
Pre-Tax Ded/n :			0.00	Post-Tax Ded/n :	0.00
Pension :			0.00		
Statutory Sick Pay :			0.00	NETT PAY (1) :	590.94
Statutory Maternity Pay :			0.00	Rounding B/F :	0.42
				NETT PAY (2) :	590.52
Total Holiday Pay :			0.00	Rounding C/F :	0.48
TAXABLE GROSS PAY :			748.80		
TOTAL GROSS PAY :			748.80	TOTAL NETT PAY :	591.00

⇨ Press **F10** to move on to the next employee and this time the cursor is against the **Basic Hourly**. Joyce has worked **150** hours this month. Enter this, press **F10** you will be presented with the screen for Rose (3).

⇨ Continue to enter one month's pay for each employee who is monthly paid but for Young (8) enter **30** hours and for English (10) enter **45** hours. When you enter the 30 hours for Claude Young you will be asked if a tax refund is to be allowed. i.e. Young's total pay this year is not sufficient to warrant paying the amount of tax that he has *already* paid. There is no reason why he should not receive this refund so press **Y** for **Yes**. When you have finished entering all these details you will returned to the Processing Payroll Menu.

⇨ Print the **Payment Summary** to ensure that it agrees with the one shown at the end of the lesson.

Check the Cumulative PAYE figure for Young (8) in Part 3 (it is highlighted for you) and compare it with the entry in the May Payment Summary. The June value is lower than the May value - by the amount of tax refund that you authorised when entering his pay this month.

⇨ If your records agree with these use the **Update Records** routine.

Double Entry Book-keeping

This section is included for the benefit of those who are studying double entry book-keeping as well as the handling of a payroll. If you are not involved in this you are advised to omit this section and move straight on to the next lesson.

Calculating the money that has to be paid to a firm's employees and what has to be sent to the Inland Revenue is merely the preliminary stage to making such payments and entering them in the firm's ledgers. Whilst there are a number of ways in which firms will keep their accounting records for the payroll Dragon Enterprise Limited chooses to do it in the following way.

When the payroll is run the firm recognises that it has two liabilities: to its employees and to the Inland Revenue. The size of these liabilities can be taken from the Payments Summary. It is going to pay its employees at the end of June £16,215.76 - the total of column 15 in Part 1. However, this understates the size of its liability to the workers for this month's work because during May the firm overpaid them by £1.78 (Col 13) (and so can now claim this back) and now intends to overpay them only £1.43 (Col 14). Its actual liability is therefore £16,215.76 + £1.78 - £1.43 = £16,216.11

It also needs to pay the Inland Revenue the total PAYE that it has deducted (Col 7) and the NIC's that the firm and its employees have made for the month. (Col 17).

These liabilities have arisen as a result of Dragon incurring the expense of employing people, the total cost of which can be found by adding the Gross Pay £21,402.20 (Col 2) and the firm's NIC's made in support of its employees £2,229.71 (Col 21).

Dragon's book-keeper can now make the necessary Journal entries as follows:

	Dr	Cr
Salaries Control		16,216.11
PAYE/NIC Control		7,415.80
Salaries Expenses Account	23,631.91	

When the firm pays its employees it must debit the Salaries Control Accounts to show that this particular liability no longer exist and it must credit its Cash Account with the payments made to the four employees who are paid in cash and credit the Bank Account with the total of the remaining payments. The Cash and Bank figures can be found from the Cash Analysis and the Giro Analysis such as you printed out in the April lesson. When Dragon sends off its cheque to the Inland Revenue for the PAYE and NIC it will debit the PAYE/NIC Control Account and credit its Bank Account.

DRAGON ENTERPRISE LIMITED
Tax month 03

Date : 300692
Page : 1

P A Y M E N T S   S U M M A R Y - P A R T 1

<< Monthly >>

Ref.	Total Gross Pay	Taxable Gross Pay	Pre-Tax Addition	Deduct'n	Pension	P.A.Y.E.	Nat.Ins.	S.S.P.	S.M.P.	Post-Tax Addition	Deduct'n	Amount B/F	C/F	Nett Pay
1	748.80	748.80	0.00	0.00	0.00	106.92	50.94	0.00	0.00	0.00	0.00	0.42	0.48	591.00
2	696.00	696.00	0.00	0.00	0.00	57.67	0.00	0.00	0.00	0.00	0.00	0.58	0.25	638.00
3	904.80	904.80	0.00	0.00	0.00	145.92	64.98	0.00	0.00	0.00	0.00	0.00	0.00	693.90
4	870.00	870.00	0.00	0.00	0.00	137.17	62.10	0.00	0.00	0.00	0.00	0.00	0.00	670.73
5	1100.00	1100.00	0.00	0.00	0.00	194.67	82.62	0.00	0.00	0.00	0.00	0.00	0.00	822.71
6	1350.00	1350.00	0.00	0.00	0.00	257.17	105.30	0.00	0.00	0.00	0.00	0.00	0.00	987.53
7	1450.00	1450.00	0.00	0.00	0.00	246.17	114.30	0.00	0.00	0.00	0.00	0.00	0.00	1089.53
8	211.50	211.50	0.00	0.00	0.00	-63.33	0.00	0.00	0.00	0.00	0.00	0.00	0.00	274.83
9	870.00	870.00	0.00	0.00	0.00	101.17	62.10	0.00	0.00	0.00	0.00	0.78	0.05	706.00
10	251.10	251.10	0.00	0.00	0.00	62.75	0.00	0.00	0.00	0.00	0.00	0.00	0.65	189.00
11	720.00	720.00	0.00	0.00	0.00	99.67	48.42	0.00	0.00	0.00	0.00	0.00	0.00	571.91
12	720.00	720.00	0.00	0.00	0.00	63.67	48.42	0.00	0.00	0.00	0.00	0.00	0.00	607.91
13	2300.00	2300.00	0.00	0.00	0.00	458.67	141.66	0.00	0.00	0.00	0.00	0.00	0.00	1699.67
14	870.00	870.00	0.00	0.00	0.00	137.17	62.10	0.00	0.00	0.00	0.00	0.00	0.00	670.73
15	500.00	500.00	0.00	0.00	0.00	0.00	28.62	0.00	0.00	0.00	0.00	0.00	0.00	471.38
16	2500.00	2500.00	0.00	0.00	0.00	632.22	225.00	0.00	0.00	0.00	0.00	0.00	0.00	1642.78
17	870.00	870.00	0.00	0.00	0.00	101.17	62.10	0.00	0.00	0.00	0.00	0.00	0.00	706.73
18	2500.00	2500.00	0.00	0.00	0.00	623.02	225.00	0.00	0.00	0.00	0.00	0.00	0.00	1651.98
19	1100.00	1100.00	0.00	0.00	0.00	194.67	82.62	0.00	0.00	0.00	0.00	0.00	0.00	822.71
20	870.00	870.00	0.00	0.00	0.00	101.17	62.10	0.00	0.00	0.00	0.00	0.00	0.00	706.73
20 employees	21402.20	21402.20	0.00	0.00	0.00	3657.71	1528.38	0.00	0.00	0.00	0.00	1.78	1.43	16215.76
	1	2	3	4	5	6	7	8	9	10	11	12	13 14	15

DRAGON ENTERPRISE LIMITED
Tax month 03

Date : 300692
Page : 2

P A Y M E N T S   S U M M A R Y – P A R T 2

<< Monthly >>

| Ref. | Name | *** NATIONAL INSURANCE *** | | | | | Employers | | Tax Code | Nat.Ins. Category |
		Standard Earnings	Total Contr'n	Emp'ees Contr'n	Con/out Earnings	Con/out Contr'n	Nat.Ins.	Pension		
1	F.Adams	746.00	115.27	50.94	0.00	0.00	64.33	0.00	344L	A
2	J.Joyce	0.00	59.86	0.00	0.00	0.00	59.86	0.00	516V	C
3	G.Rose	902.00	159.00	64.98	0.00	0.00	94.02	0.00	344L	A
4	J.Gieves	870.00	152.79	62.10	0.00	0.00	90.69	0.00	344L	A
5	B.King	1098.00	197.02	82.62	0.00	0.00	114.40	0.00	344L	A
6	W.Lansdown	1350.00	245.91	105.30	0.00	0.00	140.61	0.00	344L	A
7	A.Fisher	1450.00	265.31	114.30	0.00	0.00	151.01	0.00	516H	A
8	C.Young	0.00	0.00	0.00	0.00	0.00	0.00	0.00	516V	C
9	A.Ball	870.00	152.79	62.10	0.00	0.00	90.69	0.00	516H	A
10	M.English	0.00	11.59	0.00	0.00	0.00	11.59	0.00	BR	C
11	M.Perkins	718.00	110.34	48.42	0.00	0.00	61.92	0.00	344L	A
12	P.Corke	718.00	110.34	48.42	0.00	0.00	61.92	0.00	516H	A
13	R.Reagan	1756.00	380.86	141.66	0.00	0.00	239.20	0.00	516H	A
14	W.Tasker	870.00	152.79	62.10	0.00	0.00	90.69	0.00	344L	A
15	J.Wilson	498.00	61.62	28.62	0.00	0.00	33.00	0.00	NT	A
16	D.Carver	2500.00	540.00	225.00	0.00	0.00	315.00	0.00	189L	A
17	W.Bridges	870.00	152.79	62.10	0.00	0.00	90.69	0.00	516H	A
18	R.Long	2500.00	540.00	225.00	0.00	0.00	315.00	0.00	216L	A
19	K.Farmer	1098.00	197.02	82.62	0.00	0.00	114.40	0.00	344L	A
20	J.Nibbs	870.00	152.79	62.10	0.00	0.00	90.69	0.00	516H	A
Total values for 20 employees		19684.00	3758.09	1528.38	0.00	0.00	2229.71	0.00		
		16	17	18	19	20	21	22	23	24

DRAGON ENTERPRISE LIMITED
Tax month 03

P A Y M E N T S   S U M M A R Y - P A R T 3
=====================================

<< Monthly >>

Date : 300692
Page : 3

Ref.	Name	Total Gross Pay	Taxable Gross Pay	P.A.Y.E.	National Insurance Employees	Employers	S.S.P.	S.M.P.	Pension Employee	Employer
1	F.Adams	2188.80	2188.80	306.50	147.78	188.17	0.00	0.00	0.00	0.00
2	J.Joyce	2136.00	2136.00	185.25	0.00	183.70	0.00	0.00	0.00	0.00
3	G.Rose	2644.80	2644.80	420.50	189.18	275.40	0.00	0.00	0.00	0.00
4	J.Gieves	2610.00	2610.00	411.75	186.30	272.07	0.00	0.00	0.00	0.00
5	B.King	3300.00	3300.00	584.25	247.86	343.20	0.00	0.00	0.00	0.00
6	W.Lansdown	4050.00	4050.00	771.75	315.90	421.83	0.00	0.00	0.00	0.00
7	A.Fisher	4350.00	4350.00	738.75	342.90	453.03	0.00	0.00	0.00	0.00
8	C.Young	2411.50	2411.50	254.25	0.00	228.80	0.00	0.00	0.00	0.00
9	A.Ball	2610.00	2610.00	303.75	186.30	272.07	0.00	0.00	0.00	0.00
10	M.English	1991.10	1991.10	497.75	0.00	192.97	0.00	0.00	0.00	0.00
11	M.Perkins	2160.00	2160.00	299.25	145.26	185.76	0.00	0.00	0.00	0.00
12	P.Corke	2160.00	2160.00	191.25	145.26	185.76	0.00	0.00	0.00	0.00
13	R.Reagan	6900.00	6900.00	1376.25	424.98	717.60	0.00	0.00	0.00	0.00
14	W.Tasker	2610.00	2610.00	411.75	186.30	272.07	0.00	0.00	0.00	0.00
15	J.Wilson	1500.00	1500.00	0.00	85.86	99.00	0.00	0.00	0.00	0.00
16	D.Carver	7500.00	7500.00	1896.25	478.44	645.00	0.00	0.00	0.00	0.00
17	W.Bridges	2610.00	2610.00	303.75	186.30	272.07	0.00	0.00	0.00	0.00
18	R.Long	7500.00	7500.00	1869.05	478.44	645.00	0.00	0.00	0.00	0.00
19	K.Farmer	3300.00	3300.00	584.25	247.86	343.20	0.00	0.00	0.00	0.00
20	J.Nibbs	2610.00	2610.00	303.75	186.30	272.07	0.00	0.00	0.00	0.00
	Total values for 20 employees	67142.20	67142.20	11710.05	4181.22	6468.77	0.00	0.00	0.00	0.00

Lesson Seven (July) starts on the facing page.

Lesson Seven

Month Four - July

Statutory Sick Pay

If you need to reload the payroll records at this stage use LOAD PAYROLL AT END OF JUNE. You must remember to update the records at 300692 before you enter the payments for July.

There will be no changes in the number of hours worked by the employees this month except for two who take time off for sickness. These are numbers 6 and 7.

Statutory Sick Pay Parameters

Before making the entries for absences it will be useful to investigate the terms under which people are paid when they are off sick.

⇨ From the Main Menu go into **Government Parameters - SSP Parameters** and you will be presented with the following screen.

```
 Sage Payroll II          SSP Parameters

                            S.S.P.

         No. of waiting days :  3

       Linkage period (days) :   56

      Max. weeks SSP payable :   28

     Issue transfer form (wks) :   23

        Percentage to reclaim :  80.00

         NIC compensation rate :   0.00
```

The first two items state that no *Statutory Sick Pay (SSP)* will be paid to cover the first three days of an employee's *Period of Incapacity for Work (PIW)* through sickness or injury, but that payment of SSP will be paid after the third day. If a subsequent period of incapacity for work occurs within 56 days (8 weeks) of a previous PIW consisting of four or more days, then it will not be necessary for employees to have SSP withheld from the first three days of a second PIW.

The second pair of items is a statement that the Statutory Sick Pay will only be paid for a maximum of 28 weeks in any 3 consecutive years and that on the 23rd week of illness a form needs to be issued to the employee advising him that entitlement to SSP will soon be withdrawn. After this time if the employee is in need of income he must apply for some other form of benefit from the Benefits Agency (DSS) such as Sickness Benefit.

The final two values indicate that (a) the firm will only be entitled to reclaim 80% of the SSP that it pays to its employees from the Government and that (b) the firm gets no compensation for making this payment. You will see in Lesson Eleven (November) that the Government is more generous to firms making payments for Statutory Maternity Pay.

⇨ Press **Escape** and this time choose **SSP Rates**. You are presented with this screen.

```
┌─────────────────────────────────────────────────────────────────────┐
│  Sage Payroll II          SSP Rates                                   │
└─────────────────────────────────────────────────────────────────────┘


            No. of Thresholds :  2


        Threshold              + From +    ++ To ++    Rate

      1 :   54.00              54.00   -  189.99  :   45.30
      2 :  190.00             190.00   -  excess  :   52.50
```

This tells you that those employees with average weekly earnings below £54.00 per week are not entitled to SSP - because they will not usually make any National Insurance contributions. Those employees whose average earnings fall between £54.00 and £189.99 per week will receive £45.30 per week SSP and those whose average earnings are £190.00 and above will receive £52.50 per week. The amount to which a person is entitled is based on the average weekly earnings of the 8 weeks prior to the start of the PIW.

It is quite common for employers to supplement these basic rates to bring the pay of a sick employee up to their normal weekly or monthly pay.

⇨ Go back to the Main Menu and choose **Statutory Sick Pay - Qualifying Days**. You are presented with this screen.

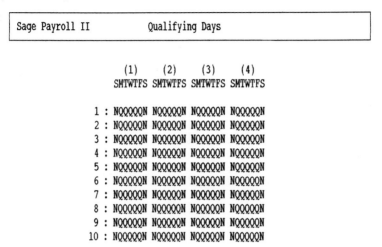

```
Sage Payroll II          Qualifying Days
```

```
                 (1)      (2)      (3)      (4)
               SMTWTFS  SMTWTFS  SMTWTFS  SMTWTFS

        1 :  NQQQQQN  NQQQQQN  NQQQQQN  NQQQQQN
        2 :  NQQQQQN  NQQQQQN  NQQQQQN  NQQQQQN
        3 :  NQQQQQN  NQQQQQN  NQQQQQN  NQQQQQN
        4 :  NQQQQQN  NQQQQQN  NQQQQQN  NQQQQQN
        5 :  NQQQQQN  NQQQQQN  NQQQQQN  NQQQQQN
        6 :  NQQQQQN  NQQQQQN  NQQQQQN  NQQQQQN
        7 :  NQQQQQN  NQQQQQN  NQQQQQN  NQQQQQN
        8 :  NQQQQQN  NQQQQQN  NQQQQQN  NQQQQQN
        9 :  NQQQQQN  NQQQQQN  NQQQQQN  NQQQQQN
       10 :  NQQQQQN  NQQQQQN  NQQQQQN  NQQQQQN
```

Along the top are four separate weeks within a month and under this the individual days; Sunday, Monday Tuesday etc. It is possible to have 10 different arrangements for what qualifies as a day off sick. Dragon however only uses one - the most common. A person who is sick on Sunday or Saturday is not entitled to claim this as a day off work with illness for which payment can be expected. Absence on the other five days of the week does qualify for SSP. It is possible to change these to suit the company. Clearly firms that operate a continental shift system will use a different and more complex arrangement of qualifying days.

⇨ Press **Escape** twice to return to the Main Menu.

Running the Payroll

⇨ Go into **Processing Payroll** and enter the date 310792. The people who are ill this month are Lansdown (6) and Fisher (7). As you go into Processing Payroll enter these two numbers as the **Lower** and **Upper Employee Nos**.

Beware! You will not be able to complete the July payroll immediately after entering these amendments. The payroll can only be updated properly if the first (1) and last (30) employee numbers are entered at this stage. Nevertheless as only two amendments are to be made this is quicker than entering employee nos. 1 and 30 and pressing F10 in order to get to these two people's details.

⇨ Choose **Enter Payments**. When Lansdown's details appear move the cursor to **Statutory Sick Pay** and press **F3**. The screen changes to the one shown below in which you are able to record the first and last day of Lansdown's absence through sickness. Lansdown's absence through illness from 8th October to 4th December 1991 is already on record. You will see from the printout that the dates of absence are from the 3rd July (**030792**) to 12th July (**120792**) and the **A** is included to indicate that the absences are legitimate and therefore qualify for SSP. Press **Enter** and **Y** for **Yes** when asked if you should **Block Fill**. **A**'s appear against the days of his absence at the bottom of the screen.

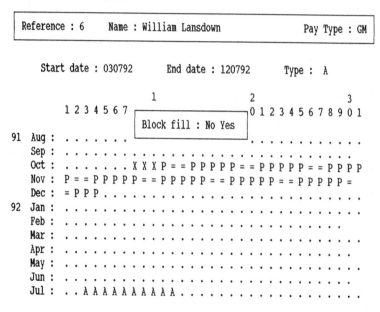

(The A's at the bottom of the screen will not appear until after you have replied **Yes** to **Block Fill**.)

⇨ Press **Escape** and you now see Lansdown's details showing his entitlement to **£31.50** SSP.

```
┌─────────────────────────────────────────────────────────────────┐
│ Reference : 6     Name : William Lansdown        Pay Type : GM    │
└─────────────────────────────────────────────────────────────────┘
```

```
    Monthly Pay :   1.0000  :   1350.00    P.A.Y.E. (TAX) :    265.16
    Basic Hourly :  0.0000  :      0.00
          Bonus :   0.0000  :      0.00    NATIONAL INS. :     107.82

          Statutory Sick Pay :  ( 31.50 )  NETT PAY (1) :     1008.52
    Statutory Maternity Pay :        0.00   Rounding B/F :        0.00

                                            NETT PAY (2) :     1008.52
          Total Holiday Pay :        0.00   Rounding C/F :        0.00

          TAXABLE GROSS PAY :      1381.50
             TOTAL GROSS PAY :     1381.50  TOTAL NETT PAY :    1008.52
```

If matters were left like this Lansdown would be receiving his monthly pay of
£1,350.00 plus his SSP of £31.50. In other words he would be better off than if he had
not been absent at all. This is clearly not what is intended.

⇨ Move the cursor to highlight **1.0000** against **Monthly Pay** and again press **F3**.
   Adjust for SSP/SMP : No Yes appears on the screen. Press **Y** for **Yes**.

Immediately Lansdown's monthly pay falls to **£1,318.50** which, when added to his SSP,
brings him up to the full pay to which he is entitled. His screen eventually appears like
this.

```
┌─────────────────────────────────────────────────────────────────┐
│ Reference : 6     Name : William Lansdown        Pay Type : GM    │
└─────────────────────────────────────────────────────────────────┘
```

```
    Monthly Pay : 0.9767    :   ( 1318.50 )  P.A.Y.E. (TAX) :    257.41
    Basic Hourly :  0.0000  :        0.00
          Bonus :   0.0000  :        0.00    NATIONAL INS. :     105.30

          Statutory Sick Pay :      31.50    NETT PAY (1) :      987.29
    Statutory Maternity Pay :        0.00    Rounding B/F :        0.00

                                             NETT PAY (2) :      987.29
          Total Holiday Pay :        0.00    Rounding C/F :        0.00

          TAXABLE GROSS PAY :      1350.00
             TOTAL GROSS PAY :     1350.00   TOTAL NETT PAY :     987.29
```

Here is a recapitulation of the procedure for entering Statutory Sick Pay *and adjusting the monthly pay to take account of this.*

> With the cursor highlighting the **SSP** cell press **F3.**
> Enter the dates of the absence on the sickness record screen
> Return to the Pay Details screen
> With the cursor against **Monthly Pay** press **F3** again.
> Answer **Yes** to the **Adjust for SSP/SMP** query.

It is now time to see the effect of these entries on Lansdown's sickness record again.

⇨ Move the cursor to **Statutory Sick Pay** and again press **F3.**

The bottom of the screen now looks like this.

```
    Feb :  . . . . . . . . . . . . . . . . . . . . . . . . . . . . . .
    Mar :  . . . . . . . . . . . . . . . . . . . . . . . . . . . . . . .
    Apr :  . . . . . . . . . . . . . . . . . . . . . . . . . . . . . . .
    May :  . . . . . . . . . . . . . . . . . . . . . . . . . . . . . . . .
    Jun :  . . . . . . . . . . . . . . . . . . . . . . . . . . . . . . .
    Jul :  . . x - - x x p p p - - . . . . . . . . . . . . . . . . . .
```

The absences have been recorded. The x's represent the three waiting days during which time Lansdown is not entitled to any SSP, the 'p's indicate the days for which Lansdown will be paid and the dashes (-) represent the Saturdays and Sundays that are not qualifying days anyway because Lansdown would not normally be expected to work on those days. Lansdown is therefore receiving SSP for three days, the 8th, 9th and 10th July, i.e. 3/5ths of £52.50 per week.

⇨ Press **Escape** and **F10** to move to Fisher's screen. Move the cursor to **Statutory Sick Pay** and press **F3.** Enter the dates of his absence: **200792** to **310792** and then **A** against **Type.** Answer **Yes** to **Block Fill.**

Fisher was absent through illness from the 20th of the month and so was available for work for the first 19 days out of the 31 days of the month. It would be possible (and normal) for the firm to adopt the same attitude towards Fisher as it did towards Lansdown. i.e. to make up his monthly pay to the normal amount. However, for the sake of these training exercises it is going to be assumed that Fisher receives the Government dictated Statutory Sick Pay when he is absent and the firm's rate of pay while he is at work but that the firm will not make his pay up to the full amount in the event of his absence.

⇨ Therefore press **Escape** to produce Fisher's payments screen and move the cursor to **Monthly Pay**. Press **F2** to bring the calculator on to the screen.

⇨ Fisher was at work for 19/31 of the month so key in **19/31=**. The value **0.612903226** appears. Press **Enter** twice and his month's pay is entered as **£888.71**. Clearly Fisher is not being treated as favourably as was Lansdown. His total pay has fallen from £1,450.00 to £888.71 plus £73.50 SSP = £962.21.

⇨ Press **Escape** twice to get back to the Main Menu and choose **Processing Payroll** again. The date is **310792** and this time accept the **1** and **30** that are offered to you.

⇨ Choose **Payment Summary** and print the details of the July Payroll. Check that yours agrees with the one at the end of the lesson and, if so, update the records.

DRAGON ENTERPRISE LIMITED   PAYMENTS SUMMARY - PART 1   Date : 310792
Tax month 04   ============================   Page : 1

                                                    << Monthly >>

Ref.	Total Gross Pay	Taxable Gross Pay	Pre-Tax Addition	Pre-Tax Deduct'n	Pension	P.A.Y.E.	Nat.Ins.	S.S.P.	S.M.P.	Post-Tax Addition	Post-Tax Deduct'n	Amount B/F	Amount C/F	Nett Pay
1	748.80	748.80	0.00	0.00	0.00	106.91	50.94	0.00	0.00	0.00	0.00	0.48	0.53	591.00
2	696.00	696.00	0.00	0.00	0.00	57.91	0.00	0.00	0.00	0.00	0.00	0.25	0.16	638.00
3	904.80	904.80	0.00	0.00	0.00	145.91	64.98	0.00	0.00	0.00	0.00	0.00	0.00	693.91
4	870.00	870.00	0.00	0.00	0.00	137.41	62.10	0.00	0.00	0.00	0.00	0.00	0.00	670.49
5	1100.00	1100.00	0.00	0.00	0.00	194.91	82.62	0.00	0.00	0.00	0.00	0.00	0.00	822.47
6	1350.00	1350.00	0.00	0.00	0.00	257.41	105.30	0.00	0.00	0.00	0.00	0.00	0.00	987.29
7	962.21	962.21	0.00	0.00	0.00	124.41	70.38	0.00	0.00	0.00	0.00	0.00	0.00	767.42
8	211.50	211.50	0.00	0.00	0.00	-63.34	0.00	31.50	0.00	0.00	0.00	0.00	0.00	274.84
9	870.00	870.00	0.00	0.00	0.00	101.41	62.10	73.50	0.00	0.00	0.00	0.05	0.56	707.00
10	251.10	251.10	0.00	0.00	0.00	62.75	0.00	0.00	0.00	0.00	0.00	0.65	0.30	188.00
11	720.00	720.00	0.00	0.00	0.00	99.91	48.42	0.00	0.00	0.00	0.00	0.00	0.00	571.67
12	720.00	720.00	0.00	0.00	0.00	63.91	48.42	0.00	0.00	0.00	0.00	0.00	0.00	607.67
13	2300.00	2300.00	0.00	0.00	0.00	458.91	141.66	0.00	0.00	0.00	0.00	0.00	0.00	1699.43
14	870.00	870.00	0.00	0.00	0.00	137.41	62.10	0.00	0.00	0.00	0.00	0.00	0.00	670.49
15	500.00	500.00	0.00	0.00	0.00	0.00	28.62	0.00	0.00	0.00	0.00	0.00	0.00	471.38
16	2500.00	2500.00	0.00	0.00	0.00	632.21	225.00	0.00	0.00	0.00	0.00	0.00	0.00	1642.79
17	870.00	870.00	0.00	0.00	0.00	101.41	62.10	0.00	0.00	0.00	0.00	0.00	0.00	706.49
18	2500.00	2500.00	0.00	0.00	0.00	623.41	225.00	0.00	0.00	0.00	0.00	0.00	0.00	1651.59
19	1100.00	1100.00	0.00	0.00	0.00	194.91	82.62	0.00	0.00	0.00	0.00	0.00	0.00	822.47
20	870.00	870.00	0.00	0.00	0.00	101.41	62.10	0.00	0.00	0.00	0.00	0.00	0.00	706.49
	20914.41	20914.41	0.00	0.00	0.00	3539.18	1484.46	105.00	0.00	0.00	0.00	1.43	1.55	15890.89

20 employees

DRAGON ENTERPRISE LIMITED
Tax month 04

Date : 310792
Page : 2

P A Y M E N T S   S U M M A R Y - P A R T   2

<< Monthly >>

*** N A T I O N A L   I N S U R A N C E ***

Ref.	Name	Standard Earnings	Total Contr'n	Emp'ees Contr'n	Con/out Earnings	Con/out Contr'n	Employers Nat.Ins.	Pension	Tax Code	Nat.Ins. Category
1	F.Adams	746.00	115.27	50.94	0.00	0.00	64.33	0.00	344L	A
2	J.Joyce	0.00	59.86	0.00	0.00	0.00	59.86	0.00	516V	C
3	G.Rose	902.00	159.00	64.98	0.00	0.00	94.02	0.00	344L	A
4	J.Gieves	870.00	152.79	62.10	0.00	0.00	90.69	0.00	344L	A
5	B.King	1098.00	197.02	82.62	0.00	0.00	114.40	0.00	344L	A
6	W.Lansdown	1350.00	245.91	105.30	0.00	0.00	140.61	0.00	344L	A
7	A.Fisher	962.00	170.64	70.38	0.00	0.00	100.26	0.00	516H	A
8	C.Young	0.00	0.00	0.00	0.00	0.00	0.00	0.00	516V	C
9	A.Ball	870.00	152.79	62.10	0.00	0.00	90.69	0.00	516H	A
10	M.English	0.00	11.59	0.00	0.00	0.00	11.59	0.00	BR	C
11	M.Perkins	718.00	110.34	48.42	0.00	0.00	61.92	0.00	344L	A
12	P.Corke	718.00	110.34	48.42	0.00	0.00	61.92	0.00	516H	A
13	R.Reagan	1756.00	380.86	141.66	0.00	0.00	239.20	0.00	516H	A
14	W.Tasker	870.00	152.79	62.10	0.00	0.00	90.69	0.00	344L	A
15	J.Wilson	498.00	61.62	28.62	0.00	0.00	33.00	0.00	NT	A
16	D.Carver	2500.00	620.00	225.00	0.00	0.00	395.00	0.00	189L	A
17	W.Bridges	870.00	152.79	62.10	0.00	0.00	90.69	0.00	516H	A
18	R.Long	2500.00	620.00	225.00	0.00	0.00	395.00	0.00	216L	A
19	K.Farmer	1098.00	197.02	82.62	0.00	0.00	114.40	0.00	344L	A
20	J.Nibbs	870.00	152.79	62.10	0.00	0.00	90.69	0.00	516H	A
	Total values for 20 employees	19196.00	3823.42	1484.46	0.00	0.00	2338.96	0.00		

DRAGON ENTERPRISE LIMITED
Tax month 04

P A Y M E N T S   S U M M A R Y - P A R T   3

<< Monthly >>

Y E A R   T O   D A T E

* Pension

Ref.	Name	Total Gross Pay	Taxable Gross Pay	P.A.Y.E.	National Insurance Employees	National Insurance Employers	S.S.P.	S.M.P.	Pension Employee	Pension Employer
1	F.Adams	2937.60	2937.60	413.41	198.72	252.50	0.00	0.00	0.00	0.00
2	J.Joyce	2832.00	2832.00	243.16	0.00	243.56	0.00	0.00	0.00	0.00
3	G.Rose	3549.60	3549.60	566.41	254.16	369.42	0.00	0.00	0.00	0.00
4	J.Gieves	3480.00	3480.00	549.16	248.40	362.76	0.00	0.00	0.00	0.00
5	B.King	4400.00	4400.00	779.16	330.48	457.60	0.00	0.00	0.00	0.00
6	W.Lansdown	5400.00	5400.00	1029.16	421.20	562.44	0.00	0.00	0.00	0.00
7	A.Fisher	5312.21	5312.21	863.16	413.28	553.29	31.50	0.00	0.00	0.00
8	C.Young	2623.00	2623.00	190.91	0.00	228.80	73.50	0.00	0.00	0.00
9	A.Ball	3480.00	3480.00	405.16	248.40	362.76	0.00	0.00	0.00	0.00
10	M.English	2242.20	2242.20	560.50	0.00	204.56	0.00	0.00	0.00	0.00
11	M.Perkins	2880.00	2880.00	399.16	193.68	247.68	0.00	0.00	0.00	0.00
12	P.Corke	2880.00	2880.00	255.16	193.68	247.68	0.00	0.00	0.00	0.00
13	R.Reagan	9200.00	9200.00	1835.16	566.64	956.80	0.00	0.00	0.00	0.00
14	W.Tasker	3480.00	3480.00	549.16	248.40	362.76	0.00	0.00	0.00	0.00
15	J.Wilson	2000.00	2000.00	0.00	114.48	132.00	0.00	0.00	0.00	0.00
16	D.Carver	10000.00	10000.00	2528.46	703.44	1040.00	0.00	0.00	0.00	0.00
17	W.Bridges	3480.00	3480.00	405.16	248.40	362.76	0.00	0.00	0.00	0.00
18	R.Long	10000.00	10000.00	2492.46	703.44	1040.00	0.00	0.00	0.00	0.00
19	K.Farmer	4400.00	4400.00	779.16	330.48	457.60	0.00	0.00	0.00	0.00
20	J.Nibbs	3480.00	3480.00	405.16	248.40	362.76	0.00	0.00	0.00	0.00
	Total values for 20 employees	88056.61	88056.61	15249.23	5665.68	8807.73	105.00	0.00	0.00	0.00

Lesson Eight

Month Five - August

A New Employee
A Bonus
Continuing Absence

If you need to reload the payroll records at this stage use LOAD PAYROLL AT END OF JULY. You must remember to update the records at 310792 before you enter the payments for August.

A New Employee

On 1st August a new employee, Martin Long, joined the firm. He had left school only a few weeks before and this was his first job.

Because he did not have a tax code he was given form P46 by Dragon to complete. The first page of this form is illustrated below.

 *Inland Revenue*

Part 1 - to be read by the employee

PAYE: Employer's notice to tax office P46

Notice to tax office of
- **employees without a P45**
- **employees previously paid below the PAYE threshold**

Why you have been given this form

Your employer has to let the tax office know about your job and work out what PAYE code to use. This form explains what you need to do and what happens next.

How to complete this form

Read statements A and B below. Then sign one if it applies to you. If neither statement applies, or you do not wish to sign, leave the form blank. If you were previously receiving full time education and both statements apply to you, sign only statement A.

If you sign either statement A or B below, your employer will tax you as a single person who has no other income or allowances. This means that you will receive a certain amount of your earnings tax free. No tax will be deducted if your pay is below the PAYE threshold.

If neither statement applies to you, or you do not wish to sign, your employer will deduct tax from all your pay at the basic rate. This means that none of your earnings from this job will be tax free.

This is my first regular job since leaving full-time education. I have not claimed unemployment benefit, or income support paid because of unemployment, since then.

Signature   *Date*

This is my only or my main job.

Signature   *Date*

Your PAYE tax code

PAYE (Pay As You Earn) is the system used by employers for calculating and collecting income tax. By deducting tax from your earnings whenever you are paid, the PAYE system helps you to avoid unexpected tax demands.

The amount of income tax you pay depends on your total income, but you may not have to pay tax on all of that income. Your PAYE tax code is used to work out the amount of tax deducted from your earnings. It is based on your allowances which depend on your personal circumstances.

What to do now

Return this form to your employer. He/she will complete part 2 and use it to notify the tax office that you have started work. **Make sure he/she knows your National Insurance (NI) number.** He/she then has to show the number on this form so that your tax office can use it as your tax reference. If your tax office does not know the number, this can cause delay in dealing with your tax affairs.

When to contact your tax office

Tell your tax office at once if you have any other income including a pension, or if you want to claim any other allowances such as married couples allowance. You can find out the address of your tax office from your employer. If you contact the tax office you will need to give your National Insurance (NI) number.

You can also contact your tax office if you need more information, for example about what allowances you may be entitled to.

Martin Long would sign this form and Dragon would send it to the Tax Office that would later notify Long and Dragon Enterprise Limited of the correct tax code to use. In the meantime Dragon must use the *Emergency Code* of 344LM1. The M1 in this tax code means that his tax will be calculated on a *Month 1* basis i.e. it will not be calculated in a cumulative manner as normal but as if each month was the first month of the tax year. You will be required to enter his correct tax code in the October lesson.

The periodic changes in the Emergency Code will have been notified to the firm by the Tax Office that will use form P7X in February if this is the predictable annual change or form P24 if there is an unexpected change (brought about by Government legislation) during the year.

The first task is to enter details of this new employee.

⇨ Go into **Employee Details - Add a New Employee**. Accept the 1 and **30** that are offered you and complete the first three screens for this employee as shown below.

```
┌─────────────────────────────────────────────────────────────────┐
│  Sage Payroll II          Add a New Employee                      │
└─────────────────────────────────────────────────────────────────┘


     Employee No. :  21      On HOLD : NO        Start Date : 010892
                                                 Leave Date :
         Forenames : Martin                  Holiday Return :
          Surname : Long

           Address :                            Tax Code : 344LM1
              .. :                          Effective from : 010892
              .. :                           N.I. Number : AC342789C
              .. :                           N.I. Category : A
                                           Contracted-Out : N
                                                SCON Ref. :  0
     Works Number : 68                     Effective from : 010892
     Payment Type : GM
      Pension Ref. :  0                     Marital Status : S
      Auto SSP/SMP : Y                       Male/Female : M
    Date of Birth : 110675                       Director : N
```

Reference : 21   Name : Martin Long   Pay Type : GM

Department :   2 : Showroom
Qualifying Days :   1 : NQQQQQN NQQQQQN NQQQQQN NQQQQQN

Rates of Pay

1 : Monthly Pay   :   520.0000
2 : Basic Hourly   :   3.2000
3 : Time and a half   :   4.8000
4 : Bonus   :   1.0000
0 : BLANK   :   0.0000

Adjustments

1 : Salary Advance
2 : Salary Refund
3 : Expenses
4 : Additions/Taxed
5 : Union Dues
0 : BLANK
0 : BLANK
0 : BLANK
0 : BLANK
0 : BLANK

Reference : 21   Name : Martin Long   Pay Type : GM

Banking Information

Bank name : Coopers Bank
Branch Address 1 : King Street
Address 2 : Benton

Branch Sort Code : 65-16-12

Account Name : M. Long
Account Number : 78294561

Previous Employment (P45)

Taxable Gross Pay :   0.00
Tax Paid :   0.00

Current Employment

Gross Pay for NI :   0.00
Rounding C/F : 0.00

⇨ Post this information by pressing **Escape** and accepting the **Post** that is offered you.

Running the Payroll

Lansdown (6) has no time off for sickness during August so his monthly pay should be amended to read 1 month.

Fisher (7) is unable to return to work this month so his monthly pay should be 0 months but he is entitled to SSP.

With the exception of the directors (16 and 18), Richard Reagan (13), Juliette Wilson (15) who is employed on a consultancy basis and the new employee Martin Long (21) all employees are to receive a bonus of 8% of their basic annual salary (or 96% of their basic monthly pay). This will cause some difficulty with the three people who are now paid on an hourly rate so these employees are to be paid a bonus equivalent to 156 hours at their basic hourly rate.

⇨ Go into **Processing Payroll** and enter the date **310892**. Choose **Enter Payments** and carry out the following instructions for Adams (1).

⇨ Move the cursor to **Bonus**. Press **F2** and key in **748.8** (Adam's monthly rate of pay) *.96= and press **Enter** twice. (Don't omit the decimal point before the 96!) The top part of the screen should appear as depicted below.

```
Reference : 1     Name : Fred Adams              Pay Type : CM


    Monthly Pay :   1.0000  :    748.80   P.A.Y.E. (TAX) :    286.92
   Basic Hourly :   0.0000  :      0.00
  Time and a half :  0.0000  :      0.00   NATIONAL INS. :    115.74
          Bonus : 718.8480  :    718.85
```

⇨ Press **F10** to move on to the screen for Joyce (2). This is slightly more difficult because the basic hourly rate does not appear on the screen to help you in the way that the basic monthly rate for Adams was there. However, this can be rectified by inserting **1** against **Basic Hourly** and immediately Joyce's hourly rate appears to the right of 1.0000; **£4.64**.

```
Reference : 2     Name : James Joyce             Pay Type : CM


        BLANK :    0.0000  :      0.00   P.A.Y.E. (TAX) :   -107.36
   Basic Hourly :   1.0000  :      4.64
  Time and a half : 0.0000  :      0.00   NATIONAL INS. :      0.00
          Bonus :    0.0000  :      0.00
```

⇨ With the cursor against **Bonus** press **F2**, press **C** to cancel the original entry on the calculator screen if necessary and key in **4.64*156=** and press **Enter** twice. A bonus of £**723.84** should appear.

Reference : 2	Name : James Joyce		Pay Type : CM
BLANK :	0.0000 :	0.00	P.A.Y.E. (TAX) : 65.67
Basic Hourly :	1.0000 :	4.64	
Time and a half :	0.0000 :	0.00	NATIONAL INS. : 0.00
Bonus :	723.8400 :	723.84	
BLANK :	0.0000 :	0.00	

⇨ The number of basic hours needs to be adjusted back to the original 150 so move the cursor back to **Basic Hourly** and key in **150** and press **Enter**. You should be left with this screen.

Reference : 2	Name : James Joyce		Pay Type : CM
BLANK :	0.0000 :	0.00	P.A.Y.E. (TAX) : 238.67
Basic Hourly :	150.0000 :	696.00	
Time and a half :	0.0000 :	0.00	NATIONAL INS. : 0.00
Bonus :	723.8400 :	723.84	
BLANK :	0.0000 :	0.00	
TAXABLE GROSS PAY :		1419.84	
TOTAL GROSS PAY :		1419.84	TOTAL NETT PAY : 1182.00

⇨ Follow the same pattern for all the other employees who are receiving a bonus. These changes are not difficult to make but you must think carefully as you make the entries. It is very, very easy to make a simple mistake. To help you a summary of the entries for each employee is given below. When you get to Fisher (7) follow the instructions given below.

Employee No.	Pay Details
1 to 5	Bonus
6	Bonus - Full month's pay
7	Bonus - No monthly pay - Absent all month
8 to 12	Bonus
13	Normal month's pay only
14	Bonus
15	Normal month's pay only
16	Normal month's pay only
17	Bonus

Employee No	Pay Details
18	Normal month's pay only
19	Bonus
20	Bonus
21	One month's pay for the first time

⇨ Fisher (7) is away all month. When entering details it is important that his monthly pay should be £0.00 although he is entitled to a bonus based upon his normal monthly pay.

⇨ In order to record his continuing absence move the cursor to **Statutory Sick Pay** on his screen and press **F3**. Enter the dates of his absence as **010892** to **310892** and type **A** and then accept **Yes** to **Block Fill**.

Before leaving that screen you will notice the X's and P's that appear against July relating to his absence during that month are now in upper case letters - previously they were in lower case letters. This change arises when the month's payroll is updated.

⇨ Press **Escape** and with the cursor still against **Statutory Sick Pay £220.50** press **F3** again.

At the bottom of the screen the A's have become p's - but lower case p's because the August payroll data has not been updated yet.

```
┌─────────────────────────────────────────────────────────────────────┐
│ Reference : 7   Name : Andrew Fisher            Pay Type : GM         │
└─────────────────────────────────────────────────────────────────────┘

        Start date :        End date :         Type :

                         1                 2                 3
                1 2 3 4 5 6 7 8 9 0 1 2 3 4 5 6 7 8 9 0 1 2 3 4 5 6 7 8 9 0 1

     91  Sep :  p . . . . . . . . . . . . . . . . . . . . . . . . . . . . . .
         Oct :  . . . . . . . . . . . . . . . . . . . . . . . . . . . . . . .
         Nov :  . . . . . . . . . . . . . . . . . . . . . . . . . . . . . . .
         Dec :  . . . . . . . . . . . . . . . . . . . . . . . . . . . . . . .
     92  Jan :  . . . . . . . . . . . . . . . . . . . . . . . . . . . . . . .
         Feb :  . . . . . . . . . . . . . . . . . . . . . . . . . . . . . . .
         Mar :  . . . . . . . . . . . . . . . . . . . . . . . . . . . . . . .
         Apr :  . . . . . . . . . . . . . . . . . . . . . . . . . . . . . . .
         May :  . . . . . . . . . . . . . . . . . . . . . . . . . . . . . . .
         Jun :  . . . . . . . . . . . . . . . . . . . . . . . . . . . . . . .
         Jul :  . . . . . . . . . . . . . . . . . . . . . . . X X X P P = = P P P P P
         Aug :  - - p p p p p - - p p p p p - - p p p p p - - p p p p p - - p
```

⇨ When all these entries have been made print the Payment Summary. Check yours with the one at the end of the lesson.

⇨ Asuming that everything is in order update your records.

Paying the Inland Revenue

Make sure that you have updated the records before proceeding with the remainder of the lessson.

Once again a Form P30 must be produced to accompany Dragon's payment to the Inland Revenue. It has been omitted from these lessons for the past two months as there were no differences to the routine that was introduced in May. However, this month Statutory Sick Pay is involved and this will affect how much has to be paid to the Inland Revenue.

⇨ From the Main Menu go into **Collector of Taxes**. Complete the screen as shown below (Tax Month **5** is August).

Sage Payroll II	Collector of Taxes			
Lower Employee No.	1		:	1
Upper Employee No.	30		:	30
By Month/Week/Date/Auto	M		:	M
Enter Tax Month from	1		:	5
Enter Tax Month to	5		:	5
Display, Print or File	D		:	P

⇨ Produce a printout similar to the one shown overleaf.

Study the Monthly Payslip Return that you have produced. £220.50 of the payment made to Fisher (7) this month was for Statutory Sick Pay (Payment Summary Part 1). 80% of this Dragon can reclaim from the Inland Revenue so £176.40 can be deducted from the Gross National Insurance figure. The remaining 20% Dragon has to pay itself. These figures must be entered on the form P30 as shown on page 8 - 9.

DRAGON ENTERPRISE LIMITED

Collector of Taxes (Monthly Payslip Returns)

Date : 310892

Record of deductions from gross National Insurance

	(1) S.S.P.	(2) NIC comp'n	(3) S.M.P.	(4) NIC comp'n	(5) Total Ded.
Weekly	0.00	0.00	0.00	0.00	0.00
2 Weekly	0.00	0.00	0.00	0.00	0.00
4 Weekly	0.00	0.00	0.00	0.00	0.00
Monthly	176.40	0.00	0.00	0.00	176.40
Totals	176.40	0.00	0.00	0.00	176.40

Record of Payments

	(1) Income Tax	(2) Gross N.I.	(3) Total Ded.	(4) Net N.I.	(5) Total Due
Weekly	0.00	0.00	0.00	0.00	0.00
2 Weekly	0.00	0.00	0.00	0.00	0.00
4 Weekly	0.00	0.00	0.00	0.00	0.00
Monthly	7060.22	6003.34	176.40	5826.94	12887.16
Totals	7060.22	6003.34	176.40	5826.94	12887.16

NIC compensation percentage

S.S.P. : 0.00   S.M.P. : 4.50

Employee range

0001 - 0030

Date range

Week : 060892 - 050992   Month : 060892 - 050992

Income Tax – Pay As You Earn
National Insurance Contributions
and
Amounts deductible from payments to Sub-Contractors in the Construction Industry

Date of issue:

(Cashier's stamp)

and initials

- **Payslip completion** ⎫
- **How to pay** ⎬ *Please see overleaf.*
- **Please write the Accounts Office reference shown below on the back of your cheque.**

Collector of Taxes
Inland Revenue Accounts Office (Shipley)
BRADFORD, West Yorkshire BD98 8AA
Telephone: Bradford (0274) 594141

P30 (BZ)(CL)

G Girobank *Trans Cash*
Girobank plc Bootle Merseyside GIR 0AA

165
215

P

Accounts Office reference _____ Year ____ Month no. ____

Employer's name *(in CAPITALS)*
DRAGON ENTERPRISE LTD

Paid in by *R. Reagan* Date *13.9.92*

(Cashier's stamp)

and initials

Fee paid

Items

Please do not fold this payslip or write or mark below this line

Payslip

610 5939

Credit account no.

Record of payment

A record should be kept of the payment made as this information will be required when you complete the Employer's Annual Statement, Declaration and Certificate.

Enter from Payslip below ▲

Accounts Office reference _____ Year Month no. ____

P

£ *7060·22*

1. Income Tax	£	
2. Gross National Insurance	£ *6003·34*	
3. Statutory Sick Pay	£ *176·40*	
4. Statutory Maternity Pay	£	
5. NIC Compensation on SSP	£	
6. NIC Compensation on SMP	£ *176·40*	
7. Total deductions (3 to 6)	£	*5826·94*
8. Net National Insurance (2 less 7)		
9. Total amount due (1 + 8)	£	*12887·16*

Cheque number ____ *417501*

How paid ⎱ Bank Giro
⎰ Girobank transfer
At the Post Office

Date paid *13.9.92*

Bank Giro Credit

Income Tax ↓ £ *7060* | *22*

Net National Insurance ↓ £ *5826* | *94*

£ *12887·16*

Total amount due (No fee payable at PO counter)

For official use only

By transfer from Girobank a/c no.

Cash

Cheques _____ *1*

10—59—39

BANK OF ENGLAND
HEAD OFFICE COLLECTION A/C
INLAND REVENUE

	12887	*16*
£	*12887*	*16*

Double Entry Book-keeping

This section is only included for those people who are studying double entry book-keeping. Other students should ignore it.

This month the situation is complicated by the fact that some of the money paid to Fisher (7) was Statutory Sick Pay and Dragon can get back 80% of this from the Inland Revenue. When calculating the liability to enter in the PAYE/NIC Control Account (i.e. the money that Dragon must send them by 19th September) the figure will be the sum of the PAYE (Col 7) - £7,060.22 plus the Total NIC (Col 17) - £6,003.34 less 80% of the Total SSP (Col 9) - £176.40.

When the cost of salaries is calculated this will be the sum of the Gross Pay (Col 2) - £35,332.68 plus the employer's NIC (Col 21) - £3,635.26 less the refund of SSP that Dragon can obtain, namely £176.40. The full figures are:

Salaries Control

Net Pay (Col 15)	25,905.59	
plus Bal b/f (Col 13)	1.55	
less Bal c/f (Col 14)	2.76	
		25,904.38

PAYE/NIC Control

PAYE (Col 7)	7,060.22	
Total NIC (Col 17)	6,003.34	
less NIC Deductions	176.40	
		12,887.16
TOTAL LIABILITIES		38,791.54

Salaries Expenses Account

Gross Pay (Col 2)	35,332.68	
Employer's NIC (Col 21)	3,635.26	
less NIC Deductions	176.40	
		38,791.54

DRAGON ENTERPRISE LIMITED   Date : 310892
Tax month 05   Page : 1

P A Y M E N T S   S U M M A R Y - P A R T 1

<< Monthly >>

Ref.	Total Gross Pay	Taxable Gross Pay	Pre-Tax Addition	Deduct'n	Pension	P.A.Y.E.	Nat.Ins.	S.S.P.	S.M.P.	Post-Tax Addition	Deduct'n	Amount B/F	C/F	Nett Pay
1	1467.65	1467.65	0.00	0.00	0.00	286.92	115.74	0.00	0.00	0.00	0.00	0.53	0.54	1065.00
2	1419.84	1419.84	0.00	0.00	0.00	238.67	0.00	0.00	0.00	0.00	0.00	0.16	0.99	1182.00
3	1773.41	1773.41	0.00	0.00	0.00	363.17	141.66	0.00	0.00	0.00	0.00	0.00	0.00	1268.58
4	1705.20	1705.20	0.00	0.00	0.00	346.17	136.98	0.00	0.00	0.00	0.00	0.00	0.00	1222.05
5	2156.00	2156.00	0.00	0.00	0.00	458.67	141.66	0.00	0.00	0.00	0.00	0.00	0.00	1555.67
6	2646.00	2646.00	0.00	0.00	0.00	581.17	141.66	0.00	0.00	0.00	0.00	0.00	0.00	1923.17
7	1612.50	1612.50	0.00	0.00	0.00	286.92	128.70	220.50	0.00	0.00	0.00	0.00	0.00	1196.88
8	1311.30	1311.30	0.00	0.00	0.00	211.42	0.00	0.00	0.00	0.00	0.00	0.00	0.00	1099.88
9	1705.20	1705.20	0.00	0.00	0.00	309.92	136.98	0.00	0.00	0.00	0.00	0.56	0.26	1258.00
10	1121.58	1121.58	0.00	0.00	0.00	280.25	0.00	0.00	0.00	0.00	0.00	0.30	0.97	842.00
11	1411.20	1411.20	0.00	0.00	0.00	272.67	110.70	0.00	0.00	0.00	0.00	0.00	0.00	1027.83
12	1411.20	1411.20	0.00	0.00	0.00	236.42	110.70	0.00	0.00	0.00	0.00	0.00	0.00	1064.08
13	2300.00	2300.00	0.00	0.00	0.00	458.67	141.66	0.00	0.00	0.00	0.00	0.00	0.00	1699.67
14	1705.20	1705.20	0.00	0.00	0.00	346.17	136.98	0.00	0.00	0.00	0.00	0.00	0.00	1222.05
15	500.00	500.00	0.00	0.00	0.00	0.00	28.62	0.00	0.00	0.00	0.00	0.00	0.00	471.38
16	2500.00	2500.00	0.00	0.00	0.00	631.82	225.00	0.00	0.00	0.00	0.00	0.00	0.00	1643.18
17	1705.20	1705.20	0.00	0.00	0.00	309.92	136.98	0.00	0.00	0.00	0.00	0.00	0.00	1258.30
18	2500.00	2500.00	0.00	0.00	0.00	623.02	225.00	0.00	0.00	0.00	0.00	0.00	0.00	1651.98
19	2156.00	2156.00	0.00	0.00	0.00	458.67	141.66	0.00	0.00	0.00	0.00	0.00	0.00	1555.67
20	1705.20	1705.20	0.00	0.00	0.00	309.92	136.98	0.00	0.00	0.00	0.00	0.00	0.00	1258.30
21	520.00	520.00	0.00	0.00	0.00	49.66	30.42	0.00	0.00	0.00	0.00	0.00	0.00	439.92
21 employees	35332.68	35332.68	0.00	0.00	0.00	7060.22	2368.08	220.50	0.00	0.00	0.00	1.55	2.76	25905.59
1	2	3	4	5	6	7	8	9	10	11	12	13	14	15

35332.68

DRAGON ENTERPRISE LIMITED   Date : 310892
Tax month 05   Page : 2

P A Y M E N T S   S U M M A R Y - P A R T 2

<< Monthly >>

*** N A T I O N A L   I N S U R A N C E ***

Ref.	Name	Standard Earnings	Total Contr'n	Emp'ees Contr'n	Con/out Earnings	Con/out Contr'n	Employers Nat.Ins.	Pension	Tax Code	Nat.Ins. Category
1	F.Adams	1466.00	268.41	115.74	0.00	0.00	152.67	0.00	344L	A
2	J.Joyce	0.00	147.68	0.00	0.00	0.00	147.68	0.00	516V	C
3	G.Rose	1756.00	326.05	141.66	0.00	0.00	184.39	0.00	344L	A
4	J.Gieves	1702.00	314.20	136.98	0.00	0.00	177.22	0.00	344L	A
5	B.King	1756.00	365.88	141.66	0.00	0.00	224.22	0.00	344L	A
6	W.Lansdown	1756.00	416.84	141.66	0.00	0.00	275.18	0.00	344L	A
7	A.Fisher	1610.00	296.35	128.70	0.00	0.00	167.65	0.00	516H	A
8	C.Young	0.00	136.45	0.00	0.00	0.00	136.45	0.00	516V	C
9	A.Ball	1702.00	314.20	136.98	0.00	0.00	177.22	0.00	516H	A
10	M.English	0.00	116.48	0.00	0.00	0.00	116.48	0.00	BR	C
11	M.Perkins	1410.00	257.55	110.70	0.00	0.00	146.85	0.00	344L	A
12	P.Corke	1410.00	257.55	110.70	0.00	0.00	146.85	0.00	516H	A
13	R.Reagan	1756.00	380.86	141.66	0.00	0.00	239.20	0.00	516H	A
14	W.Tasker	1702.00	314.20	136.98	0.00	0.00	177.22	0.00	344L	A
15	J.Wilson	498.00	61.62	28.62	0.00	0.00	33.00	0.00	NT	A
16	D.Carver	2500.00	485.00	225.00	0.00	0.00	260.00	0.00	189L	A
17	W.Bridges	1702.00	314.20	136.98	0.00	0.00	177.22	0.00	516H	A
18	R.Long	2500.00	485.00	225.00	0.00	0.00	260.00	0.00	216L	A
19	K.Farmer	1756.00	365.88	141.66	0.00	0.00	224.22	0.00	344L	A
20	J.Nibbs	1702.00	314.20	136.98	0.00	0.00	177.22	0.00	516H	A
21	M.Long	518.00	64.74	30.42	0.00	0.00	34.32	0.00	344LM1	A
	Total values for 21 employees	29202.00	6003.34	2368.08	0.00	0.00	3635.26	0.00		
		16	17	18	19	20	21	22	23	24

DRAGON ENTERPRISE LIMITED
Tax month 05

Date : 310892
Page : 3

PAYMENTS SUMMARY - PART 3

<< Monthly >>

Ref.	Name	Total Gross Pay	Taxable Gross Pay	P.A.Y.E.	YEAR TO DATE National Insurance Employees	National Insurance Employers	S.S.P.	S.M.P.	Pension Employee	Pension Employer
1	F.Adams	4405.25	4405.25	700.33	314.46	405.17	0.00	0.00	0.00	0.00
2	J.Joyce	4251.84	4251.84	481.83	0.00	391.24	0.00	0.00	0.00	0.00
3	G.Rose	5323.01	5323.01	929.58	395.82	553.81	0.00	0.00	0.00	0.00
4	J.Gieves	5185.20	5185.20	895.33	385.38	539.98	0.00	0.00	0.00	0.00
5	B.King	6556.00	6556.00	1237.83	472.14	681.82	0.00	0.00	0.00	0.00
6	W.Lansdown	8046.00	8046.00	1610.33	562.86	837.62	31.50	0.00	0.00	0.00
7	A.Fisher	6924.71	6924.71	1150.08	541.98	720.94	294.00	0.00	0.00	0.00
8	C.Young	3934.30	3934.30	402.33	0.00	365.25	0.00	0.00	0.00	0.00
9	A.Ball	5185.20	5185.20	715.08	385.38	539.98	0.00	0.00	0.00	0.00
10	M.English	3363.78	3363.78	840.75	0.00	321.04	0.00	0.00	0.00	0.00
11	M.Perkins	4291.20	4291.20	671.83	304.38	394.53	0.00	0.00	0.00	0.00
12	P.Corke	4291.20	4291.20	491.58	304.38	394.53	0.00	0.00	0.00	0.00
13	R.Reagan	11500.00	11500.00	2293.83	708.30	1196.00	0.00	0.00	0.00	0.00
14	W.Tasker	5185.20	5185.20	895.33	385.38	539.98	0.00	0.00	0.00	0.00
15	J.Wilson	2500.00	2500.00	0.00	143.10	165.00	0.00	0.00	0.00	0.00
16	D.Carver	12500.00	12500.00	3160.28	928.44	1300.00	0.00	0.00	0.00	0.00
17	W.Bridges	5185.20	5185.20	715.08	385.38	539.98	0.00	0.00	0.00	0.00
18	R.Long	12500.00	12500.00	3115.48	928.44	1300.00	0.00	0.00	0.00	0.00
19	K.Farmer	6556.00	6556.00	1237.83	472.14	681.82	0.00	0.00	0.00	0.00
20	J.Nibbs	5185.20	5185.20	715.08	385.38	539.98	0.00	0.00	0.00	0.00
21	M.Long	520.00	520.00	49.66	30.42	34.32	0.00	0.00	0.00	0.00
	Total values for 21 employees	123389.29	123389.29	22309.45	8033.76	12442.99	325.50	0.00	0.00	0.00

Lesson Nine (September) starts on the facing page

Lesson Nine

Month Six - September

Holiday Pay
Two Adjustments
Removal of Bonus
Continuing Absence

If you need to reload the payroll records at this stage use LOAD PAYROLL AT END OF AUGUST. You must remember to update the records at 310892 before you enter the payments for September.

The Changes this Month

There are two new items introduced this month; one employee is paid a month's holiday pay in advance and two employees are paid extra over and above their basic monthly pay because they have been involved in meeting some of the firm's expenses out of their own pockets. All of these are adjustments which can be dealt with semi-automatically by the Sage Payroll program.

⇨ To see how this is done go into **Company Details - Adjustment Types** to display the screen shown below.

Sage Payroll II   Adjustment Types

Description....	+/-	Tax	N.I.	Pen		Description....	+/-	Tax	N.I.	Pen
1 : Salary Advance	+	Y	Y	Y	11 : BLANK	+	Y	Y	Y
2 : Salary Refund	-	Y	Y	Y	12 : BLANK	+	Y	Y	Y
3 : Expenses	+	N	N	N	13 : BLANK	+	Y	Y	Y
4 : Additions/Taxed	+	Y	Y	N	14 : BLANK	+	Y	Y	Y
5 : Union Dues	-	N	N	N	15 : BLANK	+	Y	Y	Y
6 : BLANK	+	Y	Y	Y	16 : BLANK	+	Y	Y	Y
7 : BLANK	+	Y	Y	Y	17 : BLANK	+	Y	Y	Y
8 : BLANK	+	Y	Y	Y	18 : BLANK	+	Y	Y	Y
9 : BLANK	+	Y	Y	Y	19 : BLANK	+	Y	Y	Y
10 : BLANK	+	Y	Y	Y	20 : BLANK	+	Y	Y	Y

Dragon's payroll is set up so that five different types of adjustments can be made to people's salaries.

1: Salary Advance will be used where a salary is being paid before it is due unless this arises because of an employee is taking a holiday when he would normally be paid. A different routine, that you will be introduced to you in this lesson, exists for this purpose.

2: Salary Refund will be used for a person who has, in the past, been paid more salary than he is entitled to.

The Y's against these two items under the headings **Tax**, **NI** and **Pen**(sion) indicate that the money paid or withdrawn under either of these headings must be taken into account when calculating the tax, National Insurance contribution and pension deduction.

3: Expenses will be used when an employee incurs an expense out of his own pocket that is wholly, necessarily and exclusively for the benefit of the company. For example, a person who is driving a company car on company business and must stop and buy petrol may have the cost of that petrol refunded using this Adjustment Type. The N under **Tax**, **NI** and **Pen**sion indicate that any additional money paid under this heading will not influence the Tax, National Insurance or Pension contributions.

A firm could, of course, simply re-imburse an employee for this type of expenditure by using its Petty Cash float or expenses claim procedure.

4: Additions/Taxed will be used when, for example, a company pays towards the cost of clothing for its workers. These payments benefit the employee rather than the company. Such allowances are taxed by the Inland Revenue and the National Insurance contributions are calculated as if that money was simply a part of the salary. If the company was involved in operating a pension scheme (more of which next month) any money paid in this way would not affect the pension contribution hence the N under Pen(sion).

5: Union Dues are a deduction that Dragon can make from its employees pay and which it then passes on to the Trade Unions concerned. These will be introduced in February.

Salary Advance, Expenses and Additions/Taxed will all have the effect of increasing the total amount to be paid to an employee, hence the + sign against these. Any Salary Refund or Union Dues paid will reduce the amount to be paid, hence the - sign.

Running the Payroll

You are advised to read the whole of this part of the lesson before attempting to make any entries.

⇨ Go into **Processing Payroll** and enter the date **300992**.

You will need to go through everbody's records in order to delete the bonus. This will actually involve you in entering a bonus of **0.** There is no change in the number of hours worked by any employee this month.

Fisher (7) has still not returned to work so when you come to his screen to enter details you must record this absence from **010992** to **300992** in the same way as you did last month. You will be asked whether you wish to allow a tax refund for the month. Accept **Yes.**

The same will be true of Young (8). Allow the **Tax Refund**.

⇨ Make the entries for the first 13 employees now then read below for guidance on entering the details of Tasker's pay for the month.

Tasker (14) is taking the whole of October off as holiday. The firm has agreed to pay her October salary at the end of September. If they were to simply double her salary this month and pay her nothing during October she would be paying a different amount of National Insurance contribution than if she was paid the same amount each month. This arises because NIC's are simply calculated on each month's pay. No pay one month will involve the employee in paying no NIC for that month but a large payment the next month to compensate for this will usually require an NIC greater than would be paid in two separate months. For this reason irregular payments arising from holidays must be spread evenly over the period to which they refer.

⇨ When entering Tasker's pay delete the bonus paid last month leaving **1** month's pay as usual. Then move the cursor to the **Total Holiday Pay** field. Press **F3** to produce this Holiday Entry screen. One month's pay is to be made in advance so enter **1** against **Periods to Advance**. Press **Enter**

```
┌─────────────────────────────────────────────────────────────┐
│ Reference : 14    Name : Wendy Tasker         Holiday Entry   │
└─────────────────────────────────────────────────────────────┘
```

```
        ┌──────────────── Holiday Periods ────────────────┐
        │                                                  │
        │     Periods to Advance : 1                       │
        │                                                  │
        │                                                  │
        ├──────────────── Holiday Information ─────────────┤
        │                                                  │
        │     Payment per Period :        0.00             │
        │                                                  │
        │      Total Holiday Pay :        0.00             │
        │                                                  │
        │      Previous payments :        0.00             │
        │                                                  │
        │                                                  │
        └──────────────────────────────────────────────────┘
```

⇨ This looks like the ordinary Enter Payments screen except for the words **Holiday Entry** in the top right hand corner. Enter **1** month's salary in this screen as shown below.

```
┌─────────────────────────────────────────────────────────────┐
│ Reference : 14    Name : Wendy Tasker         Holiday Entry   │
└─────────────────────────────────────────────────────────────┘
```

Monthly Pay :	(1.0000) :	870.00	P.A.Y.E. (TAX) :	137.41
Basic Hourly :	0.0000 :	0.00		
Time and a half :	0.0000 :	0.00	NATIONAL INS. :	62.10
Bonus :	0.0000 :	0.00		
BLANK :	0.0000 :	0.00		
Pre-Tax Add/n :		0.00	Post-Tax Add/n :	0.00
Pre-Tax Ded/n :		0.00	Post-Tax Ded/n :	0.00
Pension :		0.00		
Statutory Sick Pay :		0.00	NETT PAY (1) :	670.49
Statutory Maternity Pay :		0.00	Rounding B/F :	0.00
			NETT PAY (2) :	670.49
Total Holiday Pay :		0.00	Rounding C/F :	0.00

⇨ Press **Page Up** and you see one month's salary entered as holiday pay.

```
┌─────────────────────────────────────────────────────────────┐
│ Reference : 14    Name : Wendy Tasker          Holiday Entry  │
└─────────────────────────────────────────────────────────────┘

              ┌──────────── Holiday Periods ──────────────┐
              │  Periods to Advance : 1                    │
              │      ┌──────── Holiday Information ─────────┤
              │      │                                      │
              │      │  Payment per Period :    870.00      │
              │      │                                      │
              │      │  Total Holiday Pay :     870.00      │
              │      │                                      │
              │      │  Previous payments :       0.00      │
              │      │                                      │
              └──────┴──────────────────────────────────────┘
```

⇨ Press **Escape** and you are returned to the first Enter Payments screen.

⇨ When you make the entries for Wilson (15) and Carver (16) record **£50.00 Expenses** on the second screen as shown below.

```
┌─────────────────────────────────────────────────────────────┐
│ Reference : 15    Name : Juliette Wilson      Pay Type : GM   │
└─────────────────────────────────────────────────────────────┘
```

Pre-Tax Adjustments		ANP	Post-Tax Adjustments		ANP
Salary Advance :	0.00	: +YY	Expenses :	50.00	: +NN
Salary Refund :	0.00	: -YY	Union Dues : 0.00		: -NN
Additions/Taxed :	0.00	: +YN	** :	0.00	:
** :	0.00	:	** :	0.00	:
** :	0.00	:	** :	0.00	:
** :	0.00	:	** :	0.00	:
** :	0.00	:	** :	0.00	:
** :	0.00	:	** :	0.00	:
** :	0.00	:	** :	0.00	:
** :	0.00	:	** :	0.00	:

⇨ Complete the entries for the remaining employees.

⇨ Print out the Payment Summary and if yours agrees with the one at the end of the lesson update the records.

Double Entry Book-keeping

This section is only relevant to those people studying double entry book-keeping in conjunction with this course.

This month, as with all months, the entries have to be made in Dragon's ledger but this time there is a complication. The Gross Pay (Col 2) includes the £50.00 that is being paid to Wilson (15) and Carver (16) for expenses that they incurred on behalf of the company. Such an expense should not be included in the Salaries Account but in a General Expenses Account or something similar. In this case then the Salaries Expenses Account will be debited with £21,673.20 Gross Pay (Col 2) *less* £100.00 Post-tax Additions (Col 11) plus £2,093.71 Employer's NIC (Col 21) less £184.80 (80% of £231.00 SSP). The values to be entered in the other accounts will be calculated in the same way as was described in Lesson Eight. You are advised to check that you can arrive at the figures that appear below.

The Journal entries will therefore be:

	Dr	Cr
Salaries Control		16,674.23
PAYE/NIC Control (7,092.68 less 184.80)		6,907.88
TOTAL LIABILITIES		23,582.11
Salaries Expenses Account	23,482.11	
General Expenses	100.00	
TOTAL EXPENSES	23,582.11	

DRAGON ENTERPRISE LIMITED

Tax month 06

Date : 300992
Page : 1

P A Y M E N T S   S U M M A R Y - P A R T 1

<< Monthly >>

Ref.	Total Gross Pay	Taxable Gross Pay	Pre-Tax Addition	Deduct'n	Pension	P.A.Y.E.	Nat.Ins.	S.S.P.	S.M.P.	Post-Tax Addition	Deduct'n	Amount B/F	C/F	Nett Pay
1	748.80	748.80	0.00	0.00	0.00	106.92	50.94	0.00	0.00	0.00	0.00	0.54	0.60	591.00
2	696.00	696.00	0.00	0.00	0.00	57.67	0.00	0.00	0.00	0.00	0.00	0.99	0.66	638.00
3	904.80	904.80	0.00	0.00	0.00	146.17	64.98	0.00	0.00	0.00	0.00	0.00	0.00	693.65
4	870.00	870.00	0.00	0.00	0.00	137.17	62.10	0.00	0.00	0.00	0.00	0.00	0.00	670.73
5	1100.00	1100.00	0.00	0.00	0.00	194.92	82.62	0.00	0.00	0.00	0.00	0.00	0.00	822.46
6	1350.00	1350.00	0.00	0.00	0.00	257.42	105.30	0.00	0.00	0.00	0.00	0.00	0.00	987.28
7	231.00	231.00	0.00	0.00	0.00	-58.58	0.00	231.00	0.00	0.00	0.00	0.00	0.00	289.58
8	211.50	211.50	0.00	0.00	0.00	-63.33	0.00	0.00	0.00	0.00	0.00	0.00	0.00	274.83
9	870.00	870.00	0.00	0.00	0.00	101.42	62.10	0.00	0.00	0.00	0.00	0.26	0.78	707.00
10	251.10	251.10	0.00	0.00	0.00	62.75	0.00	0.00	0.00	0.00	0.00	0.97	0.62	188.00
11	720.00	720.00	0.00	0.00	0.00	99.67	48.42	0.00	0.00	0.00	0.00	0.00	0.00	571.91
12	720.00	720.00	0.00	0.00	0.00	63.92	48.42	0.00	0.00	0.00	0.00	0.00	0.00	607.66
13	2300.00	2300.00	0.00	0.00	0.00	458.92	141.66	0.00	0.00	0.00	0.00	0.00	0.00	1699.42
14	1740.00	1740.00	0.00	0.00	0.00	274.58	124.20	0.00	0.00	0.00	0.00	0.00	0.00	1341.22
15	500.00	500.00	0.00	0.00	0.00	0.00	28.62	0.00	0.00	50.00	0.00	0.00	0.00	521.38
16	2550.00	2500.00	0.00	0.00	0.00	632.22	225.00	0.00	0.00	50.00	0.00	0.00	0.00	1692.78
17	870.00	870.00	0.00	0.00	0.00	101.42	62.10	0.00	0.00	0.00	0.00	0.00	0.00	706.48
18	2500.00	2500.00	0.00	0.00	0.00	623.02	225.00	0.00	0.00	0.00	0.00	0.00	0.00	1651.98
19	1100.00	1100.00	0.00	0.00	0.00	194.92	82.62	0.00	0.00	0.00	0.00	0.00	0.00	822.46
20	870.00	870.00	0.00	0.00	0.00	101.42	62.10	0.00	0.00	0.00	0.00	0.00	0.00	706.48
21	520.00	520.00	0.00	0.00	0.00	49.66	30.42	0.00	0.00	0.00	0.00	0.00	0.00	439.92
21 employees	21673.20	21573.20	0.00	0.00	0.00	3542.28	1506.60	231.00	0.00	100.00	0.00	2.76	2.66	16624.22
1	2	3	4	5	6	7	8	9	10	11	12	13	14	15

DRAGON ENTERPRISE LIMITED
Tax month 06

Date : 300992
Page : 2

P A Y M E N T S   S U M M A R Y – P A R T   2
==

<< Monthly >>

| Ref. | Name | Standard Earnings | *** NATIONAL INSURANCE *** | | | | Employers | | Tax Code | Nat.Ins. Category |
			Total Contr'n	Emp'ees Contr'n	Con/out Earnings	Con/out Contr'n	Nat.Ins.	Pension		
1	F.Adams	746.00	115.27	50.94	0.00	0.00	64.33	0.00	344L	A
2	J.Joyce	0.00	59.86	0.00	0.00	0.00	59.86	0.00	516V	C
3	G.Rose	902.00	159.00	64.98	0.00	0.00	94.02	0.00	344L	A
4	J.Gieves	870.00	152.79	62.10	0.00	0.00	90.69	0.00	344L	A
5	B.King	1098.00	197.02	82.62	0.00	0.00	114.40	0.00	344L	A
6	W.Lansdown	1350.00	245.91	105.30	0.00	0.00	140.61	0.00	344L	A
7	A.Fisher	0.00	0.00	0.00	0.00	0.00	0.00	0.00	516H	A
8	C.Young	0.00	0.00	0.00	0.00	0.00	0.00	0.00	516V	C
9	A.Ball	870.00	152.79	62.10	0.00	0.00	90.69	0.00	516H	A
10	M.English	0.00	11.59	0.00	0.00	0.00	11.59	0.00	BR	C
11	M.Perkins	718.00	110.34	48.42	0.00	0.00	61.92	0.00	344L	A
12	P.Corke	718.00	110.34	48.42	0.00	0.00	61.92	0.00	516H	A
13	R.Reagan	1756.00	380.86	141.66	0.00	0.00	239.20	0.00	516H	A
14	W.Tasker	1740.00	305.58	124.20	0.00	0.00	181.38	0.00	344L	A
15	J.Wilson	498.00	61.62	28.62	0.00	0.00	33.00	0.00	NT	A
16	D.Carver	2500.00	485.00	225.00	0.00	0.00	260.00	0.00	189L	A
17	W.Bridges	870.00	152.79	62.10	0.00	0.00	90.69	0.00	516H	A
18	R.Long	2500.00	485.00	225.00	0.00	0.00	260.00	0.00	216L	A
19	K.Farmer	1098.00	197.02	82.62	0.00	0.00	114.40	0.00	344L	A
20	J.Nibbs	870.00	152.79	62.10	0.00	0.00	90.69	0.00	516H	A
21	M.Long	518.00	64.74	30.42	0.00	0.00	34.32	0.00	344LM1	A
Total values for 21 employees		19622.00	3600.31	1506.60	0.00	0.00	2093.71	0.00		
		16	17	18	19	20	21	22	23	24

DRAGON ENTERPRISE LIMITED
Tax month 06

Date : 300992
Page : 3

P A Y M E N T S   S U M M A R Y - P A R T 3
==

<< Monthly >>

******************   Y E A R   T O   D A T E   ****************

Ref.	Name	Total Gross Pay	Taxable Gross Pay	P.A.Y.E.	National Insurance Employees	Employers	S.S.P.	S.M.P.	Pension Employee	Employer
1	F.Adams	5154.05	5154.05	807.25	365.40	469.50	0.00	0.00	0.00	0.00
2	J.Joyce	4947.84	4947.84	539.50	0.00	451.10	0.00	0.00	0.00	0.00
3	G.Rose	6227.81	6227.81	1075.75	460.80	647.83	0.00	0.00	0.00	0.00
4	J.Gieves	6055.20	6055.20	1032.50	447.48	630.67	0.00	0.00	0.00	0.00
5	B.King	7656.00	7656.00	1432.75	554.76	796.22	0.00	0.00	0.00	0.00
6	W.Lansdown	9396.00	9396.00	1867.75	668.16	978.23	0.00	0.00	0.00	0.00
7	A.Fisher	7155.71	7155.71	1091.50	541.98	720.94	31.50	0.00	0.00	0.00
8	C.Young	4145.80	4145.80	339.00	0.00	365.25	525.00	0.00	0.00	0.00
9	A.Ball	6055.20	6055.20	816.50	447.48	630.67	0.00	0.00	0.00	0.00
10	M.English	3614.88	3614.88	903.50	0.00	332.63	0.00	0.00	0.00	0.00
11	M.Perkins	5011.20	5011.20	771.50	352.80	456.45	0.00	0.00	0.00	0.00
12	P.Corke	5011.20	5011.20	555.50	352.80	456.45	0.00	0.00	0.00	0.00
13	R.Reagan	13800.00	13800.00	2752.75	849.96	1435.20	0.00	0.00	0.00	0.00
14	W.Tasker	6925.20	6925.20	1169.91	509.58	721.36	0.00	0.00	0.00	0.00
15	J.Wilson	3050.00	3000.00	0.00	171.72	198.00	0.00	0.00	0.00	0.00
16	D.Carver	15050.00	15000.00	3792.50	1153.44	1560.00	0.00	0.00	0.00	0.00
17	W.Bridges	6055.20	6055.20	816.50	447.48	630.67	0.00	0.00	0.00	0.00
18	R.Long	15000.00	15000.00	3738.50	1153.44	1560.00	0.00	0.00	0.00	0.00
19	K.Farmer	7656.00	7656.00	1432.75	554.76	796.22	0.00	0.00	0.00	0.00
20	J.Nibbs	6055.20	6055.20	816.50	447.48	630.67	0.00	0.00	0.00	0.00
21	M.Long	1040.00	1040.00	99.32	60.84	68.64	0.00	0.00	0.00	0.00
	Total values for 21 employees	145062.49	144962.49	25851.73	9540.36	14536.70	556.50	0.00	0.00	0.00

9-9

Lesson Ten (October) starts on the facing page.

Lesson Ten

Month Seven - October

Form P6 Received
Introduction of a Pension Scheme
Continuing Absence
Double Entry Book-keeping

If you need to reload the payroll records at this stage use LOAD PAYROLL AT END OF SEPTEMBER. You must remember to update the records at 300992 before you enter the payments for October.

⇨ You are advised to enter the date as **011092** when you load the Sage Payroll II program at the start of this lesson.

Form P6 Received

During October Dragon received a form P6 from the Tax Office. This notified them that their most recent employee, Long (21), had been given a tax code of 344L, i.e. the normal code for a single person with no special claim for allowances. It is your task to enter these new details.

⇨ Go into **Employee Details - Amend Employee Details - Full Details**. You only need access to the records for employee no. 21. Amend Long's first screen as shown below.

```
┌─────────────────────────────────────────────────────────┐
│  Sage Payroll II          Full Details                   │
└─────────────────────────────────────────────────────────┘


    Employee No. :   21      On HOLD : NO      Start Date : 010892
                                               Leave Date :
        Forenames : Martin                  Holiday Return :
          Surname : Long
                                               Tax Code : 344L
          Address :                       Effective from : 011092
              ..  :                         N.I. Number : AC342789C
              ..  :                         N.I. Category : A
              ..  :                        Contracted-Out : N
                                               SCON Ref. :  0
                                          Effective from : 010892
```

Introduction of a Pension Scheme

Dragon Enterprise Limited has negotiated the introduction of a company pension scheme for some of its employees with an insurance company. All those people who are paid by Giro monthly, with the exception of the pensioners, have agreed to join the scheme. The people who will not be joining the scheme are Adams (1), Joyce (2), Young (8), Ball (9), English (10) and Wilson (15). The other 15 employees will be contracting-out of SERPS and instead the employees will contribute 6% of their pay to a pension scheme while the firm will contribute the equivalent of 5% of each employee's pay to the scheme. The parameters within which the payroll is calculated must be altered to operate such a scheme.

Amending the Parameters and Employee Details

⇨ Go into **Company Details - Pension Schemes** and enter the 5% and 6% mentioned so that the screen will look as shown below. You must also enter the **SCON** (Scheme Contracted-Out Number) given by the Department of Social Security when it approved the company pension scheme.

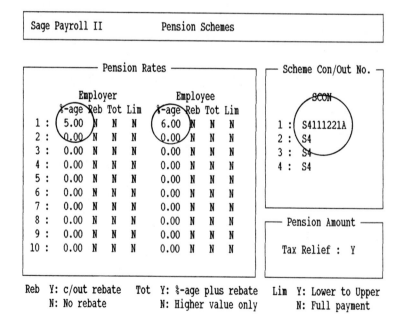

```
Sage Payroll II              Pension Schemes


────────── Pension Rates ──────────     ┌─ Scheme Con/Out No. ─┐
        Employer         Employee
       %-age Reb Tot Lim  %-age Reb Tot Lim            SCON
  1 :   5.00  N  N   N     6.00  N  N   N      1 :  S4111221A
  2 :   0.00  N  N   N     0.00  N  N   N      2 :  S4
  3 :   0.00  N  N   N     0.00  N  N   N      3 :  S4
  4 :   0.00  N  N   N     0.00  N  N   N      4 :  S4
  5 :   0.00  N  N   N     0.00  N  N   N
  6 :   0.00  N  N   N     0.00  N  N   N
  7 :   0.00  N  N   N     0.00  N  N   N
  8 :   0.00  N  N   N     0.00  N  N   N    ┌── Pension Amount ──┐
  9 :   0.00  N  N   N     0.00  N  N   N
 10 :   0.00  N  N   N     0.00  N  N   N       Tax Relief :  Y


Reb Y: c/out rebate   Tot Y: %-age plus rebate  Lim Y: Lower to Upper
    N: No rebate           N: Higher value only      N: Full payment
```

Reb(ate), **Tot**(al) and **Lim**(it) refer to conditions under which the pension scheme may operate. Schemes can be tailored to fit the wishes of firms and their employees and will not be discussed in greater detail in this course.

⇨ When you have entered this information press **Escape** to post it and return to the main menu.

It is also necessary to adjust the National Insurance Category and the Pension Reference for all those employees who will be taking advantage of this scheme. These are employees no. 3, 4, 5, 6, 7, 11, 12 13, 14, 16, 17, 18, 19, 20, and 21.

⇨ Go into **Employee Details - Amend Employee Details - Full Details**. The first employee whose details you actually have to change are Rose (3). Change the **Pension Ref** from **0** to **1** and the **National Insurance Category** from **A** to **D**. Accept the **SCON** number offered by the screen and show the effective date as **011092**. If you entered 011092 as the date when you loaded the program for this lesson you will find this date is entered for you automatically just by pressing **Enter**. A printout of how the screen should appear is given below.

```
┌──────────────────────────────────────────────────────────────┐
│ Sage Payroll II            Full Details                        │
└──────────────────────────────────────────────────────────────┘


   Employee No. :   3      On HOLD : NO        Start Date : 140891
                                               Leave Date :
          Forenames : Gladys               Holiday Return :
          Surname : Rose
                                                 Tax Code : 344L
          Address :                      Effective from : 060492
               .. :                         N.I. Number : GG121445C
               .. :                        N.I. Category : D
               .. :                       Contracted Out : Y
                                             SCON Ref. : 1
   Works Number : 220003                  Effective from : 011092
   Payment Type : GM
   Pension Ref. : 1                       Marital Status : M
   Auto SSP/SMP : Y                         Male/Female : F
   Date of Birth : 100466                      Director : N
```

⇨ Enter the same information for employees no. 4, 5, 6, 7, 11, 12 13, 14, 16, 17, 18, 19, 20, and 21.

Running the Payroll

⇨ When all the employee details have been entered in connection with the new pension scheme go into **Processing Payroll** and enter the date **311092**.

⇨ Process the payroll. All employees are to be paid at the same rate as last month. No entries need to be made when processing the payroll for the pensions. These will be included automatically as a result of the entries you have just made. However,

⇨ (a) Adams (1) is away from work on sick leave from **161092** to **271092**. Dragon is prepared to make his Statutory Sick Pay up to his normal salary of £748.80 so follow the instructions described for Lansdown (6) when he was off sick in July.

⇨ (b) Fisher (7) is still away on sick leave. He should be allowed the tax refund that is offered.

⇨ (c) When you are invited to allow a tax refund to Claude (8) this should be accepted.

⇨ (d) Tasker (14) is not entitled to a salary this month as she was paid it last month, and she does not, of course, have Holiday Pay this month.

⇨ (e) There are no expenses paid this month so those that were entered last month under **Salary Adjustments** must be removed. This affects employees 15 and 16.

⇨ (f) The tax refund should be paid to Long (21).

⇨ Print out the **Payments Summary** and if it agrees with the one at the end of the lesson update the records.

The Payments Summary

Pension Fund Contributions

Compare this month's Payments Summary with last month's. This month there is a pension contribution recorded for all those employees in the pension fund (with the exception of Tasker (14) who is not being paid this month).

National Insurance Contributions

You will notice that the NIC for those people who have joined the pension scheme is appreciably lower than the figure for previous months. People who have contracted out of SERPS pay lower contributions than those who are contracted in. These were Category A and are now Category D. The contribution rates in the two categories for employees who earn between £190.00 and £405.00 per week (£824.00 and £1,755.00 per month) are shown below.

```
              Bands            Employers       Employees
     From         To        < min   > min    < min   > min
   -----------------------   ------  ------   ------  ------
                          Category : A

     190.00  -  405.00  :    10.40   10.40    2.00    9.00

                       Category : D - con/out

     190.00  -  405.00  :    10.40    6.60    2.00    7.00
```

Using Gieves (4) as an example:

£870.00 is rounded off to £872.00 for calculation purposes. £872.00 less the first £234.00 (£54.00 per week) = £638.00.

Last month - as Category A

Employer's contribution = 10.4% of £872.00 =   £90.69
Employee's contribution = 2% of £234.00 =   £4.68
                   plus 9% of £638.00 =   £57.42
                                                                £62.10

This month - as Category D

Employer's contribution = 10.4% of £234.00 = £24.34
                   plus 6.6% of £638.00 =   £42.11
                                                                £66.45
Employee's contribution = 2% of £234.00 =   £4.68
                   plus 7% of £638.00 =   £44.66
                                                                £49.34

Directors' National Insurance Contributions

A further point to notice is the refund of NIC's made to the two directors. Because their NIC's are calculated on an annual basis and their NI category has now changed from A to D they find that they have paid too much this year already - rather like a refund of PAYE. This cannot happen with the ordinary employees as their NIC's are calculated afresh each pay day.

Tax Refund

During August and September Long (21) paid Income Tax on a Month 1 basis - a total of £99.32. All of this has been refunded during October. The reason behind this is that a person's tax liability is calculated on a cumulative basis. During the tax year 1992/93 Long has only earned a total of £1,560.00 but with a tax allowance of £3,449 per annum he is entitled to earn £2,011.91 (7/12 of £3,449) during the first seven months of the year. He hasn't earned that much yet so the tax that he has paid is returned to him.

Double Entry Book-keeping

This section should only be studied by those who are undertaking a book-keeping course at the same time as their study of the payroll.

The ledger account entries this month are further complicated by the pension contributions that the firm and its employees have made. Dragon Enterprise Limited will have to send this money to the insurance company with whom they arranged the pension. This time the running of the payroll left the firm with three liabilities: to the employees, to the Inland Revenue and to the pension organiser. The extent of these liabilities can be calculated from the Payments Summary in the following way.

Salaries Control =	Net Pay (Col 15)	£15,375.48	
	plus Bal b/f (Col 13)	£2.66	
	less Bal c/f (Col 14)	£1.53	£15,376.61
PAYE/NIC Control =	PAYE (Col 7)	£2,832.80	
	Total NIC (Col 17)	£1,114.07	£3,946.87
Pensions Control =	Pension (Col 6)	£993.35	
	plus Employer's Pension (Col 22)	£827.79	£1,821.14
TOTAL LIABILITIES			£21,144.62

These liabilites will have arisen as a result of just one expense - the cost of employing people:

Salaries Expense Account =	Gross Pay (Col 2)	£19,833.20	
	plus NIC (Col 21)	£483.63	
	plus Employer's Pension (Col 22)	£827.79	£21,144.62

Take the trouble to check each of the values listed above with your Payments Summary - it will help you to learn what the figures mean and how they are arrived at.

DRAGON ENTERPRISE LIMITED
Tax month 07

Date : 311092
Page :   1

P A Y M E N T S   S U M M A R Y - P A R T 1

<< Monthly >>

Ref.	Total Gross Pay	Taxable Gross Pay	Pre-Tax Addition	Deduct'n	Pension	P.A.Y.E.	Nat.Ins.	S.S.P.	S.M.P.	Post-Tax Addition	Deduct'n	Amount B/F	C/F	Nett Pay
1	748.80	748.80	0.00	0.00	0.00	106.91	50.94	52.50	0.00	0.00	0.00	0.60	0.65	591.00
2	696.00	696.00	0.00	0.00	0.00	57.91	0.00	0.00	0.00	0.00	0.00	0.66	0.57	638.00
3	904.80	850.51	0.00	0.00	54.29	132.41	51.58	0.00	0.00	0.00	0.00	0.00	0.00	666.52
4	870.00	817.80	0.00	0.00	52.20	124.41	49.34	0.00	0.00	0.00	0.00	0.00	0.00	644.05
5	1100.00	1034.00	0.00	0.00	66.00	178.41	65.30	0.00	0.00	0.00	0.00	0.00	0.00	790.29
6	1350.00	1269.00	0.00	0.00	81.00	237.16	82.94	0.00	0.00	0.00	0.00	0.00	0.00	948.90
7	231.00	217.14	0.00	0.00	13.86	-61.84	0.00	231.00	0.00	0.00	0.00	0.00	0.00	278.98
8	211.50	211.50	0.00	0.00	0.00	-63.34	0.00	0.00	0.00	0.00	0.00	0.00	0.00	274.84
9	870.00	870.00	0.00	0.00	0.00	101.16	62.10	0.00	0.00	0.00	0.00	0.78	0.04	706.00
10	251.10	251.10	0.00	0.00	0.00	62.75	0.00	0.00	0.00	0.00	0.00	0.62	0.27	188.00
11	720.00	676.80	0.00	0.00	43.20	89.16	38.70	0.00	0.00	0.00	0.00	0.00	0.00	548.94
12	720.00	676.80	0.00	0.00	43.20	52.91	38.70	0.00	0.00	0.00	0.00	0.00	0.00	585.19
13	2300.00	2162.00	0.00	0.00	138.00	424.16	111.22	0.00	0.00	0.00	0.00	0.00	0.00	1626.62
14	0.00	0.00	0.00	0.00	0.00	0.00	0.00	0.00	0.00	0.00	0.00	0.00	0.00	0.00
15	500.00	500.00	0.00	0.00	0.00	0.00	28.62	0.00	0.00	0.00	0.00	0.00	0.00	471.38
16	2500.00	2350.00	0.00	0.00	150.00	572.21	-68.84	0.00	0.00	0.00	0.00	0.00	0.00	1846.63
17	870.00	817.80	0.00	0.00	52.20	88.16	49.34	0.00	0.00	0.00	0.00	0.00	0.00	680.30
18	2500.00	2350.00	0.00	0.00	150.00	563.01	-68.84	0.00	0.00	0.00	0.00	0.00	0.00	1855.83
19	1100.00	1034.00	0.00	0.00	66.00	178.41	65.30	0.00	0.00	0.00	0.00	0.00	0.00	790.29
20	870.00	817.80	0.00	0.00	52.20	88.16	49.34	0.00	0.00	0.00	0.00	0.00	0.00	680.30
21	520.00	488.80	0.00	0.00	31.20	-99.32	24.70	0.00	0.00	0.00	0.00	0.00	0.00	563.42
21 employees	19833.20	18839.85	0.00	0.00	993.35	2832.80	630.44	283.50	0.00	0.00	0.00	2.66	1.53	15375.48
1	2	3	4	5	6	7	8	9	10	11	12	13	14	15

DRAGON ENTERPRISE LIMITED
Tax month 07

PAYMENTS SUMMARY - PART 2

Date : 311092
Page : 2

<< Monthly >>

Ref.	Name	Standard Earnings	*** NATIONAL INSURANCE *** Total Contr'n	Emp'ees Contr'n	Con/out Earnings	Con/out Contr'n	Employers Nat.Ins.	Pension	Tax Code	Nat.Ins. Category
1	F.Adams	746.00	115.27	50.94	0.00	0.00	64.33	0.00	344L	A
2	J.Joyce	0.00	59.86	0.00	0.00	0.00	59.86	0.00	516V	C
3	G.Rose	902.00	120.14	51.58	668.00	46.90	68.56	45.24	344L	D con/out
4	J.Gieves	870.00	115.79	49.34	636.00	44.66	66.45	43.50	344L	D con/out
5	B.King	1098.00	146.80	65.30	864.00	60.62	81.50	55.00	344L	D con/out
6	W.Lansdown	1350.00	181.07	82.94	1116.00	78.26	98.13	67.50	344L	D con/out
7	A.Fisher	0.00	0.00	0.00	0.00	0.00	0.00	11.55	516H	D con/out
8	C.Young	0.00	0.00	0.00	0.00	0.00	0.00	0.00	516V	C
9	A.Ball	870.00	152.79	62.10	0.00	0.00	90.69	0.00	516H	A
10	M.English	0.00	11.59	0.00	0.00	0.00	11.59	0.00	BR	C
11	M.Perkins	718.00	82.15	38.70	484.00	34.02	43.45	36.00	344L	D con/out
12	P.Corke	718.00	82.15	38.70	484.00	34.02	43.45	36.00	516H	D con/out
13	R.Reagan	1756.00	292.59	111.22	1522.00	106.54	181.37	115.00	516H	D con/out
14	W.Tasker	0.00	0.00	0.00	0.00	0.00	0.00	0.00	344L	D con/out
15	J.Wilson	498.00	61.62	28.62	0.00	0.00	33.00	0.00	NT	A
16	D.Carver	2500.00	-367.14	-68.84	14692.00	1028.44	-298.30	125.00	189L	D con/out
17	W.Bridges	870.00	115.79	49.34	636.00	44.66	66.45	43.50	516H	D con/out
18	R.Long	2500.00	-367.14	-68.84	14692.00	1028.44	-298.30	125.00	216L	D con/out
19	K.Farmer	1098.00	146.80	65.30	864.00	60.62	81.50	55.00	344L	D con/out
20	J.Nibbs	870.00	115.79	49.34	636.00	44.66	66.45	43.50	516H	D con/out
21	M.Long	518.00	48.15	24.70	284.00	20.02	23.45	26.00	344L	D con/out
	Total values for 21 employees	17882.00	1114.07	630.44	37578.00	2631.86	483.63	827.79		
		16	17	18	19	20	21	22	23	24

DRAGON ENTERPRISE LIMITED
Tax month 07

Date : 311092
Page : 3

P A Y M E N T S   S U M M A R Y   -   P A R T   3
===

<< Monthly >>

* *

Ref.	Name	Total Gross Pay	Taxable Gross Pay	P.A.Y.E.	National Insurance Employees	National Insurance Employers	S.S.P.	S.M.P.	Pension Employee	Pension Employer
1	F.Adams	5902.85	5902.85	914.16	416.34	533.83	52.50	0.00	0.00	0.00
2	J.Joyce	5643.84	5643.84	597.41	0.00	510.96	0.00	0.00	0.00	0.00
3	G.Rose	7132.61	7078.32	1208.16	512.38	716.39	0.00	0.00	54.29	45.24
4	J.Gieves	6925.20	6873.00	1156.91	496.82	697.12	0.00	0.00	52.20	43.50
5	B.King	8756.00	8690.00	1611.16	620.06	877.72	0.00	0.00	66.00	55.00
6	W.Lansdown	10746.00	10665.00	2104.91	751.10	1076.36	31.50	0.00	81.00	67.50
7	A.Fisher	7386.71	7372.85	1029.66	541.98	720.94	756.00	0.00	13.86	11.55
8	C.Young	4357.30	4357.30	275.66	0.00	365.25	0.00	0.00	0.00	0.00
9	A.Ball	6925.20	6925.20	917.66	509.58	721.36	0.00	0.00	0.00	0.00
10	M.English	3865.98	3865.98	966.25	0.00	344.22	0.00	0.00	43.20	36.00
11	M.Perkins	5731.20	5688.00	860.66	391.50	499.90	0.00	0.00	43.20	36.00
12	P.Corke	5731.20	5688.00	608.41	391.50	499.90	0.00	0.00	43.20	36.00
13	R.Reagan	16100.00	15962.00	3176.91	961.18	1616.57	0.00	0.00	138.00	115.00
14	W.Tasker	6925.20	6925.20	1169.91	509.58	721.36	0.00	0.00	0.00	0.00
15	J.Wilson	3550.00	3500.00	0.00	200.34	231.00	0.00	0.00	0.00	0.00
16	D.Carver	17550.00	17350.00	4364.71	1084.60	1261.70	0.00	0.00	150.00	125.00
17	W.Bridges	6925.20	6873.00	904.66	496.82	697.12	0.00	0.00	52.20	43.50
18	R.Long	17500.00	17350.00	4301.51	1084.60	1261.70	0.00	0.00	150.00	125.00
19	K.Farmer	8756.00	8690.00	1611.16	620.06	877.72	0.00	0.00	66.00	55.00
20	J.Nibbs	6925.20	6873.00	904.66	496.82	697.12	0.00	0.00	52.20	43.50
21	M.Long	1560.00	1528.80	0.00	85.54	92.09	0.00	0.00	31.20	26.00
	Total values for 21 employees	164895.69	163802.34	28684.53	10170.80	15020.33	840.00	0.00	993.35	827.79

Lesson Eleven (November) starts on the facing page.

Lesson Eleven

Month Eight - November

Two employees leave
Statutory Maternity Pay
Continuing absence

If you need to reload the payroll records at this stage use LOAD PAYROLL AT END OF OCTOBER. You must remember to update the records at 311092 before you enter the payments for November.

⇨ It is essential that you enter the date as 301192 when you load the Sage Payroll II program at the start of this lesson.

Leaving the Firm

On the 8th November Perkins (11) left Dragon Enterprise Limited. Dragon had to do two things on that day: provide her with her pay from 1st November to 8th November and give her a P45 form that she could give to her next employer. The P45 will be the way in which her new employer will know her Tax Code, how much pay she has received to date this year and how much tax she has already paid. The new employer is not allowed to simply accept Perkins' word for these details - a P45 must be produced.

After Perkins' pay has been calculated it will be necessary to remove her name from the list of current employees.

⇨ Go into **Processing Payroll** and enter the date as **081192**. Only Employee No. **11** need be dealt with at this stage so complete the screen like this.

```
┌─────────────────────────────────────────────────────────┐
│ Sage Payroll II          Processing Payroll             │
└─────────────────────────────────────────────────────────┘


        Lower Employee No.        1          :   11

        Upper Employee No.       11          :   11



            ┌─────────────────────────────────┐
            │ Clear payments file : No Yes    │
            └─────────────────────────────────┘
```

⇨ Choose **Enter Payments**.

⇨ With the cursor highlighting **Monthly Pay** press **F2** to get the calculator and key in the calculation **8/30=** and press **Enter** twice. (Obviously this refers to the 8 days she has worked and the 30 days in November, the current month). This will record the fraction of the month to which Perkins is entitled to pay. Press **F10** and allow the tax refund that is offered. The top of the screen will appear as below.

```
┌──────────────────────────────────────────────────────────────────────┐
│ Reference : 11    Name : Margaret Perkins         Pay Type : GM        │
└──────────────────────────────────────────────────────────────────────┘

       Monthly Pay : 0.2667     :    192.00   P.A.Y.E. (TAX) :     -35.08
      Basic Hourly :    0.0000  :      0.00
   Time and a half :    0.0000  :      0.00   NATIONAL INS. :        0.00
             Bonus :    0.0000  :      0.00
             BLANK :    0.0000  :      0.00
```

Until now the task of producing the payslip that is given to each employee has been omitted. It will be introduced here.

⇨ Go into **Processing Payroll - Payslips** and complete the screen as shown below by pressing **Enter** 5 times.

```
┌──────────────────────────────────────────────────────────────────────┐
│ Sage Payroll II              Payslips                                  │
└──────────────────────────────────────────────────────────────────────┘

       Lower Employee No.        11            :  11

       Upper Employee No.        11            :  11

       Input File Name           PAYSLIP.LYT   : PAYSLIP.LYT

       Printer, File or View     P             :   P

       Pause every [n] forms     11            :  11


               Switch the Printer On and Press  RETURN
```

⇨ Press **Enter** again to start the printing procedure.

⇨ You will be asked if you wish to print a **Test Pattern**. This is done to enable the operator to line up the payslips in the printer correctly. As you do not have pre-printed payslips this is not necessary so accept the **No**. You will produce a payslip for Perkins that looks like the one below.

DRAGON ENTERPRISE LIMITED

Monthly Pay :	0.2667	720.0000	192.00	P.A.Y.E. Tax	-35.08	TOTAL GROSS PAY TD	5923.20
Basic Hourly :	-	4.6400	-	National Ins.	-	Gross for Tax TD	5868.48
Time and a half :	-	6.9600	-	Pension	11.52	Tax paid TD	825.58
Bonus :	-	1.0000	-	Union Dues	-	Earnings for NI TD	5718.00
Salary Advance :	-	-	-		-	National Ins. TD	391.50
Salary Refund :	-	-	-		-	Pension TD	54.72
Expenses :	-	-	-		-		
Additions/Taxed :	-	-	-		-	====================
Sick Pay :	-	-	-		-	Earnings for NI	-
Maternity Pay :	-	-	-	Rounding B/F	-	Gross for Tax	180.48
Holiday Pay :	-	-	-	Rounding C/F	-	TOTAL GROSS PAY	192.00

8	08/11/92	1	GM	344L	11	Margaret Perkins	215.56

⇨ Go into **Payment Summary** and print out the details for this one employee. They should be as shown on the next page.

⇨ Check your printout with the one given here. If they agree go into **Processing Payroll - Update Records** and complete the usual routine for this disregarding the warning about not resetting the 'Last Update' value.

It is now time to remove Perkins from the list of current employees.

⇨ Go back to the Main Menu and choose **Employee Details - Remove an Employee.** Complete the screen as shown below.

```
┌─────────────────────────────────────────────────────────┐
│  Sage Payroll II        Remove an Employee              │
│                                                          │
└─────────────────────────────────────────────────────────┘

        Employee No. :  11

        Employee Name : Margaret Perkins

        Date of Leaving : 081192


              ┌──────────────────────────┐
              │ Is this correct : No Yes │
              └──────────────────────────┘
```

Lesson Eleven - November

DRAGON ENTERPRISE LIMITED
Tax month 08

Date : 301192
Page : 1

PAYMENTS SUMMARY - PART 1

<< Monthly >>

Ref.	Total Gross Pay	Taxable Gross Pay	Pre-Tax Addition	Pre-Tax Deduct'n	Pension	P.A.Y.E.	Nat.Ins.	S.S.P.	S.M.P.	Post-Tax Addition	Post-Tax Deduct'n	Amount B/F	C/F	Nett Pay
11	192.00	180.48	0.00	0.00	11.52	-35.08	0.00	0.00	0.00	0.00	0.00	0.00	0.00	215.56
1 employees	192.00	180.48	0.00	0.00	11.52	-35.08	0.00	0.00	0.00	0.00	0.00		0.00	215.56

PAYMENTS SUMMARY - PART 2

*** NATIONAL INSURANCE ***

Ref.	Name	Standard Earnings	Total Contr'n	Emp'ees Contr'n	Con/out Earnings	Con/out Contr'n	Employers Nat.Ins.	Employers Pension	Tax Code	Nat.Ins. Category
11	M.Perkins	0.00	0.00	0.00	0.00	0.00	0.00	9.60	344L	D con/out
Total values for 1 employees		0.00	0.00	0.00	0.00	0.00	0.00	9.60		

PAYMENTS SUMMARY - PART 3

*** YEAR TO DATE ***

Ref.	Name	Total Gross Pay	Taxable Gross Pay	P.A.Y.E.	National Insurance Employees	National Insurance Employers	S.S.P.	S.M.P.	Pension Employee	Pension Employer
11	M.Perkins	5923.20	5868.48	825.58	391.50	499.90	0.00	0.00	54.72	45.60
Total values for 1 employees		5923.20	5868.48	825.58	391.50	499.90	0.00	0.00	54.72	45.60

11 - 4

⇨ Press **Y** for **Yes,** then **Enter** twice and the printer will produce two forms.

You will obtain a P11 (not reproduced here) that lists Perkins' earnings and deductions for the year to date. This must be kept by Dragon in order that the Inland Revenue can inspect the firm's records of payments if they so wish.

So far as the new employer is concerned only the totals of pay and deductions are needed. These are provided on a P45. The second form that is printed (but not reproduced here) contains the information that must be entered on the P45 that Perkins will take to her new job. Dragon will complete the P45 as illustrated below.

P45 Details of employee leaving — Part 1

		District number	Reference number
1.	PAYE reference	415	D 9045

2.	National Insurance number	TY 93 44 45 A	

			Mr. Mrs. Miss. Ms.
3.	Surname *Use CAPITALS*	PERKINS	MISS
	First two forenames *Use CAPITALS*	MARGARET	

		Day	Month	Year
4.	Date of leaving *in figures*	8	11	19 92

			Code	Week 1 or Month 1
5.	Code at date of leaving. If Week 1 or Month 1 basis applies, please also write 'X' in the box marked 'Week 1 or Month 1'		344 L	

			Week	Month
6.	Last entries on Deductions Working Sheet *If Week 1 or Month 1 basis applies, complete item 7 instead*	Week or month number		8
		Total pay to date	£ 5868	48 p
		Total tax to date	£ 825	58 p

7.	Week 1 or Month 1 basis applies	Total pay in this employment	£	p
		Total tax in this employment	£	p

8.	Works Number	91	9. Branch, Contract Department, etc.	I

10. Employee's private address 16 LABURNUM STREET
BENTON
Postcode R38 4GQ

11. I certify that the details entered at items 1 to 9 above are correct.

Employer DRAGON ENTERPRISE LIMITED
Address MANNHEAD TRADING ESTATE
RENCHESTER
Date 8-11-92
Postcode RR9 9RR

Part 1 of the P45 will be sent by Dragon to the Tax Office and Parts 2 and 3 (copies of Part 1) will be given to Perkins for her to give to her next employer.

⇨ Just to check that the employee details now show that Perkins has left the firm go back into **Employee Details - Amend Employee Details - Full Details** and ensure that a leaving date appears on the screen for Perkins as depicted below.

```
 ┌─────────────────────────────────────────────────────────────┐
 │  Sage Payroll II            Full Details                     │
 └─────────────────────────────────────────────────────────────┘


    Employee No. :   11        On HOLD : NO        Start Date /  140189
                                                   Leave Date (: 081192
        Forenames : Margaret               Holiday Return
        Surname : Perkins
```

The other person to leave during November was Adams (1) who left on 15th November.

⇨ Follow the same procedure as shown above, i.e. run the payroll on 15th November, update the records and then remove Adams from the list of employees. While you are entering details on the Enter Payments screen place the cursor over the **Rounding C/F : 0.13** field and press **F3**. This will have the effect of ensuring that there is no rounding up of the pay this month. As Adams will not be employed next month it would not be possible for Dragon to reclaim the overpayment if it was made.

Statutory Maternity Pay

*It is essential that **301192** was entered as the date when loading the Sage Payroll II program for the following routine to operate properly.*

Betty King (5) announces that she is pregnant and intends to take maternity leave with effect from 14th November. Because she has been:

(a) continuously employed for at least 26 weeks up to the 15th week before the baby is due (the Qualifying Week),

(b) has average earnings (over the last 8 weeks) above the lower limit for National Insurance contributions,

(c) was still pregnant 11 weeks before her expected week of confinement (EWC) and

(d) has now stopped work

she is entitled to receive Statutory Maternity Pay for a maximum of 18 weeks. Her doctor or midwife has given her a form **Mat B1** on which it is stated that the expected week of her confinement (EWC) is 30th January 1993.

First you must enter the details of the anticipated absence and then you can run the payroll.

⇨ Go into **Statutory Maternity Pay - Initialise SMP Dates.** It is only employee no. **5** for whom you need to enter details.

⇨ Complete the screen as indicated below. When the cursor is against **Average Weekly Gross Pay** press **F3** and choose **Yes**. Press **Enter** after the **375.69** appears.

The information in the lower half of the screen will appear after you have entered all the information in the top half. King is not being dismissed because of her pregnancy and has not yet indicated whether or not she will be returning to work afterwards. This is what the **N** against **Fair Dismissal** refers to.

```
Reference : 5      Name : Betty King                    Pay Type : GM


   Date baby due (EWC) : 300193      Employment began : 120181
                       :                      ''  ended : 131192
  Medical evidence of EWC : Y        Min. hours per week :   37
                       :                                  :
  Average weekly gross pay :     375.69      Fair dismissal : N


      Qualifying week : 111092        Start of M.P.P. : 081192

                          S.M.P. Entitlement

      Higher rate :   6  weeks at :    338.13  :     2028.78
      Lower rate :  12  weeks at :     46.30  :      555.60
      Total due :  18  weeks      :            :     2584.38
```

In the first half you entered the **Expected Week of Confinement** and Sage calculated that 11 weeks before this would be 081192 which is when the **Maternity Pay Period (MPP)** starts. In other words, when King can take paid time off work. It also calculates the pay to which she is entitled during her absence. The first **6** weeks are paid at the higher rate of **£338.13**. The following **12** weeks are paid at the lower rate of **£46.30**.

You will recall having entered the date as 301192 when you started this lesson. This meant that when you completed the screen with the details of King's pregnancy you were able to record that she had already temporarily left her employment. The date of leaving was before the date of making the entry. This enabled the computer to accept the date because King then satisfied one of the conditions for payment of SMP - that of having already left work. It is only possible to complete this screen if all conditions for SMP are met. For example, if King's average earnings had not been sufficient to permit SMP to be paid no calculation of payment would be made. If she had not been in employment for 26 weeks the leaving date would have been rejected and a message explaining this would have appeared on the screen.

⇨ Go back to the Main Menu and choose **Government Parameters - SMP Rates**. You are presented with the following screen.

Sage Payroll II	SMP Rates

S.M.P.

Max. weeks at higher rate : 6

Max. weeks at lower rate : 12

Lower rate : 46.30

Higher rate percentage : 90.00

Percentage to reclaim : 100.00

NIC compensation rate : 4.50

This tells you that, amongst other things, the lower rate of £46.30 will be paid for a maximum of 12 weeks and that a higher rate equal to 90% of average earnings will be paid for a maximum of 6 weeks.

King's average weekly earnings are based on her having been paid £1,256.00 on 31st August and £1,100.00 on 30th September. These were the two pay days in the eight weeks immediately before 11th October (111092) - the first day of her qualifying week. The arithmetic is (£2,156.00 + £1,100.00) x 6 / 52 = £375.69 per week.

The last two items are an indication that Dragon can reclaim all of the money that it pays out in SMP from the Government plus a further 4.5% of that amount. You may remember that when the firm pays Statutory Sick Pay it is only able to reclaim 80% of the amount paid and receives no compensation for making the payment. During maternity leave neither the firm nor King is required to make National Insurance contributions unless her income from Statutory Maternity Pay places her above the lower earnings limit for NIC's.

As Betty King is not leaving Dragon's employment on a permanent basis she will not be paid until the end of the month with the rest of the employees and her name will not, of course, be removed from the records.

⇨ Go into **Processing Payroll** and enter the date **301192**. Run the rest of the payroll (employee nos. 1 to 30) ensuring that you record the following.

⇨ (a) King (5) has only worked for 13/30ths of the month.

⇨ (b) Fisher (7) has been absent all month. You should allow the tax refund to Fisher that is offered.

⇨ (c) Allow the tax refund that is offered to Young (8).

⇨ (d) Tasker (14) has worked a full month during November,

The Payments Summary

Notice that the employees who have left, Adams (1) and Perkins (11), do not appear on Parts 1 and 2, i.e. the parts that relate to this month's payroll run. They still appear in Part 3 however as their past pay is still relevant to the year-to-date figures.

Notice also that King's pay (5) includes 3 weeks Statutory Maternity Pay at £338.13 per week.

⇨ Check your printout of the Payments Summary with the one shown at the end of this lesson. If they agree update the records in the usual way.

Paying the Inland Revenue

Make sure that you have updated the records before proceeding with this section.

⇨ Go into **Processing Payroll - Collector of Taxes**. Complete the screen to indicate that it is the values for **Month 8** that you want and you will produce a printout as shown on page 11 - 11.

This records that Dragon must pay £4,237.33 to the Inland Revenue but that this would have been £1,236.44 more had the firm not paid to its employees, on the Government's behalf, £220.50 Statutory Sick Pay (of which it could reclaim £176.40) and £1,014.39 Statutory Maternity Pay. In addition though, the firm is able to reduce its payment to the Tax Office by a further £45.65 which it gets as compensation - a sort of payment - for having to make the maternity benefit payments. You will notice that no such compensation is allowed in connection with Statutory Sick Pay. Some years ago this was allowed, now it has been withdrawn.

Double Entry Book-keeping

This section is included only for those people studying double entry book-keeping in conjunction with this course.

The payment of SMP complicates the book-keeping this month. The £1,014.39 being paid can all be reclaimed from the Inland Revenue plus a further 4.5% of this as has already been explained. The calculation of the deductions from the payment to the Inland Revenue is:

80% of £220.50 SSP (Col 9)	£176.40
SMP (Col 10)	£1,014.39
4.5% of SMP	£45.65
TOTAL	£1,236.44

The ledger account entries then becomes:

Salaries Control	Net Pay (Col 15)	£14,523.97	
	plus Bal b/f (Col 13)	£0.88	
	less Bal c/f (Col 14)	£0.97	£14,523.88
PAYE/NIC Control	PAYE (Col 7)	£2,960.64	
	plus Total NIC (Col 17)	£2,500.03	
	less Inland Revenue deductions	£1,236.44	£4,224.23
Pension Control	Pension (Col 6)	£1025.18	
	plus Employer's pension (Col 22)	£854.32	£1,879.50
TOTAL LIABILITIES			£20,627.61
Salaries Expenses Account	Gross Pay (Col 2)	£19,614.96	
	less Inland Revenue deductions	£1,236.44	
	plus NIC (Col 21)	£1,394.77	
	plus Pension (Col 22)	£854.32	£20,627.61

DRAGON ENTERPRISE LIMITED

Date : 301192

Collector of Taxes (Monthly Payslip Returns)

Record of deductions from gross National Insurance

	(1) S.S.P.	(2) NIC comp'n	(3) S.M.P.	(4) NIC comp'n	(5) Total Ded.
Weekly	0.00	0.00	0.00	0.00	0.00
2 Weekly	0.00	0.00	0.00	0.00	0.00
4 Weekly	0.00	0.00	0.00	0.00	0.00
Monthly	176.40	0.00	1014.39	45.65	1236.44
Totals	176.40	0.00	1014.39	45.65	1236.44

Record of Payments

	(1) Income Tax	(2) Gross N.I.	(3) Total Ded.	(4) Net N.I.	(5) Total Due
Weekly	0.00	0.00	0.00	0.00	0.00
2 Weekly	0.00	0.00	0.00	0.00	0.00
4 Weekly	0.00	0.00	0.00	0.00	0.00
Monthly	2938.98	2534.79	1236.44	1298.35	4237.33
Totals	2938.98	2534.79	1236.44	1298.35	4237.33

NIC compensation percentage

S.S.P. : 0.00   S.M.P. : 4.50

Employee range

0001 - 0030

Date range

Week : 061192 - 051292   Month : 061192 - 051292

11 - 11

DRAGON ENTERPRISE LIMITED
Tax month 08

PAYMENTS SUMMARY - PART 1
<< Monthly >>

Date : 301192
Page : 1

Ref.	Total Gross Pay	Taxable Gross Pay	Pre-Tax Addition	Deduct'n	Pension	P.A.Y.E.	Nat.Ins.	S.S.P.	S.M.P.	Post-Tax Addition	Deduct'n	Amount B/F	C/F	Nett Pay
2	696.00	696.00	0.00	0.00	0.00	57.67	0.00	0.00	0.00	0.00	0.00	0.57	0.24	638.00
3	904.80	850.51	0.00	0.00	54.29	132.42	51.58	0.00	0.00	0.00	0.00	0.00	0.00	666.51
4	870.00	817.80	0.00	0.00	52.20	124.17	49.34	0.00	0.00	0.00	0.00	0.00	0.00	644.29
5	1491.06	1401.60	0.00	0.00	89.46	270.17	92.74	0.00	1014.39	0.00	0.00	0.00	0.00	1038.69
6	1350.00	1269.00	0.00	0.00	81.00	236.92	82.94	0.00	0.00	0.00	0.00	0.00	0.00	949.14
7	220.50	207.27	0.00	0.00	13.23	-64.33	0.00	220.50	0.00	0.00	0.00	0.00	0.00	271.60
8	211.50	211.50	0.00	0.00	0.00	-52.46	0.00	0.00	0.00	0.00	0.00	0.00	0.00	263.96
9	870.00	870.00	0.00	0.00	0.00	101.42	62.10	0.00	0.00	0.00	0.00	0.04	0.56	707.00
10	251.10	251.10	0.00	0.00	0.00	63.00	0.00	0.00	0.00	0.00	0.00	0.27	0.17	188.00
12	720.00	676.80	0.00	0.00	43.20	52.92	38.70	0.00	0.00	0.00	0.00	0.00	0.00	585.18
13	2300.00	2162.00	0.00	0.00	138.00	424.42	111.22	0.00	0.00	0.00	0.00	0.00	0.00	1626.36
14	870.00	817.80	0.00	0.00	52.20	124.17	49.34	0.00	0.00	0.00	0.00	0.00	0.00	644.29
15	500.00	500.00	0.00	0.00	0.00	0.00	28.62	0.00	0.00	0.00	0.00	0.00	0.00	471.38
16	2500.00	2350.00	0.00	0.00	150.00	572.22	175.00	0.00	0.00	0.00	0.00	0.00	0.00	1602.78
17	870.00	817.80	0.00	0.00	52.20	88.17	49.34	0.00	0.00	0.00	0.00	0.00	0.00	680.29
18	2500.00	2350.00	0.00	0.00	150.00	563.42	175.00	0.00	0.00	0.00	0.00	0.00	0.00	1611.58
19	1100.00	1034.00	0.00	0.00	66.00	178.17	65.30	0.00	0.00	0.00	0.00	0.00	0.00	790.53
20	870.00	817.80	0.00	0.00	52.20	88.17	49.34	0.00	0.00	0.00	0.00	0.00	0.00	680.29
21	520.00	488.80	0.00	0.00	31.20	0.00	24.70	0.00	0.00	0.00	0.00	0.00	0.00	464.10
19 employees	19614.96	18589.78	0.00	0.00	1025.18	2960.64	1105.26	220.50	1014.39	0.00	0.00	0.88	0.97	14523.97
	1	2	3	4	5	6	7	8	9	10	11	12	13	14	15

DRAGON ENTERPRISE LIMITED
Tax month 08

Date : 301192
Page : 2

PAYMENTS SUMMARY - PART 2

<< Monthly >>

| Ref. | Name | *** NATIONAL INSURANCE *** | | | | | Employers | | Tax Code | Nat.Ins. Category |
		Standard Earnings	Total Contr'n	Emp'ees Contr'n	Con/out Earnings	Con/out Contr'n	Nat.Ins.	Pension		
2	J.Joyce	0.00	59.86	0.00	0.00	0.00	59.86	0.00	516V	C
3	G.Rose	902.00	120.14	51.58	668.00	46.90	68.56	45.24	344L	D con/out
4	J.Gieves	870.00	115.79	49.34	636.00	44.66	66.45	43.50	344L	D con/out
5	B.King	1490.00	200.11	92.74	1256.00	88.06	107.37	74.55	344L	D con/out
6	W.Lansdown	1350.00	181.07	82.94	1116.00	78.26	98.13	67.50	344L	D con/out
7	A.Fisher	0.00	0.00	0.00	0.00	0.00	0.00	11.03	516H	D con/out
8	C.Young	0.00	0.00	0.00	0.00	0.00	0.00	0.00	516V	C
9	A.Ball	870.00	152.79	62.10	0.00	0.00	90.69	0.00	516H	A
10	M.English	0.00	11.59	0.00	0.00	0.00	11.59	0.00	BR	C
12	P.Corke	718.00	82.15	38.70	484.00	34.02	43.45	36.00	516H	D con/out
13	R.Reagan	1756.00	292.59	111.22	1522.00	106.54	181.37	115.00	516H	D con/out
14	W.Tasker	870.00	115.79	49.34	636.00	44.66	66.45	43.50	344L	D con/out
15	J.Wilson	498.00	61.62	28.62	0.00	0.00	33.00	0.00	NT	A
16	D.Carver	2500.00	340.00	175.00	2500.00	175.00	165.00	125.00	189L	D con/out
17	W.Bridges	870.00	115.79	49.34	636.00	44.66	66.45	43.50	516H	D con/out
18	R.Long	2500.00	340.00	175.00	2500.00	175.00	165.00	125.00	216L	D con/out
19	K.Farmer	1098.00	146.80	65.30	864.00	60.62	81.50	55.00	344L	D con/out
20	J.Nibbs	870.00	115.79	49.34	636.00	44.66	66.45	43.50	516H	D con/out
21	M.Long	518.00	48.15	24.70	284.00	20.02	23.45	26.00	344L	D con/out
Total values for 19 employees		17680.00	2500.03	1105.26	13738.00	963.06	1394.77	854.32		
		16	17	18	19	20	21	22	23	24

DRAGON ENTERPRISE LIMITED

Tax month 08

Date : 301192
Page : 3

PAYMENTS SUMMARY - PART 3
==================================

<< Monthly >>

Ref.	Name	Total Gross Pay	Taxable Gross Pay	P.A.Y.E.	YEAR TO DATE National Insurance		S.S.P.	S.M.P.	Pension	
					Employees	Employers			Employee	Employer
1	F.Adams	6277.25	6277.25	927.58	433.80	551.13	52.50	0.00	0.00	0.00
2	J.Joyce	6339.84	6339.84	655.08	0.00	570.82	0.00	0.00	0.00	0.00
3	G.Rose	8037.41	7928.83	1340.58	563.96	784.95	0.00	0.00	108.58	90.48
4	J.Gieves	7795.20	7690.80	1281.08	546.16	763.57	0.00	0.00	104.40	87.00
5	B.King	10247.06	10091.60	1881.33	712.80	985.09	0.00	1014.39	155.46	129.55
6	W.Lansdown	12096.00	11934.00	2341.83	834.04	1174.49	31.50	0.00	162.00	135.00
7	A.Fisher	7607.21	7580.12	965.33	541.98	720.94	976.50	0.00	27.09	22.58
8	C.Young	4568.80	4568.80	223.20	0.00	365.25	0.00	0.00	0.00	0.00
9	A.Ball	7795.20	7795.20	1019.08	571.68	812.05	0.00	0.00	0.00	0.00
10	M.English	4117.08	4117.08	1029.25	0.00	355.81	0.00	0.00	0.00	0.00
11	M.Perkins	5923.20	5868.48	825.58	391.50	499.90	0.00	0.00	54.72	45.60
12	P.Corke	6451.20	6364.80	661.33	430.20	543.35	0.00	0.00	86.40	72.00
13	R.Reagan	18400.00	18124.00	3601.33	1072.40	1797.94	0.00	0.00	276.00	230.00
14	W.Tasker	7795.20	7743.00	1294.08	558.92	787.81	0.00	0.00	52.20	43.50
15	J.Wilson	4050.00	4000.00	0.00	228.96	264.00	0.00	0.00	0.00	0.00
16	D.Carver	20050.00	19700.00	4936.93	1259.60	1426.70	0.00	0.00	300.00	250.00
17	W.Bridges	7795.20	7690.80	992.83	546.16	763.57	0.00	0.00	104.40	87.00
18	R.Long	20000.00	19700.00	4864.93	1259.60	1426.70	0.00	0.00	300.00	250.00
19	K.Farmer	9856.00	9724.00	1789.33	685.36	959.22	0.00	0.00	132.00	110.00
20	J.Nibbs	7795.20	7690.80	992.83	546.16	763.57	0.00	0.00	104.40	87.00
21	M.Long	2080.00	2017.60	0.00	110.24	115.54	0.00	0.00	62.40	52.00
	Total values for 21 employees	185077.05	182947.00	31623.51	11293.52	16432.40	1060.50	1014.39	2030.05	1691.71

Lesson Twelve

Month Nine - December

Tax Code Changes
Overtime
Continuing Absence
Issuing a Change Over Form (SSP1)

If you need to reload the payroll records at this stage use LOAD PAYROLL AT END OF NOVEMBER. You must remember to update the records at 301192 before you enter the payments for December.

During the month the Tax Office changed Corke's tax code from 516H to 344L as he had not replied to an enquiry that they had sent him. (In such ways does the Tax Office encourage co-operation!)

During December the tax code of two employees was changed. Carver (16) got married and notified the Inland Revenue to this effect. As a result he was given a new Tax Code of 246H. It is not the responsibility of the firm to produce a revised tax code for any of its employees. It must just accept the ones notified to it by the Tax Office.

An explanation of how the new tax code for Carver was arrived at is given at the end of this month's details.

⇨ Go into **Employee Details - Amend Employee Details - Full Details** and post the new tax code of **344L** for Corke (12) as illustrated below and **246H** for Carver (16).

```
┌────────────────────────────────────────────────────────────────┐
│  Sage Payroll II            Full Details                         │
└────────────────────────────────────────────────────────────────┘


   Employee No. :   12      On HOLD : NO        Start Date : 300982
                                                Leave Date :
      Forenames : Paul                       Holiday Return :
        Surname : Corke
                                                 Tax Code : 344L
        Address :                          Effective from : 311292
             .. :                             N.I. Number : GG136445A
             .. :                            N.I. Category : D
             .. :                           Contracted-Out : Y
                                                SCON Ref. : 1
   Works Number :   24                      Effective from : 011092
```

```
┌──────────────────────────────────────────────────────────────────┐
│  Sage Payroll II            Full Details                           │
└──────────────────────────────────────────────────────────────────┘
```

Employee No. : 16   On HOLD : NO   Start Date : 230188
                                              Leave Date :
      Forenames : David   Holiday Return :
        Surname : Carver
                                                 Tax Code : 246H
        Address :   Effective from : 311292
             .. :   N.I. Number : RR557445C
             .. :   N.I. Category : D
             .. :   Contracted-Out : Y
                                             SCON Ref. : 1
   Works Number : 41   Effective from : 011092

During December a number of employees worked overtime. For most people these extra hours are paid at time and a half. The extra hours undertaken by Young however did not bring his hours up to a full month (you will remember that he has been working only 30 hours a month lately) so all his hours (48 this month) are paid at the Basic Hourly rate. A summary of the hours and rates of pay is given below.

Employee	Hours O'time	Rate of pay
Rose (3)	12	Time and a half
Young (8)	18 (plus 30)	Basic rate
Corke (12)	17	Time and a half
Tasker (14)	12	Time and a half
Long (21)	18	Time and a half

⇨ Go into **Processing Payroll** and enter the date **311292**. Make the appropriate entries for each employee noting, in addition to their overtime, the following.

⇨ (a) A printout of the overtime entry for Rose (3) is given at the end of these instructions.

⇨ (b) King (5) is, of course, away on maternity leave and therfore not entitled to any pay. Her SMP will be calculated automatically.

⇨ (c) Fisher (7) is still off work and should be paid his tax refund. After you have entered Fisher's absence this message will appear on the screen.

```
┌─────────────────────────────────────┐ ┌──────────────────────────────────┐
│                                      │ │ Have you issued a TRANSFER form  │
│  Reference : 7      Name : Andrew Fisher                                   │
│                                      │ │ Hit any key to continue          │
└─────────────────────────────────────┘ └──────────────────────────────────┘

        Start date :           End date :             Type :
```

You will need to return to this task when you have run the payroll.

⇨ (d) The tax refund for Young (8) should be allowed.

```
┌──────────────────────────────────────────────────────────────────────────┐
│  Reference : 3      Name : Gladys Rose                    Pay Type : GM    │
└──────────────────────────────────────────────────────────────────────────┘
```

Monthly Pay :	1.0000 :	904.80	P.A.Y.E. (TAX) :	156.92
Basic Hourly :	0.0000 :	0.00		
Time and a half :	12.0000 :	104.46	NATIONAL INS. :	58.86
Bonus : 0.0000	:	0.00		
BLANK :	0.0000 :	0.00		
Pre-Tax Add/n :		0.00	Post-Tax Add/n :	0.00
Pre-Tax Ded/n :		0.00	Post-Tax Ded/n :	0.00
Pension :		60.56		

⇨ Print the Payment Summary and check it against the one that appears at the end of the lesson. *Do not update the records yet.*

Change-over Forms (SSP1)

During December Fisher will have been away on sick leave for the 23rd week. He is only permitted a total of 28 weeks Statutory Sick Pay. It is important that he is warned that he is nearing the end of this entitlement. The Sage Payroll II program is able to warn when this is imminent and to produce a warning notice.

⇨ From the Main Menu go into **Statutory Sick Pay - Transfer & Exclusion Forms** and produce a printout similar to the one below.

DRAGON ENTERPRISE LIMITED   Transfer and Exclusion Report

No.	Employee Name	Form type	Start of PIW	End of PIW	Reason for Issue
----	-----------------	---------	------	------	-----------------
7	Fisher	SSP1(T)	200792	311292	Transfer form limit of 23 weeks exceeded.

The **End of PIW, 311292,** is not the last day for which Fisher could be paid SSP - it is the latest day for which his absence has already been recorded. It is, however, more than 23 weeks since the start of Fisher's PIW. 28 weeks (196 days) from 20th July 1992 is 3rd February 1993 so this is the date that must appear on the Change-over Form (SSP1) that Dragon must send him.

⇨ You should now update the records.

Tax Code Change Calculations

Carver got married 8/12ths of the way through the year. He was using a tax code of 189 during this period. For the remaining 4/12ths of the year he is entitled to a married person's allowance of £1720 so his tax code for the last four months will be 189 + 172 = 361. However, if his code was simply to be changed to the new figure in December he would effectively be awarded this code for the whole year as the calculations are always based upon the cumulative pay for the year to date. To overcome this the Inland Revenue calculates a *weighted average* tax code for the year. The calculation is made as follows.

	189 x 8/12 =	126
plus	361 x 4/12 =	<u>120</u>
equals		246

Carver's suffix changes from L to H because he is now married.

Payments Summary

The effect of the two tax code changes can be seen clearly this month. Whilst Corke's (12) gross pay rose in December by £118.32 his PAYE increased by £352.25. This has arisen because the Tax Office has withdrawn (perhaps temporarily) his married person's allowance.

For Carver (16) the change is in the opposite direction. His PAYE this month is £171.20 less than last month - a reflection of the married person's allowance that he is now receiving that he did not receive before.

DRAGON ENTERPRISE LIMITED   Date : 311292
Tax month 09   Page : 1

P A Y M E N T S   S U M M A R Y - P A R T 1
==

<< Monthly >>

Ref.	Total Gross Pay	Taxable Gross Pay	Pre-Tax Addition	Pre-Tax Deduct'n	Pension	P.A.Y.E.	Nat.Ins.	S.S.P.	S.M.P.	Post-Tax Addition	Post-Tax Deduct'n	Amount B/F	Amount C/F	Nett Pay
2	696.00	696.00	0.00	0.00	0.00	57.92	0.00	0.00	0.00	0.00	0.00	0.24	0.16	638.00
3	1009.26	948.70	0.00	0.00	60.56	156.92	58.86	0.00	0.00	0.00	0.00	0.00	0.00	732.92
4	870.00	817.80	0.00	0.00	52.20	124.17	49.34	0.00	0.00	0.00	0.00	0.00	0.00	644.29
5	1060.69	997.05	0.00	0.00	63.64	168.92	62.50	0.00	1060.69	0.00	0.00	0.00	0.00	765.63
6	1350.00	1269.00	0.00	0.00	81.00	237.17	82.94	0.00	0.00	0.00	0.00	0.00	0.00	948.89
7	241.50	227.01	0.00	0.00	14.49	-59.58	5.10	241.50	0.00	0.00	0.00	0.00	0.00	281.49
8	338.40	338.40	0.00	0.00	0.00	-18.60	0.00	0.00	0.00	0.00	0.00	0.00	0.00	357.00
9	870.00	870.00	0.00	0.00	0.00	101.17	62.10	0.00	0.00	0.00	0.00	0.56	0.83	707.00
10	251.10	251.10	0.00	0.00	0.00	62.75	0.00	0.00	0.00	0.00	0.00	0.17	0.82	189.00
12	838.32	788.02	0.00	0.00	50.30	405.17	47.10	0.00	0.00	0.00	0.00	0.00	0.00	335.75
13	2300.00	2162.00	0.00	0.00	138.00	424.17	111.22	0.00	0.00	0.00	0.00	0.00	0.00	1626.61
14	977.64	918.98	0.00	0.00	58.66	149.67	56.62	0.00	0.00	0.00	0.00	0.00	0.00	712.69
15	500.00	500.00	0.00	0.00	0.00	0.00	28.62	0.00	0.00	0.00	0.00	0.00	0.00	471.38
16	2500.00	2350.00	0.00	0.00	150.00	401.02	74.27	0.00	0.00	0.00	0.00	0.00	0.00	1874.71
17	870.00	817.80	0.00	0.00	52.20	88.42	49.34	0.00	0.00	0.00	0.00	0.00	0.00	680.04
18	2500.00	2350.00	0.00	0.00	150.00	563.02	74.27	0.00	0.00	0.00	0.00	0.00	0.00	1712.71
19	1100.00	1034.00	0.00	0.00	66.00	178.42	65.30	0.00	0.00	0.00	0.00	0.00	0.00	790.28
20	870.00	817.80	0.00	0.00	52.20	88.42	49.34	0.00	0.00	0.00	0.00	0.00	0.00	680.04
21	606.40	570.02	0.00	0.00	36.38	0.00	30.86	0.00	0.00	0.00	0.00	0.00	0.00	539.16
	19749.31	18723.68	0.00	0.00	1025.63	3129.15	907.78	241.50	1060.69	0.00	0.00	0.97	1.81	14687.59

19 employees

DRAGON ENTERPRISE LIMITED

Tax month 09

Date : 311292
Page : 2

PAYMENTS SUMMARY - PART 2

<< Monthly >>

| Ref. | Name | Standard Earnings | *** NATIONAL INSURANCE *** | | | | Employers | | Tax Code | Nat.Ins. Category |
			Total Contr'n	Emp'ees Contr'n	Con/out Earnings	Con/out Contr'n	Nat.Ins.	Pension		
2	J.Joyce	0.00	59.86	0.00	0.00	0.00	59.86	0.00	516V	C
3	G.Rose	1006.00	134.28	58.86	772.00	54.18	75.42	50.46	344L	D con/out
4	J.Gieves	870.00	115.79	49.34	636.00	44.66	66.45	43.50	344L	D con/out
5	B.King	1058.00	141.36	62.50	824.00	57.82	78.86	53.03	344L	D con/out
6	W.Lansdown	1350.00	181.07	82.94	1116.00	78.26	98.13	67.50	344L	D con/out
7	A.Fisher	238.00	15.91	5.10	4.00	0.42	10.81	12.08	516H	D con/out
8	C.Young	0.00	15.64	0.00	0.00	0.00	15.64	0.00	516V	C
9	A.Ball	870.00	152.79	62.10	0.00	0.00	90.69	0.00	516H	A
10	M.English	0.00	11.59	0.00	0.00	0.00	11.59	0.00	BR	C
12	P.Corke	838.00	111.44	47.10	604.00	42.42	64.34	41.92	344L	D con/out
13	R.Reagan	1756.00	292.59	111.22	1522.00	106.54	181.37	115.00	516H	D con/out
14	W.Tasker	974.00	129.93	56.62	740.00	51.94	73.31	48.88	344L	D con/out
15	J.Wilson	498.00	61.62	28.62	0.00	0.00	33.00	0.00	NT	A
16	D.Carver	1061.00	293.96	74.27	1061.00	74.27	219.69	125.00	246H	D con/out
17	W.Bridges	870.00	115.79	49.34	636.00	44.66	66.45	43.50	516H	D con/out
18	R.Long	1061.00	293.96	74.27	1061.00	74.27	219.69	125.00	216L	D con/out
19	K.Farmer	1098.00	146.80	65.30	864.00	60.62	81.50	55.00	344L	D con/out
20	J.Nibbs	870.00	115.79	49.34	636.00	44.66	66.45	43.50	516H	D con/out
21	M.Long	606.00	68.93	30.86	372.00	26.18	38.07	30.32	344L	D con/out
Total values for 19 employees		15024.00	2459.10	907.78	10848.00	760.90	1551.32	854.69		

DRAGON ENTERPRISE LIMITED
Tax month 09

Date : 311292
Page : 3

P A Y M E N T S   S U M M A R Y - P A R T 3

<< Monthly >>

Ref.	Name	Total Gross Pay	Taxable Gross Pay	P.A.Y.E.	National Insurance Employees	National Insurance Employers	S.S.P.	S.M.P.	Pension Employee	Pension Employer
1	F.Adams	6277.25	6277.25	927.58	433.80	551.13	52.50	0.00	0.00	0.00
2	J.Joyce	7035.84	7035.84	713.00	0.00	630.68	0.00	0.00	0.00	0.00
3	G.Rose	9046.67	8877.53	1497.50	622.82	860.37	0.00	0.00	169.14	140.94
4	J.Gieves	8665.20	8508.60	1405.25	595.50	830.02	0.00	0.00	156.60	130.50
5	B.King	11307.75	11088.65	2050.25	775.30	1063.95	0.00	0.00	219.10	182.58
6	W.Lansdown	13446.00	13203.00	2579.00	916.98	1272.62	0.00	2075.08	243.00	202.50
7	A.Fisher	7848.71	7807.13	905.75	547.08	731.75	31.50	0.00	41.58	34.66
8	C.Young	4907.20	4907.20	204.60	0.00	380.89	1218.00	0.00	0.00	0.00
9	A.Ball	8665.20	8665.20	1120.25	633.78	902.74	0.00	0.00	0.00	0.00
10	M.English	4368.18	4368.18	1092.00	0.00	367.40	0.00	0.00	0.00	0.00
11	M.Perkins	5923.20	5868.48	825.58	391.50	499.90	0.00	0.00	54.72	45.60
12	P.Corke	7289.52	7152.82	1066.50	477.30	607.69	0.00	0.00	136.70	113.92
13	R.Reagan	20700.00	20286.00	4025.50	1183.62	1979.31	0.00	0.00	414.00	345.00
14	W.Tasker	8772.84	8661.98	1443.75	615.54	861.12	0.00	0.00	110.86	92.38
15	J.Wilson	4550.00	4500.00	0.00	257.58	297.00	0.00	0.00	0.00	0.00
16	D.Carver	22550.00	22050.00	5337.95	1333.87	1646.39	0.00	0.00	450.00	375.00
17	W.Bridges	8665.20	8508.60	1081.25	595.50	830.02	0.00	0.00	156.60	130.50
18	R.Long	22500.00	22050.00	5427.95	1333.87	1646.39	0.00	0.00	450.00	375.00
19	K.Farmer	10956.00	10758.00	1967.75	750.66	1040.72	0.00	0.00	198.00	165.00
20	J.Nibbs	8665.20	8508.60	1081.25	595.50	830.02	0.00	0.00	156.60	130.50
21	M.Long	2686.40	2587.62	0.00	141.10	153.61	0.00	0.00	98.78	82.32
	Total values for 21 employees	204826.36	201670.68	34752.66	12201.30	17983.72	1302.00	2075.08	3055.68	2546.40

Lesson Thirteen

Month Ten - January

Two New Employees; one with a P45, one without
A Futher Absence

If you need to reload the payroll records at this stage use LOAD PAYROLL AT END OF DECEMBER. You must remember to update the records at 311292 before you enter the payments for January.

On 5th January 1993 two new employees joined the firm. Linda Baker arrived with the P45 she had been given by her previous employer, Jack Dark, a labourer who is to be employed on an hourly basis and paid in cash, said that he didn't have one but he knew he was entitled to a married man's allowance. Richard Reagan, who is responsible for the firm's payroll, was not interested. If Dark starts without a P45 Dragon *must* use an emergency tax code as they did when Long (21) started working for the firm.

Dragon will provide Dark with a P46 form. If Dark cannot find his P45 (that should have been given to him by his previous employer when he left) he should fill in this form and send it to the Tax Office. If the Tax Office needs to know more information about Dark before they can give him a new tax code thet will send him a Form P91 to complete. If Dark is able to find his P45 he can disregard the P46.

⇨ Go into **Employee Details - Add a New Employee**. Press **Enter** twice and record all the details of the new employees from the following printouts of the screens. There are no details that can be entered on the third screen for Dark (23) as (a) he is being paid in cash so Dragon does not need to know about his bank account and (b) because Dark could not produce a P45 Dragon does not know how much his gross pay has been in the past, his taxable pay, or how much tax he has been stopped.

```
┌──────────────────────────────────────────────────────────────────┐
│  Sage Payroll II           Add a New Employee                      │
└──────────────────────────────────────────────────────────────────┘
```

```
Employee No. :   22      On HOLD : NO           Start Date : 050193
                                               Leave Date :
      Forenames : Linda                     Holiday Return :
        Surname : Baker
                                                Tax Code : 344L
        Address :                       Effective from : 060492
           ..   :                         N.I. Number : GG563129C
           ..   :                        N.I. Category : D
           ..   :                       Contracted-Out : Y
                                             SCON Ref. : 1
Works Number : 69                       Effective from : 220188
Payment Type : GM
Pension Ref. : 1                        Marital Status : M
Auto SSP/SMP : Y                           Male/Female : F
Date of Birth : 221070                        Director : N
```

```
┌──────────────────────────────────────────────────────────────────┐
│  Reference : 22     Name : Linda Baker           Pay Type : GM     │
└──────────────────────────────────────────────────────────────────┘
```

```
┌──────────────────────────────────────────────────────────────────┐
│       Department :   2 : Showroom                                  │
│   Qualifying Days :   1 : NQQQQQN NQQQQQN NQQQQQN NQQQQQN           │
│                                                                    │
└──────────────────────────────────────────────────────────────────┘
```

```
┌─────────── Rates of Pay ───────────┐   ┌──────── Adjustments ────────┐
│                                     │   │                             │
│   1 : Monthly Pay      :  870.0000  │   │   1 : Salary Advance        │
│   2 : Basic Hourly     :    5.5800  │   │   2 : Salary Refund         │
│   3 : Time and a half  :    8.3700  │   │   3 : Expenses              │
│   4 : Bonus            :    1.0000  │   │   4 : Additions/Taxed       │
│   0 : BLANK            :    0.0000  │   │   5 : Union Dues            │
│                                     │   │   0 : BLANK                 │
│                                     │   │   0 : BLANK                 │
│                                     │   │   0 : BLANK                 │
│                                     │   │   0 : BLANK                 │
│                                     │   │   0 : BLANK                 │
│                                     │   │                             │
└─────────────────────────────────────┘   └─────────────────────────────┘
```

```
┌─────────────────────────────────────────────────────────────────────┐
│  Reference : 22    Name : Linda Baker              Pay Type : GM      │
└─────────────────────────────────────────────────────────────────────┘

      ┌──────────────────── Banking Information ───────────────────┐
      │                                                            │
      │           Bank name : Midfield Bank                        │
      │     Branch Address 1 : Arch Street                         │
      │           Address 2 : Renchester                           │
      │                                                            │
      │      Branch Sort Code : 12-12-33                           │
      │                                                            │
      │         Account Name : L. Baker                            │
      │       Account Number : 62390123                            │
      │                                                            │
      └────────────────────────────────────────────────────────────┘

  ┌── Previous Employment (P45) ──┐  ┌──── Current Employment ────┐
  │                               │  │                            │
  │ Taxable Gross Pay :  7200.00  │  │ Gross Pay for NI :   0.00  │
  │         Tax Paid :  1053.25   │  │     Rounding C/F :   0.00  │
  │                               │  │                            │
  └───────────────────────────────┘  └────────────────────────────┘


  ┌────────────────────────────────────────────────────────────────┐
  │  Sage Payroll II          Add a New Employee                     │
  └────────────────────────────────────────────────────────────────┘
```

```
Employee No. :  23      On HOLD : NO          Start Date : 050193
                                              Leave Date :
    Forenames : Jack                       Holiday Return :
      Surname : Dark
                                                Tax Code : 344LM1
      Address :                          Effective from : 050193
           .. :                             N.I. Number : RD784219B
           .. :                           N.I. Category : A
           .. :                          Contracted-Out : N
                                              SCON Ref. : 0
 Works Number : 70                       Effective from : 050193
 Payment Type : CM
 Pension Ref. : 0                         Marital Status : S
 Auto SSP/SMP : Y                           Male/Female : M
Date of Birth : 131242                         Director : N
```

⇨ Note that the **Payment Type** is **CM** - Cash Monthly - here.

```
┌─────────────────────────────────────────────────────────────────┐
│  Reference : 23    Name : Jack Dark              Pay Type : CM     │
└─────────────────────────────────────────────────────────────────┘
```

```
┌─────────────────────────────────────────────────────────────────┐
│                                                                   │
│       Department :   1  : Printshop                               │
│    Qualifying Days :  1  : NQQQQQN NQQQQQN NQQQQQN NQQQQQN         │
│                                                                   │
└─────────────────────────────────────────────────────────────────┘
```

```
┌────────── Rates of Pay ──────────┐   ┌────── Adjustments ──────┐
│                                  │   │                          │
│  2 : Basic Hourly   :   5.3000   │   │  1 : Salary Advance      │
│  0 : BLANK          :   0.0000   │   │  2 : Salary Refund       │
│  0 : BLANK          :   0.0000   │   │  3 : Expenses            │
│  0 : BLANK          :   0.0000   │   │  4 : Additions/Taxed     │
│  0 : BLANK          :   0.0000   │   │  5 : Union Dues          │
│                                  │   │  0 : BLANK               │
│                                  │   │  0 : BLANK               │
│                                  │   │  0 : BLANK               │
│                                  │   │  0 : BLANK               │
│                                  │   │  0   : BLANK             │
│                                  │   │                          │
└──────────────────────────────────┘   └──────────────────────────┘
```

⇨ Go into **Processing Payroll** and enter the date **310193**. Complete the entries for all employees bearing in mind the following:

⇨ (a) Nobody worked overtime so last month's overtime pay must be removed from employees 3, 8 12, 14 and 21.

⇨ (b) King (5) is still away on Maternity Leave. She should not be given her tax refund as she asked if this could wait until the end of the tax year when she could get the refund in a large lump sum.

⇨ (c) Fisher (7) is still absent and should be given his tax refund.

⇨ (d) Young (8) worked for 30 hours at the Basic Hourly rate. He should be given his tax refund when this is offered.

⇨ (e) Corke (12) is absent from 4th January until 17th January inclusive. This means that he is entitled to 17/31 of the month's pay. Dragon will *not* make his pay up to his normal amount but he should be allowed his tax refund.

⇨   (f) Linda Baker (22) only worked 27/31ths of the month.

⇨   (g) Jack Dark (23) worked for 121.5 hours during the month. All of these
      hours were at the basic rate.

⇨   Print the Payment Summary and if it agrees with the one at the end of the
      lesson update the records.

DRAGON ENTERPRISE LIMITED
Tax month 10

PAYMENTS SUMMARY - PART 1

Date : 310193
Page : 1

<< Monthly >>

Ref.	Total Gross Pay	Taxable Gross Pay	Pre-Tax Addition	Deduct'n	Pension	P.A.Y.E.	Nat.Ins.	S.S.P.	S.M.P.	Post-Tax Addition	Deduct'n	Amount B/F	C/F	Nett Pay
2	696.00	696.00	0.00	0.00	0.00	57.66	0.00	0.00	0.00	0.00	0.00	0.16	0.82	639.00
3	904.80	850.51	0.00	0.00	54.29	132.41	51.58	0.00	0.00	0.00	0.00	0.00	0.00	666.52
4	870.00	817.80	0.00	0.00	52.20	124.41	49.34	0.00	0.00	0.00	0.00	0.00	0.00	644.05
5	231.50	217.61	0.00	0.00	13.89	0.00	0.00	0.00	231.50	0.00	0.00	0.00	0.00	217.61
6	1350.00	1269.00	0.00	0.00	81.00	236.91	82.94	0.00	0.00	0.00	0.00	0.00	0.00	949.15
7	220.50	207.27	0.00	0.00	13.23	-64.34	0.00	220.50	0.00	0.00	0.00	0.00	0.00	271.61
8	211.50	211.50	0.00	0.00	0.00	-44.00	0.00	0.00	0.00	0.00	0.00	0.00	0.00	255.50
9	870.00	870.00	0.00	0.00	0.00	101.41	62.10	0.00	0.00	0.00	0.00	0.83	0.34	706.00
10	251.10	251.10	0.00	0.00	0.00	62.75	0.00	0.00	0.00	0.00	0.00	0.82	0.47	188.00
12	458.26	430.76	0.00	0.00	27.50	27.41	20.50	63.42	0.00	0.00	0.00	0.00	0.00	382.85
13	2300.00	2162.00	0.00	0.00	138.00	424.41	111.22	0.00	0.00	0.00	0.00	0.00	0.00	1626.37
14	870.00	817.80	0.00	0.00	52.20	124.16	49.34	0.00	0.00	0.00	0.00	0.00	0.00	644.30
15	500.00	500.00	0.00	0.00	0.00	0.00	28.62	0.00	0.00	0.00	0.00	0.00	0.00	471.38
16	2500.00	2350.00	0.00	0.00	150.00	553.01	0.00	0.00	0.00	0.00	0.00	0.00	0.00	1796.99
17	870.00	817.80	0.00	0.00	52.20	88.16	49.34	0.00	0.00	0.00	0.00	0.00	0.00	680.30
18	2500.00	2350.00	0.00	0.00	150.00	563.01	0.00	0.00	0.00	0.00	0.00	0.00	0.00	1786.99
19	1100.00	1034.00	0.00	0.00	66.00	178.16	65.30	0.00	0.00	0.00	0.00	0.00	0.00	790.54
20	870.00	817.80	0.00	0.00	52.20	88.16	49.34	0.00	0.00	0.00	0.00	0.00	0.00	680.30
21	520.00	488.80	0.00	0.00	31.20	40.40	24.70	0.00	0.00	0.00	0.00	0.00	0.00	423.70
22	757.74	712.28	0.00	0.00	45.46	122.91	41.22	0.00	0.00	0.00	0.00	0.00	0.00	548.15
23	643.95	643.95	0.00	0.00	0.00	80.66	41.58	0.00	0.00	0.00	0.00	0.00	0.29	522.00
	19495.35	18515.98	0.00	0.00	979.37	2897.66	727.12	283.92	231.50	0.00	0.00	1.81	1.92	14891.31

21 employees

DRAGON ENTERPRISE LIMITED
Tax month 10

Date : 310193
Page : 3

PAYMENTS SUMMARY - PART 3

<< Monthly >>

Ref.	Name	Total Gross Pay	Taxable Gross Pay	P.A.Y.E.	National Insurance Employees	National Insurance Employers	S.S.P.	S.M.P.	Pension Employee	Pension Employer
1	F.Adams	6277.25	6277.25	927.58	433.80	551.13	52.50	0.00	0.00	0.00
2	J.Joyce	7731.84	7731.84	770.66	0.00	690.54	0.00	0.00	0.00	0.00
3	G.Rose	9951.47	9728.04	1629.91	674.40	928.93	0.00	0.00	223.43	186.18
4	J.Gieves	9535.20	9326.40	1529.66	644.84	896.47	0.00	0.00	208.80	174.00
5	B.King	11539.25	11306.26	2050.25	775.30	1063.95	0.00	2306.58	232.99	194.16
6	W.Lansdown	14796.00	14472.00	2815.91	999.92	1370.75	31.50	0.00	324.00	270.00
7	A.Fisher	8069.21	8014.40	841.41	547.08	731.75	1438.50	0.00	54.81	45.69
8	C.Young	5118.70	5118.70	160.60	0.00	380.89	0.00	0.00	0.00	0.00
9	A.Ball	9535.20	9535.20	1221.66	695.88	993.43	0.00	0.00	0.00	0.00
10	M.English	4619.28	4619.28	1154.75	0.00	378.99	0.00	0.00	0.00	0.00
11	M.Perkins	5923.20	5868.48	825.58	391.50	499.90	0.00	0.00	54.72	45.60
12	P.Corke	7747.78	7583.58	1093.91	497.80	629.46	63.42	0.00	164.20	136.83
13	R.Reagan	23000.00	22448.00	4449.91	1294.84	2160.68	0.00	0.00	552.00	460.00
14	W.Tasker	9642.84	9479.78	1567.91	664.88	927.57	0.00	0.00	163.06	135.88
15	J.Wilson	5050.00	5000.00	0.00	286.20	330.00	0.00	0.00	0.00	0.00
16	D.Carver	25050.00	24400.00	5890.96	1333.87	1906.39	0.00	0.00	600.00	500.00
17	W.Bridges	9535.20	9326.40	1169.41	644.84	896.47	0.00	0.00	208.80	174.00
18	R.Long	25000.00	24400.00	5990.96	1333.87	1906.39	0.00	0.00	600.00	500.00
19	K.Farmer	12056.00	11792.00	2145.91	815.96	1122.22	0.00	0.00	264.00	220.00
20	J.Nibbs	9535.20	9326.40	1169.41	644.84	896.47	0.00	0.00	208.80	174.00
21	M.Long	3206.40	3076.42	40.40	165.80	177.06	0.00	0.00	129.98	108.32
22	L.Baker	7957.74	7912.28	1176.16	41.22	45.18	0.00	0.00	45.46	37.89
23	J.Dark	643.95	643.95	80.66	41.58	55.38	0.00	0.00	0.00	0.00
	Total values for 23 employees	231521.71	227386.66	38703.57	12928.42	19540.00	1585.92	2306.58	4035.05	3362.55

13 - 7

DRAGON ENTERPRISE LIMITED
Tax month 10

Date : 310193
Page : 2

P A Y M E N T S   S U M M A R Y   –   P A R T   2

<< Monthly >>

| Ref. | Name | *** NATIONAL INSURANCE *** | | | | | Employers | | Tax Code | Nat.Ins. Category |
		Standard Earnings	Total Contr'n	Emp'ees Contr'n	Con/out Earnings	Con/out Contr'n	Nat.Ins.	Pension		
2	J.Joyce	0.00	59.86	0.00	0.00	0.00	59.86	0.00	516V	C
3	G.Rose	902.00	120.14	51.58	668.00	46.90	68.56	45.24	344L	D con/out
4	J.Gieves	870.00	115.79	49.34	636.00	44.66	66.45	43.50	344L	D con/out
5	B.King	0.00	0.00	0.00	0.00	0.00	0.00	11.58	344L	D con/out
6	W.Lansdown	1350.00	181.07	82.94	1116.00	78.26	98.13	67.50	344L	D con/out
7	A.Fisher	0.00	0.00	0.00	0.00	0.00	0.00	11.03	516H	D con/out
8	C.Young	0.00	0.00	0.00	0.00	0.00	0.00	0.00	516V	C
9	A.Ball	870.00	152.79	62.10	0.00	0.00	90.69	0.00	516H	A
10	M.English	0.00	11.59	0.00	0.00	0.00	11.59	0.00	BR	C
12	P.Corke	458.00	42.27	20.50	224.00	15.82	21.77	22.91	344L	D con/out
13	R.Reagan	1756.00	292.59	111.22	1522.00	106.54	181.37	115.00	516H	D con/out
14	W.Tasker	870.00	115.79	49.34	636.00	44.66	66.45	43.50	344L	D con/out
15	J.Wilson	498.00	61.62	28.62	0.00	0.00	33.00	0.00	NT	A
16	D.Carver	0.00	260.00	0.00	0.00	0.00	260.00	125.00	246H	D con/out
17	W.Bridges	870.00	115.79	49.34	636.00	44.66	66.45	43.50	516H	D con/out
18	R.Long	0.00	260.00	0.00	0.00	0.00	260.00	125.00	216L	D con/out
19	K.Farmer	1098.00	146.80	65.30	864.00	60.62	81.50	55.00	344L	D con/out
20	J.Nibbs	870.00	115.79	49.34	636.00	44.66	66.45	43.50	516H	D con/out
21	M.Long	518.00	48.15	24.70	284.00	20.02	23.45	26.00	344L	D con/out
22	L.Baker	754.00	86.40	41.22	520.00	36.54	45.18	37.89	344L	D con/out
23	J.Dark	642.00	96.96	41.58	0.00	0.00	55.38	0.00	344LM1	A
	Total values for 21 employees	12326.00	2283.40	727.12	7742.00	543.34	1556.28	816.15		

Lesson Fourteen

Month Eleven - February

An Employee Leaves
Ex Gratia Payment
Salary Refund
Missing P45 Received
More Adjustments

If you need to reload the payroll records at this stage use LOAD PAYROLL AT END OF JANUARY. You must remember to update the records at 310193 before you enter the payments for February.

During the month Dark (23) was able to get hold of his missing P45. A copy of this is shown below. Dragon will complete Part 3 of this and send it to the Tax Office. Part 2 will be kept in Dragon's records.

P45 Employee leaving   Part 2
Copy of employer's certificate

1. Previous PAYE reference	415 G3760	
2. National Insurance number	RD 78 42 19 B	

		Mr. Mrs. Miss. Ms.
3. Surname	DARK	MR
First two forenames	JACK	

	Day	Month	Year
4. Date of leaving	31	12	19 92

		Code	Week 1 or Month 1
5. Code at date of leaving 'X' means Week 1 or Month 1 basis	516	H	

6. Last entries on Deductions Working Sheet	Week or Month number	Week	Month 9
If there is an 'X' at item 5, there will be no entries here	Total pay to date	£ 5632	12 p
	Total tax to date	£ 362	00 p

Employee — This form is important. *Do not lose it.*
You cannot get a duplicate. *Do not separate the two parts*

The tax code for Dark (23) must now be entered.

⇨ Go into **Employee Details - Amend Employee Details - Full Details.** It is only employee no. 23 whose details need to be amended. Complete the first screen to record his correct tax code and the third screen to enter the **Taxable Gross Pay** and **Tax Paid** in his previous employment as illustrated below.

```
┌─────────────────────────────────────────────────────────────────────┐
│ Sage Payroll II              Full Details                             │
└─────────────────────────────────────────────────────────────────────┘


   Employee No. :   23      On HOLD : NO        Start Date : 050193
                                                Leave Date :
        Forenames : Jack                     Holiday Return :
          Surname : Dark
                                                  Tax Code : 516H
          Address :                        Effective from : 280293
               .. :                            N.I. Number : RD784219B
               .. :                          N.I. Category : A
               .. :                         Contracted-Out : N
                                                 SCON Ref. :  0
   Works Number : 70                       Effective from : 050193
   Payment Type : CM
   Pension Ref. :  0                       Marital Status : S
   Auto SSP/SMP : Y                          Male/Female : M
  Date of Birth : 131242                       Director : N
```

```
┌─────────────────────── Banking Information ───────────────────────┐
│                                                                    │
│                    Bank name :                                     │
│            Branch Address 1 :                                      │
│                  Address 2 :                                       │
│                                                                    │
│            Branch Sort Code : 00-00-00                             │
│                                                                    │
│                 Account Name :                                     │
│              Account Number :                                      │
│                                                                    │
└────────────────────────────────────────────────────────────────────┘
```

```
┌─ Previous Employment (P45) ─┐    ┌─── Current Employment ───┐
│ Taxable Gross Pay :  5632.12 │    │ Gross Pay for NI :   643.95 │
│        Tax Paid :    362.00 │    │    Rounding C/F :     0.29  │
└─────────────────────────────┘    └─────────────────────────────┘
```

Continuing ill health has forced Fisher (7) to leave the firm. This takes effect from 28th February 1993. He has not been receiving any pay from Dragon for the past few months but in recognition of his past service the Board of Directors agreed to pay him a parting bonus of £500.00. Because this bonus is not a part of the normal pay structure used by Dragon it is not taxable.

At the moment there is no means by which Dragon can make non-taxable payments to its employees using the payroll procedure. The easiest way in which this can be done is for Dragon to write a cheque and send it to Fisher and make no entries in the payroll records. The alternative would be to create a new type of Pay Adjustment called Additions/Non Taxable. The objections to this are that it not only makes more work for the Accounts Office but by including such an adjustment in the payroll program Dragon is implying that it represents a *normal,* if infrequent, method of pay. It is because this is a payment to which no employee would consider himself *automatically* entitled that it can be paid free of tax. It is for these reasons that Dragon chooses to make the payment not using the payroll program.

There is therefore no further reference to this payment now that you are ready to use the Processing Payroll routine.

⇨ Go into **Processing Payroll** and key in the date **280293**. Run the payroll for February taking the following information into account. To help you certain screen printouts are displayed where appropriate.

⇨ (a) Employees Rose (3), Lansdown (6), Corke (12), Tasker (14), Farmer (19) and Nibbs (20) are all members of a trade union. At the employees' request Dragon has agreed to deduct £6.50 per month from their pay and pass this on to the union. The same employees are each to be paid £10 per month towards the cost of protective clothing (they all work in the printshop). This must be entered as an Adjustment **4: Additions/Taxed.**

```
 Reference : 3      Name : Gladys Rose                Pay Type : GM


       Pre-Tax Adjustments        ANP      Post-Tax Adjustments        ANP

  Salary Advance : 0.00        : +YY     Expenses :    0.00  : +NN
  Salary Refund :        0.00  : -YY     Union Dues :   6.50  -NN
  Additions/Taxed :     10.00  : +YN        ** :       0.00  :
```

⇨ (b) King (5) is still away on Maternity Leave and is not to be paid her tax refund.

⇨ (c) Record Fisher's (7) continued absence until 28th February 1993. He should be given his tax refund.

You will notice that this month his Statutory Sick Pay is only £31.50. In other words he has been away from work for more than the 28 weeks during which this is paid. While you are making these entries you will be reminded to issue an *Exclusion Form.* These are no longer used and in December Dragon notified Fisher that he would soon come to the end of his entitlement to Statutory Sick Pay. Instead Fisher should be given a Form SSP1(L) as he has received more than 4 days SSP in the 8 weeks prior to his leaving Dragon's employment. He should also be given a Form SSP1 as he was away on sick leave at the time of leaving.

⇨ (d) Young (8) has worked for 50 hours this month. His tax refund should be allowed.

⇨ (e) Corke (12) has worked a full month.

⇨ (f) Baker (22) has worked a full month.

⇨ (g) Dark (23) has worked for 96 hours this month. However, it was discovered that he had only worked for 111.5 hours last month, not the 121.5 hours for which he had been paid. This represented an overpayment (before deductions) of £53.00. When entering this month's hours you must enter this salary refund. His tax refund should be allowed.

```
 ┌──────────────────────────────────────────────────────────────────┐
 │  Reference : 23    Name : Jack Dark              Pay Type : CM    │
 └──────────────────────────────────────────────────────────────────┘


        Pre-Tax Adjustments        ANP        Post-Tax Adjustments         ANP

   Salary Advance :     0.00    : +YY        Expenses :      0.00  : +NN
    Salary Refund :    53.00    : -YY      Union Dues :      0.00  : -NN
 Additions/Taxed : 0.00         : +YN            ** :       0.00  :
```

⇨ Produce a Payment Summary and if it agrees with the one at the end of the lesson update the records.

⇨ Record that Fisher (7) left Dragon Enterprise Limited on 28th February 1993. The instructions for how to do this were given in the November lesson.

Payments Summary

For the first time this year there are Pre-tax and Post-tax additions and Post-tax deductions involved.

You will notice that Dark (23) this month receives a tax refund of £38.08. This arises because last month he paid tax at a higher rate than he should have because his Tax Code was assumed to be 344 rather than his correct rate of 516. The calculation behind this is:

Total earnings to 28th Feb 1993		£6,731.87
less Tax free pay (11/12 of £2,589 + £2,589) (see page 2 - 8)		£4,746.50
		£1,985.37
25% of £1,985.00	£496.25	
less 5% of £2000 x 11/12	£91.67	
Tax due to date		£404.58
Tax paid in prior employment	£362.00	
plus tax paid last month	£80.66	
Total tax paid to date		£442.66
Tax refund due		£38.08

Double Entry Book-keeping

This section is only included for those people studying double entry book-keeping.

The calculations this month are affected by a new liability to the Trade Union and an additional expense of clothing that Dragon has decided not to include in the Salaries Expenses Account. The calculation of the NIC deductions that Dragon is enjoying this month are:

80% of £31.50 SSP	25.20
SMP	185.20
4.5% compensation fro SMP	8.33
TOTAL	218.73

The remaining calculations are:

Salaries Control

Net Pay (Col 15)	15,038.79	
plus Bal b/f (Col 13)	1.92	
less Bal c/f (Col 14)	1.54	15,039.17

PAYE/NIC Control

	PAYE (Col 7)	2,840.32	
plus Total NIC (Col 17)		2,334.60	
less NIC Deductions		218.73	4,956.19

Pensions Control

Pension (Col 6)		987.69	
plus Employer's pension (Col 22)		823.08	1,810.77

Trade Union Control   (Col 12)   39.00

TOTAL LIABILITIES   21,845.13

Salaries Expenses Account

Gross Pay (Col 2)		19,699.90	
plus NIC (Col 21)		1,593.88	
plus Pensions (Col 22)		823.08	
less Pre-tax Adds (Col 4)		60.00	
less Deductions (Col 5)		53.00	
less NIC Deductions		218.73	21,785.13

Clothing Expenses Account   (Col 4)   60.00

TOTAL EXPENSES   21,845.13

DRAGON ENTERPRISE LIMITED
Tax month 11

P A Y M E N T S   S U M M A R Y - P A R T 1
===

<< Monthly >>

Date : 280293
Page : 1

Ref.	Total Gross Pay	Taxable Gross Pay	Pre-Tax Addition	Deduct'n	Pension	P.A.Y.E.	Nat.Ins.	S.S.P.	S.M.P.	Post-Tax Addition	Deduct'n	Amount B/F	C/F	Nett Pay
2	696.00	696.00	0.00	0.00	0.00	57.92	0.00	0.00	0.00	0.00	0.00	0.82	0.74	638.00
3	914.80	860.51	10.00	0.00	54.29	134.92	52.42	0.00	0.00	0.00	6.50	0.00	0.00	666.67
4	870.00	817.80	0.00	0.00	52.20	124.17	49.34	0.00	0.00	0.00	0.00	0.00	0.00	644.29
5	185.20	174.09	0.00	0.00	11.11	0.00	0.00	0.00	185.20	0.00	6.50	0.00	0.00	174.09
6	1360.00	1279.00	10.00	0.00	81.00	239.67	83.50	0.00	0.00	0.00	6.50	0.00	0.00	949.33
7	31.50	29.61	0.00	0.00	1.89	-108.83	0.00	31.50	0.00	0.00	0.00	0.00	0.00	138.44
8	352.50	352.50	0.00	0.00	0.00	-15.80	0.00	0.00	0.00	0.00	0.00	0.00	0.00	368.30
9	870.00	870.00	0.00	0.00	0.00	101.17	62.10	0.00	0.00	0.00	0.00	0.34	0.61	707.00
10	251.10	251.10	0.00	0.00	0.00	62.75	0.00	0.00	0.00	0.00	0.00	0.47	0.12	188.00
12	730.00	686.80	10.00	0.00	43.20	91.42	39.54	0.00	0.00	0.00	6.50	0.00	0.00	549.34
13	2300.00	2162.00	0.00	0.00	138.00	424.17	111.22	0.00	0.00	0.00	0.00	0.00	0.00	1626.61
14	880.00	827.80	10.00	0.00	52.20	126.67	49.90	0.00	0.00	0.00	6.50	0.00	0.00	644.73
15	500.00	500.00	0.00	0.00	0.00	0.00	28.62	0.00	0.00	0.00	0.00	0.00	0.00	471.38
16	2500.00	2350.00	0.00	0.00	150.00	553.02	0.00	0.00	0.00	0.00	0.00	0.00	0.00	1796.98
17	870.00	817.80	0.00	0.00	52.20	88.17	49.34	0.00	0.00	0.00	0.00	0.00	0.00	680.29
18	2500.00	2350.00	0.00	0.00	150.00	563.02	0.00	0.00	0.00	0.00	0.00	0.00	0.00	1786.98
19	1110.00	1044.00	10.00	0.00	66.00	180.92	66.14	0.00	0.00	0.00	6.50	0.00	0.00	790.44
20	880.00	827.80	10.00	0.00	52.20	90.67	49.90	0.00	0.00	0.00	6.50	0.00	0.00	680.73
21	520.00	488.80	0.00	0.00	31.20	40.20	24.70	0.00	0.00	0.00	0.00	0.00	0.00	423.90
22	870.00	817.80	0.00	0.00	52.20	124.17	49.34	0.00	0.00	0.00	0.00	0.00	0.00	644.29
23	508.80	455.80	0.00	53.00	0.00	-38.08	24.66	0.00	0.00	0.00	0.00	0.29	0.07	469.00
21 employees	19699.90	18659.21	60.00	53.00	987.69	2840.32	740.72	31.50	185.20	0.00	39.00	1.92	1.54	15038.79
1	2	3	4	5	6	7	8	9	10	11	12	13	14	15

DRAGON ENTERPRISE LIMITED
Tax month 11

Date : 280293
Page : 2

PAYMENTS SUMMARY - PART 2

<< Monthly >>

| Ref. | Name | *** NATIONAL INSURANCE *** | | | | | Employers | | Tax Code | Nat.Ins. Category |
		Standard Earnings	Total Contr'n	Emp'ees Contr'n	Con/out Earnings	Con/out Contr'n	Nat.Ins.	Pension		
2	J.Joyce	0.00	59.86	0.00	0.00	0.00	59.86	0.00	516V	C
3	G.Rose	914.00	121.77	52.42	680.00	47.74	69.35	45.24	344L	D con/out
4	J.Gieves	870.00	115.79	49.34	636.00	44.66	66.45	43.50	344L	D con/out
5	B.King	0.00	0.00	0.00	0.00	0.00	0.00	9.26	344L	D con/out
6	W.Lansdown	1358.00	182.16	83.50	1124.00	78.82	98.66	67.50	344L	D con/out
7	A.Fisher	0.00	0.00	0.00	0.00	0.00	0.00	1.58	516H	D con/out
8	C.Young	0.00	16.19	0.00	0.00	0.00	16.19	0.00	516V	C
9	A.Ball	870.00	152.79	62.10	0.00	0.00	90.69	0.00	516H	A
10	M.English	0.00	11.59	0.00	0.00	0.00	11.59	0.00	BR	C
12	P.Corke	730.00	83.56	39.54	496.00	34.86	44.02	36.00	344L	D con/out
13	R.Reagan	1756.00	292.59	111.22	1522.00	106.54	181.37	115.00	516H	D con/out
14	W.Tasker	878.00	116.88	49.90	644.00	45.22	66.98	43.50	344L	D con/out
15	J.Wilson	498.00	61.62	28.62	0.00	0.00	33.00	0.00	NT	A
16	D.Carver	0.00	260.00	0.00	0.00	0.00	260.00	125.00	246H	D con/out
17	W.Bridges	870.00	115.79	49.34	636.00	44.66	66.45	43.50	516H	D con/out
18	R.Long	0.00	260.00	0.00	0.00	0.00	260.00	125.00	216L	D con/out
19	K.Farmer	1110.00	148.43	66.14	876.00	61.46	82.29	55.00	344L	D con/out
20	J.Nibbs	878.00	116.88	49.90	644.00	45.22	66.98	43.50	516H	D con/out
21	H.Long	518.00	48.15	24.70	284.00	20.02	23.45	26.00	344L	D con/out
22	L.Baker	870.00	115.79	49.34	636.00	44.66	66.45	43.50	344L	D con/out
23	J.Dark	454.00	54.76	24.66	0.00	0.00	30.10	0.00	516H	A
Total values for 21 employees		12574.00	2334.60	740.72	8178.00	573.86	1593.88	823.08		
		16	17	18	19	20	21	22	23	24

DRAGON ENTERPRISE LIMITED
Tax month 11

Date : 280293
Page : 3

P A Y M E N T S   S U M M A R Y   -   P A R T   3

<< Monthly >>

Ref.	Name	Total Gross Pay	Taxable Gross Pay	P.A.Y.E.	National Insurance Employees	National Insurance Employers	S.S.P.	S.M.P.	Pension Employee	Pension Employer
1	F.Adams	6277.25	6277.25	927.58	433.80	551.13	52.50	0.00	0.00	0.00
2	J.Joyce	8427.84	8427.84	828.58	0.00	750.40	0.00	0.00	0.00	0.00
3	G.Rose	10866.27	10588.55	1764.83	726.82	998.28	0.00	0.00	277.72	231.42
4	J.Gieves	10405.20	10144.20	1653.83	694.18	962.92	0.00	0.00	261.00	217.50
5	B.King	11724.45	11480.35	2050.25	775.30	1063.95	0.00	0.00	244.10	203.42
6	W.Lansdown	16156.00	15751.00	3055.58	1083.42	1469.41	31.50	2491.78	405.00	337.50
7	A.Fisher	8100.71	8044.01	732.58	547.08	731.75	1470.00	0.00	56.70	47.27
8	C.Young	5471.20	5471.20	144.80	0.00	397.08	0.00	0.00	0.00	0.00
9	A.Ball	10405.20	10405.20	1322.83	757.98	1084.12	0.00	0.00	0.00	0.00
10	M.English	4870.38	4870.38	1217.50	0.00	390.58	0.00	0.00	54.72	45.60
11	M.Perkins	5923.20	5868.48	825.58	391.50	499.90	0.00	0.00	207.40	172.83
12	P.Corke	8477.78	8270.38	1185.33	537.34	673.48	63.42	0.00	690.00	575.00
13	R.Reagan	25300.00	24610.00	4874.08	1406.06	2342.05	0.00	0.00	215.26	179.38
14	W.Tasker	10522.84	10307.58	1694.58	714.78	994.55	0.00	0.00	0.00	0.00
15	J.Wilson	5550.00	5500.00	0.00	314.82	363.00	0.00	0.00	750.00	625.00
16	D.Carver	27550.00	26750.00	6443.98	1333.87	2166.39	0.00	0.00	261.00	217.50
17	W.Bridges	10405.20	10144.20	1257.58	694.18	962.92	0.00	0.00	750.00	625.00
18	R.Long	27500.00	26750.00	6553.98	1333.87	2166.39	0.00	0.00	330.00	275.00
19	K.Farmer	13166.00	12836.00	2326.83	882.10	1204.51	0.00	0.00	261.00	217.50
20	J.Nibbs	10415.20	10154.20	1260.08	694.74	963.45	0.00	0.00	161.18	134.32
21	M.Long	3726.40	3565.22	80.60	190.50	200.51	0.00	0.00	97.66	81.39
22	L.Baker	8827.74	8730.08	1300.33	90.56	111.63	0.00	0.00	0.00	0.00
23	J.Dark	6784.87	6731.87	404.58	66.24	85.48	0.00	0.00	0.00	0.00
	Total values for 23 employees	256853.73	251677.99	41905.89	13669.14	21133.88	1617.42	2491.78	5022.74	4185.63

14 - 9

Lesson Fifteen (March) starts on the facing page.

Lesson Fifteen

Month Twelve - March

Save As You Earn
Payroll Giving
Year End Reports

If you need to reload the payroll records at this stage use LOAD PAYROLL AT END OF FEBRUARY. It is not necessary to update the records before you enter the payments for March - this has already been done.

Save as you Earn (SAYE)

Three of Dragon's employees have persuaded the company to operate a Save as you Earn scheme. The firm has agreed to stop £80 per month from the pay of Lansdown (6), Reagan (13) and Bridges (17). This money will then be sent to Ironstone Trust Ltd who will use it to invest in PEP's on behalf of these three people. Dragon Enterprise Limited is only involved in deducting this money from the pay packets and passing it on to Ironstone. They have no financial commitment to the scheme. There are no tax implications of this scheme. All savings will be made *after* PAYE and NIC have been calculated. Obviously a new Pay Adjustment must be entered in the payroll program. You will do this after learning about the other new scheme to be introduced.

Payroll Giving

In order to encourage donations to charity the Government allows employees to have regular deductions made from their salaries (up to a maximum amount that varies each year) which the employer will then pass on to the Agency Charity concerned. These deductions will be made *before* the calculation of PAYE just like pension contributions but NIC's are still assessed on the gross pay without any allowance for such deductions. The directors, Carver (16) and Long (18) are the two people involved in this.

Altering the Payroll Parameters

⇨ From the main menu go into **Company Details - Adjustment Types** and enter adjustments **6** and **7** as shown below to prepare for the Save as you Earn and Payroll Giving schemes described above. Both, of course, are deductions hence the - signs, but whereas SAYE has no effect on Tax, NIC or Pension, Payroll Giving is shown as affecting income tax liability.

```
┌─────────────────────────────────────────────────────────────┐
│ Sage Payroll II          Adjustment Types                    │
└─────────────────────────────────────────────────────────────┘
```

	Description....	+/-	Tax	N.I.	Pen		Description....	+/-	Tax	N.I.	Pen
1 :	Salary Advance	+	Y	Y	Y	11 :	BLANK	+	Y	Y	Y
2 :	Salary Refund	-	Y	Y	Y	12 :	BLANK	+	Y	Y	Y
3 :	Expenses	+	N	N	N	13 :	BLANK	+	Y	Y	Y
4 :	Additions/Taxed	+	Y	Y	N	14 :	BLANK	+	Y	Y	Y
5 :	Union Dues	-	N	N	N	15 :	BLANK	+	Y	Y	Y
6 :	S.A.Y.E	-	N	N	N	16 :	BLANK	+	Y	Y	Y
7 :	Payroll Giving	-	Y	N	N	17 :	BLANK	+	Y	Y	Y
8 :	BLANK	+	Y	Y	Y	18 :	BLANK	+	Y	Y	Y
9 :	BLANK	+	Y	Y	Y	19 :	BLANK	+	Y	Y	Y
10 :	BLANK	+	Y	Y	Y	20 :	BLANK	+	Y	Y	Y

⇨ Press Escape to get back to the Main Menu.

Altering the Employee Details

It is now necessary to include these two Adjustment Types in the details of the employees who are involved.

⇨ Go into **Employee Details - Amend Employee Details - Table Selections**. Choose nos. **6** and **18** as the **Lower** and **Upper Employee No.**

⇨ Include Adjustment **6** as illustrated below for Lansdown (6), Reagan (13) and Bridges (17).

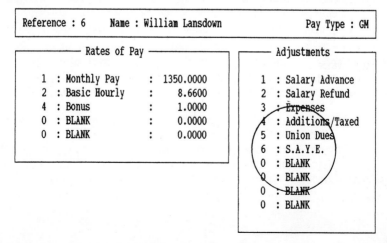

```
┌─────────────────────────────────────────────────────────────┐
│ Reference : 6    Name : William Lansdown        Pay Type : GM │
└─────────────────────────────────────────────────────────────┘
┌──────── Rates of Pay ────────┐   ┌──── Adjustments ────┐
│  1 : Monthly Pay  : 1350.0000 │   │ 1 : Salary Advance  │
│  2 : Basic Hourly :    8.6600 │   │ 2 : Salary Refund   │
│  4 : Bonus        :    1.0000 │   │ 3 : Expenses        │
│  0 : BLANK        :    0.0000 │   │ 4 : Additions/Taxed │
│  0 : BLANK        :    0.0000 │   │ 5 : Union Dues      │
│                               │   │ 6 : S.A.Y.E.        │
│                               │   │ 0 : BLANK           │
│                               │   │ 0 : BLANK           │
│                               │   │ 0 : BLANK           │
│                               │   │ 0 : BLANK           │
└───────────────────────────────┘   └─────────────────────┘
```

⇨ Include Adjustment **7** as illustrated below for Carver (16) and Long (18).

```
┌─────────────────────────────────────────────────────────────────────┐
│  Reference : 16    Name : David Carver              Pay Type : GM     │
├─────────────────────────────────────────────────────────────────────┤
│  ┌──────── Rates of Pay ────────┐    ┌──── Adjustments ────┐          │
│                                                                       │
│    1  : Monthly Pay   :  2500.0000      1 : Salary Advance            │
│    4  : Bonus         :     1.0000      2 : Salary Refund             │
│    0  : BLANK         :     0.0000      3 : Expenses                  │
│    0  : BLANK         :     0.0000      4 : Additions/Taxed           │
│    0  : BLANK         :     0.0000      5 : Union Dues                │
│                                         7 : Payroll Giving            │
│                                         0 : BLANK                     │
│                                         0 : BLANK                     │
└─────────────────────────────────────────────────────────────────────┘
```

You are now in a position to run the March payroll.

Running the Payroll

⇨ Go into **Processing Payroll** and enter the date **310393**. Run the payroll. Do not make any alterations to the entries made last month except:

⇨ (a)   Allow the tax refund to King (5), who is, of course, still away on Maternity Leave, and Young (8).

⇨ (b)   Enter the SAYE of £80.00 for Lansdown (6), Reagan (13) and Bridges (17) and a charitable gift of £25.00 by Carver (16) and Long (18) as depicted in the two sample printouts below.

Pre-Tax Adjustments		ANP	Post-Tax Adjustments		ANP
Salary Advance : 0.00		: +YY	Expenses :	0.00	: +NN
Salary Refund :	0.00	: -YY	Union Dues :	6.50	: -NN
Additions/Taxed :	10.00	: +YN	S.A.Y.E. :	80.00	: -NN

Pre-Tax Adjustments		ANP	Post-Tax Adjustments		ANP
Salary Advance : 0.00		: +YY	Expenses :	0.00	: +NN
Salary Refund :	0.00	: -YY	Union Dues :	0.00	: -NN
Additions/Taxed :	0.00	: +YN	** :	0.00	:
Payroll Giving :	25.00	: -NN	** :	0.00	:

⇨ (c) Dark (23) does not have a pay refund this month as he did in February.

```
┌─────────────────────────────────────────────────────────────────────┐
│  Reference : 23    Name : Jack Dark                Pay Type : CM      │
└─────────────────────────────────────────────────────────────────────┘

         Pre-Tax Adjustments        ANP      Post-Tax Adjustments      ANP

    Salary Advance :        0.00   : +YY        Expenses :    0.00  : +NN
    Salary Refund :         0.00   : -YY      Union Dues :    0.00  : -NN
    Additions/Taxed : 0.00         : +YN              ** :    0.00  :
```

⇨ Ensure that your Payment Summary agrees with the one at the end of the lesson and update the records.

Year End Routine

It is now the end of the Tax Year and, inevitably, certain procedures have to be completed as described below.

⇨ From the Opening Menu go into **Utilities - Year End**. You are presented with this menu.

```
┌─────────────────────────────────────────────────────────────────────┐
│  Sage Payroll II          Year End Routines                          │
└─────────────────────────────────────────────────────────────────────┘


              ┌──────────────────────────────┐
              │                              │
              │   P35 Year End Summary       │
              │   P11 Deduction Form         │
              │   P14/P60 Certificate        │
              │   Clear Year-TD Totals       │
              │                              │
              └──────────────────────────────┘
```

You need to print the **P35, P11** and **P14/60** forms.

⇨ Choose **P35 Year End Summary**. Press **Enter** three times and print this report. As you can see this is a summary of the Tax, NIC, SSP and SMP affecting each employee.

⇨ Choose **P14/60 Certificate** and print one of these just for Gieves (4). You will be offered the chance of printing a **Test Pattern** but you can reply **No** to this as it would only apply if you had pre-printed stationery that you needed to align in your printer correctly.

Three-part pre-printed stationery is essential in the real world for this task as all three parts of the form are needed for different purposes.

It is also necessary to print a P11 for each employee and if you were to choose this option here you would automatically print out 23 forms - one for each person. This would be rather wasteful as this is only a training exercise so instead you should produce a P11 for just one employee using the different routine described below.

⇨ From the Main Payroll Menu choose **Employee Details - P11 Deduction Form** and indicate that you want to print a P11 for Gieves (4).

When Dragon is happy that these printouts are correct the firm will send the P35 (more formally known as the Employer's Annual Statement, Declaration and Certificate) together with Parts 1 and 2 of the P14/60's to the Tax Office. These must arrive by May 19th. The third part of the P14's (which are P60's) will be given to each employee that still works for Dragon. For employees who left the firm during the Tax Year the third part of the P14's (the P60) must be destroyed. Dragon will keep the P11's on file in case the Inland Revenue wish to inspect the firm's records in the future.

Preparing for the Next Year

Everything that it is necessary to do to run the payroll for a year has now been done. All that remains is to clear the entries from the computer so that you can start anew for the 1993/94 Tax Year.

⇨ Choose **Utilities - Year End - Clear Year-TD Totals**. Press **Enter** four times.

⇨ There are no records of pay in the computer now. Check this for yourself by going into **Employee Details - Amend Employee Details - Cumulative Values**. There is now no record of Adams or Perkins who have left and no values for payments for any remaining employees.

Dragon is now in a position to start the next year's payroll run. Before the end of the 1992/93 Tax Year Dragon may have received a form P9 from the Tax Office notifying changes to some tax codes. These would now be entered using the Employee Details - Amend Employee Details - Full Details routine. The majority of employees will not be so affected and will continue to use last year's tax code until Dragon receives a form P7X in May authorising it to change the tax code of all employees with the more common H, L, P and V suffixes. Employees whose tax code has a suffix of T will have their code changes notified by the use of a form P9.

Double Entry Book-keeping

A final study of the Payments Summary for December produces the following values to be entered in Dragon's ledger accounts. Firstly the liabilities:

Salary Control	Nett Pay (Col 15)	£14,662.25	
	plus Bal b/f (Col 14)	£1.54	
	less Bal c/f (Col 13)	£1.84	£14,661.95
PAYE/NIC Control	PAYE (Col 7)	£2,859.20	
	NIC (Col 17)	£2,342.71	£5,201.91
Pension Control	Employer's (Col 22)	£816.87	
	Employee's (Col 6)	£980.25	£1,797.12
Union Control	Post-tax Ded. (Col 12)		£39.00
S.A.Y.E. Control	Post-tax Ded. (Col 12)		£240.00
Agency Charity Control	(Col 5)		£50.00
			£21,989.98

These liabilities arise from the following expenses:

General Expenses Account			
	Pre-tax Adds (Col 4)		£60.00
Salaries Expenses Account			
	Gross Pay (Col 2)	£19,575.80	
	less Pre-tax Add (Col 4)	£60.00	(Expenses - not pay)
	plus Pension (Col 22)	£816.87	
	plus NIC (Col 21)	£1,597.31	£21,929.98
			£21,989.98

Notice how the Post-tax deductions now include two different types of entry: SAYE and Union Dues.

In due course Dragon will clear the Salaries Control Account by paying cash and issuing bank giros for its employees and will send cheques to the Inland Revenue, the insurance company running the pension scheme and the trade union involved. A cheque for £240.00 will be sent to the Ironstone Trust Limited for the S.A.Y.E. and £50.00 will be sent to the Agency Charity.

The expense account entries will, of course, be added to the records of previous salary and general expenses incurred during the year and will eventually find their way into Dragon's Profit and Loss Account.

Payments Summary

Being the end of the year it should now be possible to take one person's salary for the past twelve months and analyse all the deductions. For this purpose Gieves (4) will be considered. Study the entries in Part 3 of the Payments Summary.

Tax

His tax is calculated as follows.

Gross Pay	£11,275.00
less Pension	£313.20
Taxable pay	£10,961.80
less Tax free pay	£3,449.00
	£7,512.80
25% of £7512	£1,878.00
less 5% of £2,000	£100.00
Total tax paid	£1,778.00

National Insurance Contributions

It is not possible to take a person's total pay for the year and calculate his total NIC. This is because each pay period is treated separately, not summated. The only method of calculating Gieve's total NIC would be to take each month's gross pay separately. If you study the P11 that you produced for Gieves you will see that he earned the same amount during each of eleven months and paid the same NIC during each of these. If you look at his PAYE deductions there are slight variations each month as you have come to expect..

For the month in which Gieves received his Bonus his NIC increased considerably of course.

DRAGON ENTERPRISE LIMITED

Date : 310393
Page : 1

Tax month 12

P A Y M E N T S   S U M M A R Y - P A R T   1
==

<< Monthly >>

Ref.	Total Gross Pay	Taxable Gross Pay	Pre-Tax Addition	Deduct'n	Pension	P.A.Y.E.	Nat.Ins.	S.S.P.	S.M.P.	Post-Tax Addition	Deduct'n	Amount B/F	C/F	Nett Pay
2	696.00	696.00	0.00	0.00	0.00	57.67	0.00	0.00	0.00	0.00	0.00	0.74	0.41	638.00
3	914.80	860.51	10.00	0.00	54.29	135.17	52.42	0.00	0.00	0.00	6.50	0.00	0.00	666.42
4	870.00	817.80	0.00	0.00	52.20	124.17	49.34	0.00	0.00	0.00	0.00	0.00	0.00	644.29
5	92.60	87.04	0.00	0.00	5.56	-120.75	0.00	0.00	92.60	0.00	0.00	0.00	0.00	207.79
6	1360.00	1279.00	10.00	0.00	81.00	239.42	83.50	0.00	0.00	0.00	86.50	0.00	0.00	869.58
8	352.50	352.50	0.00	0.00	0.00	-15.80	0.00	0.00	0.00	0.00	0.00	0.00	0.00	368.30
9	870.00	870.00	0.00	0.00	0.00	101.42	62.10	0.00	0.00	0.00	0.00	0.61	0.13	706.00
10	251.10	251.10	0.00	0.00	0.00	62.75	0.00	0.00	0.00	0.00	0.00	0.12	0.77	189.00
12	730.00	686.80	0.00	0.00	43.20	91.67	39.54	0.00	0.00	0.00	6.50	0.00	0.00	549.09
13	2300.00	2162.00	0.00	0.00	138.00	424.42	111.22	0.00	0.00	0.00	80.00	0.00	0.00	1546.36
14	880.00	827.80	10.00	0.00	52.20	126.92	49.90	0.00	0.00	0.00	6.50	0.00	0.00	644.48
15	500.00	500.00	0.00	0.00	0.00	0.00	28.62	0.00	0.00	0.00	0.00	0.00	0.00	471.38
16	2500.00	2325.00	0.00	25.00	150.00	543.42	0.00	0.00	0.00	0.00	80.00	0.00	0.00	1781.58
17	870.00	817.80	0.00	0.00	52.20	88.42	49.34	0.00	0.00	0.00	0.00	0.00	0.00	600.04
18	2500.00	2325.00	0.00	25.00	150.00	553.42	0.00	0.00	0.00	0.00	0.00	0.00	0.00	1771.58
19	1110.00	1044.00	10.00	0.00	66.00	180.67	66.14	0.00	0.00	0.00	6.50	0.00	0.00	790.69
20	880.00	827.80	10.00	0.00	52.20	90.92	49.90	0.00	0.00	0.00	6.50	0.00	0.00	680.48
21	520.00	488.80	0.00	0.00	31.20	40.20	24.70	0.00	0.00	0.00	0.00	0.00	0.00	423.90
22	870.00	817.80	0.00	0.00	52.20	124.17	49.34	0.00	0.00	0.00	0.00	0.00	0.00	644.29
23	508.80	508.80	0.00	0.00	0.00	10.92	29.34	0.00	0.00	0.00	0.00	0.07	0.53	469.00
20 employees	19575.80	18545.55	60.00	50.00	980.25	2859.20	745.40	0.00	92.60	0.00	279.00	1.54	1.84	14662.25
	1	2	3	4	5	6	7	8	9	10	11	12	13 14	15

DRAGON ENTERPRISE LIMITED
Tax month 12

Date : 310393
Page : 2

P A Y M E N T S   S U M M A R Y - P A R T 2

<< Monthly >>

Ref.	Name	*** NATIONAL INSURANCE ***					Employers		Tax Code	Nat.Ins. Category
		Standard Earnings	Total Contr'n	Emp'ees Contr'n	Con/out Earnings	Con/out Contr'n	Nat.Ins.	Pension		
2	J.Joyce	0.00	59.86	0.00	0.00	0.00	59.86	0.00	516V	C
3	G.Rose	914.00	121.77	52.42	680.00	47.74	69.35	45.24	344L	D con/out
4	J.Gieves	870.00	115.79	49.34	636.00	44.66	66.45	43.50	344L	D con/out
5	B.King	0.00	0.00	0.00	0.00	0.00	0.00	4.63	344L	D con/out
6	W.Lansdown	1358.00	182.16	83.50	1124.00	78.82	98.66	67.50	344L	D con/out
8	C.Young	0.00	16.19	0.00	0.00	0.00	16.19	0.00	516V	C
9	A.Ball	870.00	152.79	62.10	0.00	0.00	90.69	0.00	516H	A
10	M.English	0.00	11.59	0.00	0.00	0.00	11.59	0.00	BR	C
12	P.Corke	730.00	83.56	39.54	496.00	34.86	44.02	36.00	344L	D con/out
13	R.Reagan	1756.00	292.59	111.22	1522.00	106.54	181.37	115.00	516H	D con/out
14	W.Tasker	878.00	116.88	49.90	644.00	45.22	66.98	43.50	344L	D con/out
15	J.Wilson	498.00	61.62	28.62	0.00	0.00	33.00	0.00	NT	A
16	D.Carver	0.00	260.00	0.00	0.00	0.00	260.00	125.00	246H	D con/out
17	W.Bridges	870.00	115.79	49.34	636.00	44.66	66.45	43.50	516H	D con/out
18	R.Long	0.00	260.00	0.00	0.00	0.00	260.00	125.00	216L	D con/out
19	K.Farmer	1110.00	148.43	66.14	876.00	61.46	82.29	55.00	344L	D con/out
20	J.Nibbs	878.00	116.88	49.90	644.00	45.22	66.98	43.50	516H	D con/out
21	M.Long	518.00	48.15	24.70	284.00	20.02	23.45	26.00	344L	D con/out
22	L.Baker	870.00	115.79	49.34	636.00	44.66	66.45	43.50	344L	D con/out
23	J.Dark	506.00	62.87	29.34	0.00	0.00	33.53	0.00	516H	A
	Total values for 20 employees	12626.00	2342.71	745.40	8178.00	573.86	1597.31	816.87		
		16	17	18	19	20	21	22	23	24

DRAGON ENTERPRISE LIMITED

Tax month 12

Date : 310393
Page : 3

P A Y M E N T S S U M M A R Y - P A R T 3

<< Monthly >>

Ref.	Name	Total Gross Pay	Taxable Gross Pay	P.A.Y.E.	National Insurance Employees	Employers	S.S.P.	S.M.P.	Pension Employee	Employer
1	F.Adams	6277.25	6277.25	927.58	433.80	551.13	52.50	0.00	0.00	0.00
2	J.Joyce	9123.84	9123.84	886.25	0.00	810.26	0.00	0.00	0.00	0.00
3	G.Rose	11781.07	11449.06	1900.00	779.24	1067.63	0.00	0.00	332.01	276.66
4	J.Gieves	11275.20	10962.00	1778.00	743.52	1029.37	0.00	0.00	313.20	261.00
5	B.King	11817.05	11567.39	1929.50	775.30	1063.95	0.00	2584.38	249.66	208.05
6	W.Lansdown	17516.00	17030.00	3295.00	1166.92	1568.07	31.50	0.00	486.00	405.00
7	A.Fisher	8100.71	8044.01	732.58	547.08	731.75	1470.00	0.00	56.70	47.27
8	C.Young	5823.70	5823.70	129.00	0.00	413.27	0.00	0.00	0.00	0.00
9	A.Ball	11275.20	11275.20	1424.25	820.08	1174.81	0.00	0.00	0.00	0.00
10	M.English	5121.48	5121.48	1280.25	0.00	402.17	0.00	0.00	0.00	0.00
11	M.Perkins	5923.20	5868.48	825.58	391.50	499.90	0.00	0.00	54.72	45.60
12	P.Corke	9207.78	8957.18	1277.00	576.88	717.50	63.42	0.00	250.60	208.83
13	R.Reagan	27600.00	26772.00	5298.50	1517.28	2523.42	0.00	0.00	828.00	690.00
14	W.Tasker	11402.84	11135.38	1821.50	764.68	1061.53	0.00	0.00	267.46	222.88
15	J.Wilson	6050.00	6000.00	0.00	343.44	396.00	0.00	0.00	0.00	0.00
16	D.Carver	30050.00	29075.00	6987.40	1333.87	2426.39	0.00	0.00	900.00	750.00
17	W.Bridges	11275.20	10962.00	1346.00	743.52	1029.37	0.00	0.00	313.20	261.00
18	R.Long	30000.00	29075.00	7107.40	1333.87	2426.39	0.00	0.00	900.00	750.00
19	K.Farmer	14276.00	13880.00	2507.50	948.24	1286.80	0.00	0.00	396.00	330.00
20	J.Nibbs	11295.20	10982.00	1351.00	744.64	1030.43	0.00	0.00	313.20	261.00
21	M.Long	4246.40	4054.02	120.80	215.20	223.96	0.00	0.00	192.38	160.32
22	L.Baker	9697.74	9547.88	1424.50	139.90	178.08	0.00	0.00	149.86	124.89
23	J.Dark	7293.67	7240.67	415.50	95.58	119.01	0.00	0.00	0.00	0.00
	Total values for 23 employees	276429.53	270223.54	44765.09	14414.54	22731.19	1617.42	2584.38	6002.99	5002.50

This is the structure of the menu system used by Sage Sterling Payroll II. Only those items referred to in the course are displayed.

Payroll	Employee Details	Amend Employee Details	Full Details
			Personal Details
			Table Selections
			Bank/P45 Information
			Cumulative Values
		Add a New Employee	
		Remove an Employee	
	Processing Payroll	Enter Payments	
		Payment Summary	
		Cash Analysis	
		Giro Analysis	
		Payslips	
		Collector of Taxes	
		Update Records	
	Statutory Sick Pay	Transfer & Exclusion Forms	
		Qualifying Days	
		Initialise SSP Diary	
	Statutory Maternity Pay	Initialise SSP Dates	
	Government Parameters	Tax Bandwidths & Rates	
		NI Bandwidths	
		NI Categories	
		NI Rates	
		SSP Parameters	
		SSP Rates	
		SMP Rates	
	Company Details	Company Information	
		Pension Schemes	
		Department Names	
		Payment Types	
		Adjustment Types	
Utilities		Year End	P35 Year End Summary
			P11 Deduction Form
			P14/60 Certificates
			Clear Year-TD Totals

These are the parameters within which the payroll is operating at the beginning of the course. The only changes that occur during the course are the introduction of schemes for a company pension, Save as You Earn and Payroll Giving.

```
--------------------------------------------------------------------------------
                              Company Details
--------------------------------------------------------------------------------


                        Initialised for 30 employees


          Company Name : DRAGON ENTERPRISE LIMITED
             Address 1 : UNIT 10
                     2 : MANNHEAD TRADING ESTATE
                     3 : RENCHESTER
                     4 : RR9 9RR


             Bank name : Midfield Bank plc
             Address 1 : Arch Street
                     2 : Renchester

             Sort Code : 12-12-33
          Account Name : Dragon Enterprise Ltd-No.1 A/c
        Account Number : 20899901


         Tax Reference : 415/D9045
       Cash Rounding To :       1.00


         Retirement Age - Women :  60    Men :  65



--------------------------------------------------------------------------------
                                Departments
--------------------------------------------------------------------------------
      1 : Printshop              11 : BLANK
      2 : Showroom               12 : BLANK
      3 : Management             13 : BLANK
```

```
----------------------------------------------------------------------------------
                    Pension Rates                    Cash Analysis Limits
----------------------------------------------------------------------------------
           Employer          Employee
        %-age Reb Tot Lim  %-age Reb Tot Lim     Scheme        ---  Pounds  ---
        ------------------ ------------------  Contracted-Out  50 :   0
  1 :   0.00  N   N   N    0.00  N   N   N        Number       20 :   0
  2 :   0.00  N   N   N    0.00  N   N   N         SCON        10 :   0
  3 :   0.00  N   N   N    0.00  N   N   N      --------------  5 :   0
  4 :   0.00  N   N   N    0.00  N   N   N     1. S4            1 :   0
  5 :   0.00  N   N   N    0.00  N   N   N     2. S4
  6 :   0.00  N   N   N    0.00  N   N   N     3. S4          ---  Pence  ---
  7 :   0.00  N   N   N    0.00  N   N   N     4. S4          50 :   0
  8 :   0.00  N   N   N    0.00  N   N   N                    20 :   0
  9 :   0.00  N   N   N    0.00  N   N   N                    10 :   0
 10 :   0.00  N   N   N    0.00  N   N   N                     5 :   0
                                                              2 :   0
              Tax relief on pension : Y                       1 :   0
```

```
----------------------------------------------------------------------------------
                            Payment Types
----------------------------------------------------------------------------------
```

	Tax	Nat.Ins.	Pension
1 : Monthly Pay	Y	Y	Y
2 : Basic Hourly	Y	Y	Y
3 : Time and a half	Y	Y	Y
4 : Bonus	Y	Y	N

```
----------------------------------------------------------------------------------
                            Adjustment Types
----------------------------------------------------------------------------------
```

	Add /Ded	Tax	Nat.Ins.	Pension
1 : Salary Advance	+	Y	Y	Y
2 : Salary Refund	-	Y	Y	Y
3 : Expenses	+	N	N	N
4 : Additions/Taxed	+	Y	Y	N
5 : Union Dues	-	N	N	N

```
--------------------------------------------------------------------------
                           Tax Bandwidths and Rates
--------------------------------------------------------------------------

         No. of Bandwidths :  2              Basic Rate Band :  2


              Bandwidth        ++ From ++      +++ To +++     %-Tax
              ----------       ----------     ----------     -----
      1 :     2000.00               0.01  -     2000.00      20.00
      2 :    21700.00            2000.01  -    23700.00      25.00
      3 :  * excess *           23700.01  -  * excess *      40.00


--------------------------------------------------------------------------
                              N.I. Bandwidths
--------------------------------------------------------------------------

                      No. of Bandwidths :  3


                     Limits                    Factors
                     -------                   -------
            Lower :   54.00       Weekly B/W :   1.00
           Band 1 :   90.00       Weekly R/F :   1.00
           Band 2 :  135.00
           Band 3 :  190.00      Monthly B/W :   4.00
            Upper :  405.01      Monthly R/F :   1.00


--------------------------------------------------------------------------
                              N.I. Categories
--------------------------------------------------------------------------

                        Category   Contracted
                         Letter       -out
                        ------       ----
                  1 :      A           N
                  2 :      B           N
                  3 :      C           N
                  4 :      C           Y
                  5 :      D           Y
                  6 :      E           Y
                  7 :      X           N
```

```
--------------------------------------------------------------------------------
                            National Insurance Rates
--------------------------------------------------------------------------------
```

Category : A

++++++ Bands ++++++			Employers		Employees	
From		To	< min	> min	< min	> min
54.00	-	89.99 :	4.60	4.60	2.00	9.00
90.00	-	134.99 :	6.60	6.60	2.00	9.00
135.00	-	189.99 :	8.60	8.60	2.00	9.00
190.00	-	405.01 :	10.40	10.40	2.00	9.00
405.02	-	excess :	10.40	10.40	0.00	0.00

Category : B

++++++ Bands ++++++			Employers		Employees	
From		To	< min	> min	< min	> min
54.00	-	89.99 :	4.60	4.60	3.85	3.85
90.00	-	134.99 :	6.60	6.60	3.85	3.85
135.00	-	189.99 :	8.60	8.60	3.85	3.85
190.00	-	405.01 :	10.40	10.40	3.85	3.85
405.02	-	excess :	10.40	10.40	0.00	0.00

Category : C

++++++ Bands ++++++			Employers		Employees	
From		To	< min	> min	< min	> min
54.00	-	89.99 :	4.60	4.60	0.00	0.00
90.00	-	134.99 :	6.60	6.60	0.00	0.00
135.00	-	189.99 :	8.60	8.60	0.00	0.00
190.00	-	405.01 :	10.40	10.40	0.00	0.00
405.02	-	excess :	10.40	10.40	0.00	0.00

Category : C - con/out

++++++ Bands ++++++			Employers		Employees	
From		To	< min	> min	< min	> min
54.00	-	89.99 :	4.60	0.80	0.00	0.00
90.00	-	134.99 :	6.60	2.80	0.00	0.00
135.00	-	189.99 :	8.60	4.80	0.00	0.00
190.00	-	405.01 :	10.40	6.60	0.00	0.00
405.02	-	excess :	10.40	6.60	0.00	0.00

```
-------------------------------------------------------------------------------
                         National Insurance Rates
-------------------------------------------------------------------------------
```

Category : D - con/out

++++++ Bands ++++++		Employers		Employees	
From	To	< min	> min	< min	> min
54.00 -	89.99 :	4.60	0.80	2.00	7.00
90.00 -	134.99 :	6.60	2.80	2.00	7.00
135.00 -	189.99 :	8.60	4.80	2.00	7.00
190.00 -	405.01 :	10.40	6.60	2.00	7.00
405.02 -	excess :	10.40	6.60	0.00	0.00

Category : E - con/out

++++++ Bands ++++++		Employers		Employees	
From	To	< min	> min	< min	> min
54.00 -	89.99 :	4.60	0.80	3.85	3.85
90.00 -	134.99 :	6.60	2.80	3.85	3.85
135.00 -	189.99 :	8.60	4.80	3.85	3.85
190.00 -	405.01 :	10.40	6.60	3.85	3.85
405.02 -	excess :	10.40	6.60	0.00	0.00

Category : X

++++++ Bands ++++++		Employers		Employees	
From	To	< min	> min	< min	> min
54.00 -	89.99 :	0.00	0.00	0.00	0.00
90.00 -	134.99 :	0.00	0.00	0.00	0.00
135.00 -	189.99 :	0.00	0.00	0.00	0.00
190.00 -	405.01 :	0.00	0.00	0.00	0.00
405.02 -	excess :	0.00	0.00	0.00	0.00

This is a list of the employees and their details at the opening of the course or when the employee joined Dragon Enterprise Limited.

No	Forenames	Surname	W/No	P/Tp	P/Rf	SSP/SMP	DoB	Start	T/Cde	From	NI No	NI/CtCn/O	From	M/tl	M/F	Dir
1	Fred	Adams	31	CM	0	Y	130571	160491	344L	060492	RD121345A	A N	060492	S	M	N
2	James	Joyce	48	CM	0	Y	120325	170368	516V	060492	AR921345A	A C in N	300691	M	M	N
3	Gladys	Rose	22	GM	0	Y	100466	140891	344L	060492	GG121445C	A N	310884	M	F	N
4	Jean	Gieves	56	GM	0	Y	150769	150690	344L	060492	TF982356D	A N	191087	M	F	N
5	Betty	King	33	GM	0	Y	100670	120181	344L	060492	AA133345A	A N	120181	S	M	N
6	William	Lansdown	76	GM	0	Y	200937	140676	344L	060492	FR335672C	A N	140676	S	M	N
7	Andrew	Fisher	45	GM	0	Y	291239	101082	516H	060492	RD121453D	A N	140676	M	M	N
8	Claude	Young	63	GM	0	Y	111123	300982	516V	060492	FD121724F	A C in N	101082	M	M	N
9	Arthur	Ball	28	CM	0	Y	141142	270582	516H	060492	SS287345A	A N	300982	M	M	N
10	Mollie	English	44	CM	0	Y	311025	140169	BR	060492	TF654327C	A C in N	311085	S	F	N
11	Margaret	Perkins	91	GM	0	Y	190469	140189	344L	060492	TY934445A	A N	140189	S	F	N
12	Paul	Corke	24	GM	0	Y	191268	300982	516H	060492	GG136445A	A N	140189	M	M	N
13	Richard	Reagan	51	GM	0	Y	170135	140788	516H	060492	ET777422B	A N	300982	M	M	N
14	Wendy	Tasker	28	GM	0	Y	150236	191091	344L	060492	WE499674B	A N	140788	M	F	N
15	Juliette	Wilson	82	GM	0	Y	300938	141277	NT	060492	PI121444A	A N	191091	M	F	N
16	David	Carver	41	GM	0	Y	210938	230188	189L	060492	RR557445C	A N	141277	S	M	Y
17	Wilbur	Bridges	72	GM	0	Y	141173	191077	516H	060492	DT33345A	A N	230188	M	M	N
18	Rachel	Long	30	GM	0	Y	150642	120181	216L	060492	TD784445B	A N	191081	S	F	Y
19	Kirstie	Farmer	42	GM	0	Y	230933	191077	344L	060492	GR133645A	A N	120181	S	F	N
20	John	Nibbs	67	GM	0	Y	220470	191077	516H	060492	WW773334A	A N	191077	M	M	N
21	Martin	Long	68	GM	0	Y	110675	010892	344L	010892	AC342789C	A N	010892	S	M	N
22	Linda	Baker	69	GM	1	Y	220170	050193	344L	060492	GG563129C	D Y	050193	M	F	N
23	Jack	Dark	70	CM	0	Y	131242	050193	344LM1	050193	RD784219B	A N	191071	M	M	N

No	Forenames	Surname	Dpt	Q/Dy	Rates	Amounts Month	Basic Hr	Time + 0.5	Bonus
1	Fred	Adams	1	1	1-2-3-4	720.00	4.64	6.96	1.00
2	James	Joyce	1	1	1-2-3-4	720.00	4.64	6.96	1.00
3	Gladys	Rose	1	1	1-2-3-4	870.00	5.58	8.37	1.00
4	Jean	Gieves	2	1	1-2-3-4	870.00	5.58	8.37	1.00
5	Betty	King	1	1	1-2-3-4	1100.00	7.05	10.57	1.00
6	William	Lansdown	1	1	1-2-4	1350.00	8.66		1.00
7	Andrew	Fisher	2	1	1-2-4	1450.00	9.30		1.00
8	Claude	Young	2	1	1-2-3-4	1100.00	7.05	10.57	1.00
9	Arthur	Ball	2	1	1-2-3-4	870.00	5.58	8.37	1.00
10	Mollie	English	1	1	1-2-3-4	870.00	5.58	8.37	1.00
11	Margaret	Perkins	1	1	1-2-3-4	720.00	4.64	6.96	1.00
12	Paul	Corke	1	1	1-2-3-4	720.00	4.64	6.96	1.00
13	Richard	Reagan	3	1	1-4	2300.00			1.00
14	Wendy	Tasker	1	1	1-2-3-4	870.00	5.58	8.37	1.00
15	Juliette	Wilson	1	1	1-4	500.00			1.00
16	David	Carver	3	1	1-4	2500.00			1.00
17	Wilbur	Bridges	2	1	1-2-3-4	870.00	5.58	8.37	1.00
18	Rachel	Long	3	1	1-4	2500.00			1.00
19	Kirstie	Farmer	1	1	1-2-4	1100.00	7.05		1.00
20	John	Nibbs	1	1	1-2-3-4	870.00	5.58	8.37	1.00
21	Martin	Long	2	1	1-2-3-4	520.00	3.20	4.80	1.00
22	Linda	Baker	2	1	1-2-3-4	870.00	5.58	8.37	1.00
23	Jack	Dark	1	1	2		5.30		1.00

		Adjust	Bank	Sort Code	Acc Name	Acc No.
1	Fred Adams	1-2-3-4-5	Midfield Bank, Arch Street, Renchester	12-12-33	G. Rose	33380934
2	James Joyce	1-2-3-4-5	Midfield Bank, Arch Street, Renchester	12-12-33	J. Gieves	23784491
3	Gladys Rose	1-2-3-4-5	Barland Bank, May Road, Benton	01-05-32	B. King	23986343
4	Jean Gieves	1-2-3-4-5	Midfield Bank, Arch Street, Renchester	12-12-33	W. Lansdow	99734563
5	Betty King	1-2-3-4-5	Eastern Bank, High Road, Renchester	09-10-43	A. Fisher	33982487
6	William Lansdown	1-2-3-4-5	Midfield Bank, Arch Street, Renchester	12-12-33	C. Young	22324567
7	Andrew Fisher	1-2-3-4-5				
8	Claude Young	1-2-3-4-5				
9	Arthur Ball	1-2-3-4-5				
10	Mollie English	1-2-3-4-5				
11	Margaret Perkins	1-2-3-4-5	Eastern Bank, High Road, Renchester	09-10-43	M. Perkins	45627682
12	Paul Corke	1-2-3-4-5	Eastern Bank, High Road, Renchester	09-10-43	P. Corke	27893345
13	Richard Reagan	1-2-3-4-5	Midfield Bank, Arch Street, Renchester	12-12-33	R. Reagan	20202011
14	Wendy Tasker	1-2-3-4-5	Barland Bank, May Road, Benton	01-05-32	W. Tasker	32145123
15	Juliette Wilson	1-2-3-4-5	Barland Bank, May Road, Benton	01-05-32	J. Wilson	39902334
16	David Carver	1-2-3-4-5	Midfield Bank, Arch Street, Renchester	12-12-33	D. Carver	22248971
17	Wilbur Bridges	1-2-3-4-5	Coopers Bank, King Street, Benton	65-16-12	W. Bridges	28978712
18	Rachel Long	1-2-3-4-5	Coopers Bank, King Street, Benton	65-16-12	R. Long	78782456
19	Kirstie Farmer	1-2-3-4-5	Midfield Bank, Arch Street, Renchester	12-12-33	K. Farmer	33351212
20	John Nibbs	1-2-3-4-5	Midfield Bank, Arch Street, Renchester	12-12-33	J. Nibbs	26549812
21	Martin Long	1-2-3-4-5	Coopers Bank, King Street, Benton	65-16-12	M. Long	78294561
22	Linda Baker	1-2-3-4-5	Midfield Bank, Arch Street, Renchester	12-12-33	L. Baker	62390123
23	Jack Dark	1-2-3-4-5				

Notes

Notes